D1360279

From the participants who attended our Trainings and learned what you are about to learn in this book:

"I had a belief that I didn't deserve to be rich, that I couldn't have what I wanted. Money was always for someone else. Your dynamic visualizations were very powerful for me, and they helped me get where I am. This year I increased my income by 30%. Now I have the freedom to receive, and I am really welcoming abundance."

—Eve Gage,
Emmy Award–winning film editor

"Last year my sales were extraordinarily off. I was very concerned that I would be looking for a new job.

Learning this material turned out to be probably the best thing that ever happened to me. It forced me to look in a new direction, to examine an area of my life I had never delved into: my relationship to money and developing a prosperity consciousness. As a result, I surpassed my sales plan by a significant amount—by over 20%. Today I am responsible for three out of the four largest sales deals in my region. I am absolutely convinced that it is the result of releasing the obstacles that I had to accepting prosperity."

—Anthony Yim,
corporate sales

"I am a singer and a saxophone player and I work in a band. And recently I took over as the leader of the group.

I acquired so many tools from you, and I have a new mindset for believing and leading. Every day and every week I am making progress. I am feeling really great. Next to my saxophone, [getting your information] was the best money I ever spent in my life."

—Lisa McLeod,
singer and saxophonist

"I had been relatively successful, but it was hit or miss. I was a multiple six-figure income earner for about four or five years, but then I found I didn't have a nest egg anymore. I'd just get to where things started working and I'd move away. I believed I didn't deserve it, that I wasn't good enough. All that changed with your help. In August my income was $4,900 per month. This month it's $20,000."

—Greg Hillman,
network marketing and oil and gas sales

"I am making more money than I ever have in my life. And I feel I am worth it. My beliefs have changed to feeling that I have value, that I can contribute."

—Ken Cross,
home improvement contractor

"You taught me that I can be the cause of everything in my life. I can plan for things and make things happen and trust that they will. I take responsibility for what's going on in my life. And when I am not getting the results that I want, I now have tools that I can use to change myself, so I can get what I want. I don't feel that I am at the whim of anybody or anything else. You guys have the tools that take the rust right off and get down to the good stuff, and very quickly."

—Dr. Tom Leutner,
www.AmericanHypnosis.com

"At the beginning, I was pretty resistant—still hanging onto the idea of having a job as my salvation. Then I was laid off, without severance or benefits. Now my business is generating about double what my job did. This is the first time in my life ever where I wake up in the morning and don't mind going to work."

—Miguel Soares,
information technology executive

WEALTH WITHOUT A JOB

WEALTH WITHOUT A JOB

THE ENTREPRENEUR'S GUIDE TO FREEDOM AND SECURITY BEYOND THE 9 TO 5 LIFESTYLE

Phil Laut
Andy Fuehl

WILEY

John Wiley & Sons, Inc.

Published by John Wiley & Sons, Inc., Hoboken, New Jersey.
Published simultaneously in Canada.

For general information on our other products and services, or technical support, please contact our Customer Care Department within the United States at 800-762-2974, outside the United States at 317-572-3993 or fax 317-572-4002.

Wiley also publishes its books in a variety of electronic formats. Some content that appears in print may not be available in electronic books.

For more information about Wiley products, visit our web site at www.wiley.com.

Library of Congress Cataloging-in-Publication Data
Laut, Phil.
    Wealth without a job : the entrepreneur's guide to freedom and security beyond the 9 to 5 lifestyle / Phil Laut and Andy Fuehl.
        p.   cm.
    Includes index.
    ISBN 0-471-65645-3 (cloth)
    1. New business enterprises.   2. Entrepreneurship.   3. Job satisfaction.
4. Success in business.   I. Fuehl, Andy, 1962–   II. Title.
HD62.5.L38 2004
658.1'1—dc22

                                                                                2004002226

Printed in the United States of America.

10   9   8   7   6   5   4   3   2   1

CONTENTS

ACKNOWLEDGMENTS

We extend our heartfelt thanks to the many people who have aided and inspired us in the creation of this book:

Linda Konner, our literary agent, for her guidance and wisdom.

Jeffery Combs, for his ideas and example.

Debra Englander and the fine folks at John Wiley & Sons.

Joellen Handley, Andy's sister-in-law, for her conscientious, thorough, and speedy editing.

Richard Bandler and John Grinder, for inventing Neuro Linguistic Programming (NLP).

Lisa Kitter, for her inspiring example.

Tony Robbins, for leading the way.

And our many students and clients, who enrich our lives in many ways.

Phil extends his personal thanks to his sister, Lisa Van Rossum, for her help in some dark times.

Thanks also to Jim Leonard for his good ideas.

Andy extends his personal thanks to his wife, Tamar, for love, support, patience, and understanding through this entire process.

And thanks to:

Bob Proctor, for providing self-understanding that moves him forward regardless of circumstances.

Dr. Dolf de Roos, for his valuable time and guidance in real estate investing and his friendship.

Elisabeth and Josef Fuehl, loving parents who provided core values, a good example, and too much else to mention here.

Douglas Raymond, my friend and coauthor of *Why Wait—Selling with Active Confidence.*

Ashok Patil, for starting me on the quest to live life to the fullest and being a great friend.

And Brad Hoeck, my friend and coauthor of my first book, *Profiting in Turbulent Times.*

INTRODUCTION

This is a book about know-how.

If you are like most people, you have probably heard plenty of instructions. Your boss, your spouse and family members, church leaders, the advertising media, the government, and a wide variety of financial advisors continuously offer advice. A common characteristic of this advice is that it tells you *what* to do.

This book is different. It is our firm conviction that knowing *how* to do anything is the essential element. If you only know what to do but not how to do it, then you are left with trial and error as a method for accomplishment. Trial and error greatly increases the risk of doing anything new to the degree that many people accept the limitations of the status quo rather than risking the action to get the changes they want.

Entrepreneurship is not taught in the government-dominated education system or in private schools, either. For this reason, most entrepreneurs learn through baptism by fire—a method that can be both expensive and time-consuming. We don't presume to know the exact business that is best for you. Instead, we will show you how to discover your true purpose so that you can choose a business that expresses your own values and calls forth your passion.

The difference in this book is that you learn *how* to do things from the inside out—not just *what* to do. We refer to this as the *real* interior decoration. We decorate our homes and our bodies in ways that please us. Why not decorate your mind (your internal reality) in ways that please you? In ways that move you ahead, in ways that make your work more meaningful than merely making money, in ways that bring forth personal resources that you may not be aware of at this point?

We go beyond materialism in this book. Money can't buy happiness. The paradox is that poverty surely produces unhappiness, anxiety, and dissatisfaction.

But we cover more than your personal psychology and mind-set. After reading this book, you will understand the fundamental structural changes that have occurred in the economy that have destroyed the once-common expectation that working for someone else offers the possibility of improving your standard of living and gaining financial security.

Earning the income you want from work you love: yes, that's what you'll learn to do in this book. Although it may seem a distant dream to you now, you will learn how to identify and then prosper at work that is an expression of your true purpose.

We have taught courses about earning the income you want from work you love in many parts of the world for quite some time. From this experience, we can anticipate some of the hesitations that you may have in using this material. Your mind may be saying something like "I never thought of myself as an entrepreneur or a business owner, so aren't I just lying to myself by using this book?" This is an important question. Entrepreneurship is natural and instinctive. Most kids do not have to be told about earning money, and many spontaneously open lemonade stands. What you are really doing by using this material is returning to your instinctive method of earning an income. We know it is a lie that you must rely on a single source or a job for income. It is a big mistake to leave the decision of how much you are worth to a corporate or institutional bureaucracy. Most jobholders do not think about it this way, but in today's job market, you are leaving even the decision of *whether* you get paid to your employer.

People who earn lots of money from work they do not enjoy experience dissatisfaction because the money is never enough. They may face credit card problems from attempts to find in consumption the satisfaction missing at work. Yet people who enjoy their work but who earn so little that they are continually beset by financial problems sooner or later find that the problems overwhelm the enjoyment.

Work you love obviously possesses the potential of providing far greater intangible rewards, such as joy in doing and the satisfaction of contribution. Unless you are blessed with a trust fund to pay your bills, it's essential to devise a way for the work you love to provide an abundant income.

Earning the income you want from work you love ranks close to good health, fulfilling personal relationships, and a clear conscience as essential elements for a satisfying life. There is an infinite variety of ways to earn the income you want from work you love. Deciding how much income you want and choosing the work you love are personal determinations. Although we make suggestions about how you might find answers to these questions, the final decision is up to you.

We have observed some important characteristics about wealthy people, which we present here to get you more comfortable with the prospect of greater wealth for yourself. A common observation is that wealthy people are different. Yes, that's right. However, the money they possess is the smallest of these differences. What are some of the important differences?

Wealthy people are decisive. This is because they have an enduring vision to guide their decisions and actions. This vision provides the framework for making decisions quickly and free of second thoughts.

Wealthy people take prudent risks. Poor people tend to be dominated by fear of loss or fear of making a mistake, so they rarely take risks. Poor people seem to be willing to settle for the misperceived safety of enduring struggle.

Wealthy people take responsibility. They do not blame their financial situation on themselves or anyone or anything else. Instead, they take the steps necessary to change their own thinking and behavior to move ahead.

Wealthy people don't work for money. Rather, they develop a self-benefiting mind-set about money and receiving and do work that suits them, motivated by their sense of accomplishment and service.

Wealthy people are good for the economy. They pay most of the taxes and make most of the charitable contributions. If you have need of a job, surely you wouldn't ask a poor person to hire you.

Wealthy people do not rely on luck. Less than 2 percent of American millionaires have inherited trust funds, and even a smaller percentage has won lotteries.

Wealth is voluntary. You have to sign up. Are you ready? If you have had enough of living with the financial results of preconditioned thinking about money and want to take a giant step forward, then you are in the right place to succeed.

Psychology, particularly thoughts and feelings, is the focus of this book. From more than 20 years of teaching people, in groups and individually, to earn the income they want from work they love, we know that the obstacles that truly stand in the way are internal. These obstacles are the result of limited conditioning learned during 20,000 meals with parents who gave conflicting messages about money. The methods you will be learning here bring to the surface personal psychological patterns you may have denied or suppressed. You will learn to make profitable use of the energy and thinking that previously stood in your way, turning stumbling blocks into stepping-stones.

Starting one's own business has always been an option for people wanting to take charge of their future and escape the trap of income stagnation. Financial experts traditionally suggest a nest egg consisting of six months to two years of expenses before quitting a job to start a business. With the advent of wireless communications, laptop computers, and the Internet, such a nest egg is no longer necessary. Modern technology can empower you to start most businesses while you keep your job or if you are currently unemployed.

What to Do If You Are Unemployed

Here in my adopted hometown of Charlotte, North Carolina, I (PL) belong to a Toastmasters Club with about 30 members. Half our membership is entrepreneurs and the rest have jobs, at least until they're downsized. This happens to a couple of people each year. I always ask the newly unemployed person about his or her plans. "Find another job," they say. "Why?" I ask. "To pay the bills," they respond.

We think you would agree that how much you are paid and even *whether* you are paid is far too important a decision to leave to corporate bureaucracy. If you are unemployed, then you can make a better choice than these people. With this book, you are not just another unemployed person. You have in your hands the information required to start and build your own full- or part-time business. Here is the road to financial security. No more vulnerability to income loss because of the mistakes of others. The business owner derives income from multiple sources—a structure that enhances security. The business owner relies on his or her wits, initiative, and creativity for income, a far more reliable source than any employer.

If you are unemployed, then take the best job you can find that pays more than unemployment benefits. Once your unemployment benefits have run out, this will be pretty easy to do. Make sure it is a job that involves selling, so you gain or polish your selling skills. Make it your goal to become the top salesperson in the organization within six months. At the same time, start using the information and practicing the skills in this book to build an entrepreneurial mind-set. During this period, start your own business, part time at first, until you are ready to move to full time.

I (AF) worked in corporate America for more than 15 years at Fortune 500 and Fortune 50 companies. I was climbing the corporate ladder to lead and manage global space and land-based telecommunications programs with budgets in the range of several hundred million dollars. I was the person responsible for developing the plans, bringing in the resources, getting team collaboration from other groups, and managing the programs for success.

During the time I was working for a company, I always had the urge to serve others through my own business. I was never quite content with where I was and with what was happening around me. I felt that being on my own could be much more satisfying. Then I, not someone else, would be in control of my own destiny.

In the corporate world, I generated and saved the companies hundreds of millions of dollars and received very little compensation in comparison. In addition, I dealt with many people who really hated their jobs and despised the company they worked for. At times it was depressing to listen to these people, which made working for a company that much more challenging.

I continued to look for a better way. I always told myself that working for a company gave me security. This illusion of security was holding me back from achieving what I was really meant to do. Six months prior to being laid off, I knew the company was in trouble. I thought this would be the push I required to venture on my own. The safety net would be removed and I would be forced to take action. So I prepared for the moment with anticipation. I re-created my mind-set about being on my own without a job. At first it was a bit scary and sometimes even frightening, but I got over that quickly. I was facing a big step: going from receiving a big steady paycheck whether I made or saved the company money or not that week to having to go out and sell myself on a daily basis. Now my paycheck would be based solely on my efforts. That was a big change in thinking for me.

During those six months, I had to change my thinking and my internal representations for my new life that was coming. From different books I had read and from working with Phil and many others, I learned that I had to create the vision of what I wanted. I envisioned what life was going to be like without a job. I created every detail about what I wanted and what I was going to do. I improved the vision on a daily basis and made it more clear and detailed in my mind. I wrote out empowering affirmations using the methods in Chapter 9 that would move me forward and clear my mind of chatter. By doing this I was able to think clearly. I still was not sure what I was going to do, but I knew that it would come to me at the right time.

I kept my faith and followed my heart. I read many different books, listened to tapes, and went to seminars. I knew that by changing my mind-set I would become the person I had to be. I really enjoyed the process, although it was not easy at times. Doubts crept in that caused fear and anxiety. When I realized these were imaginary, I let them go. I continued working on myself because I knew that this was the path to my dreams. This felt empowering! For the first time in a very long time, I really felt alive.

Two weeks prior to the layoffs, I cleared out my desk, preparing for the moment just in case I was targeted. Actually I hoped that I was. Finally the layoffs started—an ugly two-day period. But I was mentally prepared to leave. My belongings were packed and my mind was checked out. I was only waiting for the official word.

The first day, everyone who had been with the company less than 10 years was laid off. You could feel the tension in the air. I hoped it would end quickly. Unfortunately, I had been with the company for more than 10 years, so I had to wait until the next day. I had decided that if they did not call me that day, I would volunteer to leave. When my manager, the director of program management and engineering, approached me and said, "Would you please come to my office? I would like to talk to you," I knew what was coming.

I was excited because I knew from this point forward I would be in charge of my life. I knew with certainty that it would improve dramatically. Even though I did not know specifically what I was going to do, I was ready for the challenge and the change.

I went into my manager's office. He began, "I'm so sorry, but we have to let you go. We appreciate your many years of service, but the economic times mandate we let you go, blah, blah blah. . . ." I stopped listening. My mind was on the bright future I had envisioned. I was ecstatic. I had a smile on my face from ear to ear and I replied, "Thank you so much. You have no idea what you did for me. You have removed the shackles that have been holding me back. Thank you." My manager looked at me as if I were psychotic. He had expected me to break down; he did not expect me to be happy. I knew the layoff meant nothing about *me*. In my mind, I knew that I was worth much more than they were paying me. I considered this a gift of freedom to earn the money I desired and do what I love instead of what I have to do to survive.

My manager continued to apologize, saying "I feel sorry for you that this had to happen this way." I replied, "Don't feel sorry for me. This is the best day of my life. I feel sorry for *you*." He looked puzzled and shocked. I continued, "You're still here and have to deal with the aftermath." This is not what he expected! Then I asked him, "How fast can I get out of here?" Off we went to human resources to process the paperwork.

The story was similar at human resources. They too apologized and felt sorry for me. When I said the same things I had said to my manager, the human resources person got nervous. He thought I was losing my mind. He could not understand how anyone could possibly be so happy about being laid off. I had fun with that person, as well.

When I passed the security gate and entered the parking lot, I was more relieved than I ever had been. The shackles were off; I felt free. I knew that what had happened was meant to be and that life from that point forward would not be the same. It was going to be much better. My mind was clear and there was no chatter.

Doing what I had to was finally over; I could make a fresh start. When I arrived at home with my box beneath my arm, my wife, Tamar, knew exactly what had happened. I said, "Tonight we are going out to celebrate my new freedom."

Job loss is devastating. 100 percent of my income disappeared overnight. I am very grateful that I used the methods in this book during the months that followed. I have compassion for those of my former colleagues who were laid off at the same time (three years ago), but remain devastated by their loss. Despite the intense object lesson in the instability of working for someone else, many of these people still are seeking jobs to produce income.

At first I felt disoriented by my newfound freedom. This lasted only a short time until I began systematic use of the methods in this book. I had already established my purpose in life. Now I was free to express my own purpose—rather than that of my former employer—through the goals I chose. Just as important, I was free to choose my business associates instead of accepting those whom the company had provided.

Since my involuntary departure from corporate America, I have published my first book *Profiting in Turbulent Times*, have written this book with Phil, and am working on another partnership with Dolf de Roos. Dolf is the author of the bestseller *Real Estate Riches*. He and I spent about six weeks together over the period of a year. During this time, I had the privilege of watching him review hundreds of possible real-estate purchases and observing the procedures he uses to create wealth. Moreover, I learned and wrote about his underlying mind-set and unconscious awareness. While less obvious, these internal ingredients are just as essential to his spectacular success as the tangible procedures. For this reason, our upcoming book is entitled, *Revealed: Hidden Strategies of a Real Estate Tycoon*. Now, I am well on my way to becoming a real estate tycoon myself. In addition, I have three other books in the works. My consulting business has grown and I have the privilege of combining talents and abilities with Phil to deliver Trainings and products which help people quickly and permanently overcome their obstacles.

Since becoming unemployed almost three years ago, I have become a millionaire. It has been a delightfully challenging transition. I repeatedly used the methods in this book to overcome the psychological obstacles that often paralyze other people. I do not mention this to impress you but to impress upon you what *you* can accomplish.

We believe this story is important to those of you who are concerned about job security—and rightfully so. This book will prepare you to take the next step and move beyond dependence on a job. There is much more to life than working for someone else. Mind-set is the key issue to success. Our thoughts and internal focus directly create results. I'm not suggesting you quit your job tomorrow. Rather, prepare yourself for the greater things you are capable of. When you have the proper mind-set, you will take the necessary action to express your purpose in life.

The Organization Man is dead. People who place help wanted advertisements confide that the stack of resumes they receive in response to each ad is too overwhelming to even glance at all of them. They grab an arbitrary handful of 25 or so for examination and throw away the rest, sometimes hundreds. Anyone over 45 (especially if white and male) engaged in an involuntary job search is certain to be looking for a very long time. Then there is the depressing discovery that salary offers are lower than the job that was left, even though pointing this out may not be politically correct.

A so-called side business can offer benefits far beyond the income that it produces. Some of these benefits are:

- It can be a prudent first step toward a full-time business of your own.

- It can increase your job satisfaction by reducing dependency on your job.
- It can be a risk-free way to learn a new occupation.
- It can be a way to discover if you would enjoy some new occupation.
- It can be a way to grow and expand your mind, discover your true potential and who you really are.

Additionally, the fact that job security has disappeared means that you are likely to be in the job market several times during a career, sometimes willingly and other times not. "No jobs will be lost as a result of this merger" has replaced "The check is in the mail" as the cliché falsehood.

In this book you will learn essential entrepreneurial skills that will aid you in your own business, in job advancement, and in job search. Most people discover that business ownership is very, very different from employment. In a job your success depends on how good you are at what you do; in your own business your success depends on how good you are at business. With a job there is someone to tell you what to do and someone to motivate you. An internally generated purpose is less important than willingness to surrender to the company purpose. The process of receiving and expanding income is somewhat remote in a job. If, as an employee, your pay is automatically deposited in your bank account, then the experience of receiving money is more distant and abstract than in your own business, where customers pay you directly.

The biggest difference, however, is the degree of emotional and psychological involvement in the actual production of income. With a job, it is easy to conclude that others determine your pay and that extraordinary performance may or may not produce increased income, especially in the near term. Your personal involvement with the creation of your income in a job is far more operational and behavioral than emotional and psychological. Owning your own business changes all of this. It quickly becomes profoundly evident that your own consciousness about money is intimately related to your income. Issues such as unconscious dependency, resentment of rich people, motivation by disapproval, fear of rejection, fear of loss, and others come to the fore in ways they never would in a job.

How to make the internal emotional and psychological adjustments required for entrepreneurship is a topic that is not covered anywhere by the educational system. School produces expectations of a job. In school other people made goals for you. In school other people told you what time to do things. Schools have a well-defined measurement system, and someone else lets you know how you are doing. On tests all you must do is pick out the correct answer from alternatives offered (rather than creating your own solutions).

Time is of the essence. The essential challenge of learning entrepreneurship is whether you can learn how to do it successfully before you go broke. You have in your hands the source of the tools that will speed your learning. The emotional and psychological changes the methods in this book create for you will put an end to your struggles and move you forward far more quickly than you may have imagined.

This is a book you will read more than once. Sprinkled throughout are very important methods to move your mind immediately to building an entrepreneurial mind-set. Act on these methods as you read, rather than waiting until you have completed the entire book. The methods are indicated by the symbol shown in Figure I.1.

FIGURE I.1

When you see this symbol, complete the method immediately before continuing. These methods were designed and placed in each section intentionally to assist you in producing your desired success. Skipping the methods altogether will limit the value of this book to what you paid for it. However, actually engaging your mind so that the changes these methods make for you do occur produces limitless value. The choice is yours.

We placed the first method in the appendix so as not to interrupt the flow of the book at this early stage. It is entitled "How to Feel Better Instantly without Years of Therapy." Do this exercise now.

Specifically, you will learn to put events which have upset you in the past into the proper perspective so they no longer affect your productivity. You will learn to access the infinite power of your creativity whenever you want it, instead of passively waiting for inspiration. You will have a consciously declared purpose for your life that integrates your activities and provides the motivation necessary to accomplish things you never thought you could.

EARNING THE
INCOME YOU WANT
FROM WORK YOU LOVE

Discover devastating effects of doing work you don't like, just for the money. Work you don't like may feed you, but it will never nourish you. Working just for the money produces people who feel cheated, people who know the cost of everything and the value of nothing. Earning the income you want from work you love is an act of defiance—it defies both parental conditioning and societal conditioning.

Financial success means earning the income you want doing work you love. One without the other falls short. Earning the income you want from work you don't like greatly reduces your satisfaction and enjoyment.

All of us know people who spend 40 or so hours per week working in an office, where they lift nothing heavier than file folders and telephones. On Friday they go home for the weekend moaning about how tired they are and how hard they have been working. On Saturday they play a vigorous tennis match for two hours, expending more energy than they did all week long. Yet after the tennis match, they say they feel invigorated—tired but invigorated.

Obviously there are two kinds of tiredness. The stress kind of tiredness results from the work of holding in our feelings. In this case it is the feelings about the work we don't like. Five hundred years ago, most people were killed by microscopic organisms, primarily smallpox, plague, and influenza. Today stress-related diseases, primarily heart disease, cause most deaths. The exertion kind of tiredness is far healthier and results from expending mental and physical energy in ways we enjoy.

Doing the work you love must produce a sufficient income. Otherwise, sooner or later, you will feel helpless. People in this situation often are quite skilled at their profession but don't possess the business skills required to turn talent into a reliable and abundant cash flow. Such people sometimes are referred to as starving artists. Unfortunately, the stress and uncertainty associated with meeting financial obligations disrupts focus on work and can transform even the most satisfying occupation into drudgery.

What Change May Be Like for You

Change is almost always scary—even change for the better, because it intensifies the basic fear of the unknown. It follows then that fear is the cause of procrastination. No matter how unacceptable your current situation may be, it's known to you. Anything different is not. For this reason, moving forward and making progress toward your goals is *supposed* to feel uncomfortable. Change does not have to be agony, but it certainly will activate uncomfortable feelings.

Remember the Dilbert cartoon that says, "Change is good. You go first"? Fear is chronically linked to change. Unacknowledged fear causes procrastination. At the beginning of an important project, there is fear of failure or fear that you will not be able to reach completion. Toward the end of the project, as success gets closer and more certain, the emotional experience tends to shift to fear about what success may mean. Expect to feel a little uncomfortable about making changes. The discomfort is natural and does not mean that you are doing something wrong. A compulsive desire for emotional comfort can defeat your desire to make the changes you want, if you allow it to.

Misperception of Risk

Most of us realize that change involves risk. The status quo involves risk, too, although that risk is much less noticeable. The current status quo once represented a change from whatever came before it. However, we naturally perceive the risks associated with change to be greater than those of the status quo. Risk is a subjective perception, which cannot be quantified. Figure 1.1 illustrates how most people's perception of risk is distorted. It is different depending on whether we are contemplating a change to a new situation or contemplating the status quo.

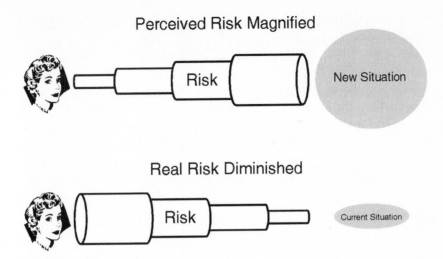

FIGURE 1.1   Misperceptions of Risk

When we contemplate any new situation, we tend to magnify the risk. This isn't logical. Our biggest fear is of the unknown, even in cases where there is no danger. In situations that we have been accustomed to, our minds tend to minimize the risks. In other words, we perceive risk by looking through the large end of the telescope. It's not necessarily bad that our minds do this. However, if you are not aware that your mind is doing this, *any* change is going to seem to be so risky that you will never attempt it.

But risks must be taken. Playing it safe may be the riskiest strategy of all. People who risk nothing may avoid pain and disappointment temporarily, but they don't learn, feel, change, grow, love—live. Chained by their fear, they are slaves, having forfeited freedom.

It's quite possible that *any* change—getting married or divorced, moving to another city or changing careers—will appear to be riskier than maintaining the status quo. In terms of job security, having a job may appear less risky than having your own business, but this perception may be distorted by the risk telescope shown in Figure 1.1. One common perception is that having a job in the private sector is more risky than a career in the military. In 1968 I (PL) left the military to attend graduate school and got a job in the computer business. By the early 1990s career military people were being phased out of the service due to force reductions. In 1976 I left my job at a major American computer manufacturer to start my own business. Most people would perceive having your own business as much riskier than having a job. By the 1980s the computer manufacturer had laid off more than 30,000 of its workers. These are both examples of misperceptions of risk.

Owning your own business transforms you into a capitalist. If you have always had a job in the past, then your participation in the capitalist system has been as a provider of labor. As a business owner, you negotiate for yourself on a frequent basis; you decide which people to hire and fire; and you invest your capital, your time, and your energy. Most important, you must sell to your customers the products and services you provide. In today's world of downsizing, temporary jobs, and part-time employment, even people who stay in the job market are pretty close to entrepreneurship anyway.

Use Technology to Speed Up and to Multiply Your Work

If you are still a technophobe, get over it. Technophobia is expensive, and today's computers are friendly enough that anyone can learn. Today computer literacy is taken for granted. Surveys show that people with a home-based business who do not use a personal computer make an average income of $40,000, while those who use personal computers make an average income of $69,100 per year. Even if these surveys are wrong, you can purchase a personal computer today and learn how to use it for a lot less than the $29,000 difference between these averages.

Do Work You Love

Nothing can compare to performing work you love. Most of us spend 40 or more of our approximately 100 waking hours every week providing an income for ourselves and our family. Other than the possible exception of good health, doing work you love will do more to increase your enjoyment and satisfaction in life than finding the ideal mate, winning the lottery, or owning your dream house.

Work you don't like can never provide the satisfaction that makes life enjoyable and worthwhile. Work you don't like may provide an abundant income, but it never seems to be enough, because the income represents such a meager return on the struggle and self-denial you invest to create it.

Work you don't enjoy fails to provide the sense of satisfaction that comes from the joyous accomplishment derived from favorite hobbies. Without this, no amount of pay is ever enough. Life is mostly process and a little bit of outcome. If the process is not en-

joyable, then the outcome cannot be. Working just for money produces people who feel cheated, people who know the cost of everything and the value of nothing.

Doing work you don't like leaves you obsessed by results. Without enjoyment of the process, no success ever seems enough. Each
failure, even temporary setbacks, becomes intolerable. Work you
don't like is the functional equivalent of high-paid slavery.

Work you don't like may feed you, but it will never nourish you.
Compulsive spending is a common futile attempt to satisfy this
hunger. If your current work doesn't satisfy you and doesn't include
expression of your creativity and important values, you may try to
fill these needs by buying things. Advertisers use this tendency by
trying to convince you that your life will be better if you were to
switch to a particular brand of beer or car.

Work you don't enjoy also has negative effects on your loving relationships. If you arrive home on Friday after a week at work you
don't like, then you will feel you have made a sacrifice, have little
left to give, and thus expect your spouse to take care of you. If both
members of a couple are doing this, the relationship soon becomes
a hollow shell without much energy for each other.

Working just for the money eventually twists a person's view of
him- or herself and his or her worth. In such a distorted and materi-
alistic value system, a successful person is one who can earn money
faster than his or her family can spend it.

Determining the income you want requires independent thinking because you cannot judge from appearances. Some folks use
their wealth (or high credit rating) to impress others. They struggle to make the mortgage payment on a half-million-dollar home
and the lease payments on two luxury cars. Conversely lots of millionaires live in ordinary houses and drive secondhand Chevys.
The value system of conspicuous consumption comes up empty,
because there never seems to be enough. In some cases, people
who realize there is never enough to be satisfied conclude "that
there is no reason to try to get any more." If this is your situation,
you'll achieve both higher income and more satisfaction by choosing work you love that supports your purpose beyond gaining the
approval of others.

Work you love will make you more alive, healthier, more enthusiastic, and therefore more successful. Work you love provides an
outlet for your creativity and permits you to express your important
values. It possesses an intrinsic satisfaction independent of your ex-

ternal success or financial results. Unless your chosen work is very strenuous physically, you can look forward to doing it as long as you want to, instead of counting the days until retirement.

But even with work you love, a balance is required. Sixty hours per week at work you love will burn you out, just not as quickly as 60 hours per week at work you don't like.

The possibility of actually deriving income from an activity you find pleasurable may be an alien concept for some. You may be imprisoned by views that associate work with struggle and unpleasantness—thinking it is necessary to do a lot of what you don't like in order to get a little of what you do like. If you look around, you can find someone who derives income from just about any activity you can imagine. You have the *choice* to do something more suited to your personality and talents.

Work you love isn't completely free of stress and frustration. Professional golfers sometimes curse and bend a club over their knees. However, the personal passion and satisfaction from work you love eases and speeds the recovery from any setback.

Clearly it is impossible to suggest a single method of identifying a perfect career that will work for everyone, because there is such a wide variety of starting points on the issue of career satisfaction. We authors are not suggesting you quit your day job as soon as you finish reading this book to become an aspiring actor, business owner, self-employed accountant, landscape artist, or something else. This book will show you several ways to make the transition with far less risk than abruptly quitting your day job.

You can reduce the difficulty of transition with a "test drive" of your intended new career while keeping your day job. Do this either by accepting a part-time position or by giving away your services to see how you like it. Just because you enjoy playing golf doesn't mean you will enjoy teaching golf, for example. If you intend to purchase a restaurant franchise or a picture-framing store, then take a part-time position in such a place to see how you like it first.

Staying in a Job

Across-the-board salary increases are a thing of the past. It doesn't matter whether you are an accountant, baker, chemist, doctor, or zoologist; your advancement will depend far more on your ability to sell yourself and your organization than your occupational competency within your field. If you intend to remain as an employee in today's turbulent job market, the entrepreneurial skills in this book will be extremely useful, both in securing advancement in your current company and in a job search, should one be required.

As an employee, you create your greatest success by making your boss a hero in the eyes of his or her boss. Do this repeatedly and you will move up rapidly. The skills of negotiation, selling, and planning that this book teaches will help you greatly in moving up in the organization of current and future employers.

Moving yourself to earning the income you want from work you love is a process that will occur over time. Here are seven helpful hints that will get you started immediately and accelerate your progress.

1. *Beware of addictions.* Bad habits cost you twice. The worse the habit, the greater the cost. Stop wasting both your energy and your money by giving up your worst habits now.
2. *Stop complaining.* Don't wait until you feel grateful to start giving thanks.
3. *Stop hanging out with negative people.* Do everything possible to minimize your contact with the naysaying, hopeless victims of the world who (well meaning or not) sabotage and enfeeble your efforts to improve.
4. *Stop listening to music with negative lyrics.* This rules out most country western and most rap.
5. *Accept your feelings.* It is OK to have them. If you fight against them, then they have you. They don't mean anything. In particular, they don't mean anything about you. They are like internal weather.
6. *Realize that your parents did not give you useful training about money.* It's not their fault, and it's your responsibility to give yourself the proper training.
7. *Live below your means.* Money is better used to express your true purpose than to impress others.

The next two chapters deal with the current economic situation and trends related to prospects for your income in the United States and the European Community. If you detest economics, you may jump ahead to Chapter 4, but you'll miss the explanation, not available in the financial press, of why even dual-income families find it difficult to make ends meet.

CHAPTER 2

THE OLD METHODS NO LONGER WORK IN TODAY'S ECONOMY

Learn the nasty truth about jobs and wages. American wages have been declining in purchasing power for more than 20 years. If the American dream is to do better than your parents, then the prospects of fulfilling this dream with a job are far slimmer than they once were.

This chapter offers a brief historical perspective of today's economic conditions to inspire you with a sense of urgency.

Figure 2.1 presents a startling graph showing the purchasing power of the average weekly wage income of the American worker, adjusted for inflation, since 1959.

Here you can see the gradual decline in real wages since 1973. (Real wages are adjusted for inflation and thus reflect purchasing power.) Despite the fact that current dollar wages have been increasing, these gains have been outstripped by inflation since 1973, resulting in a gradual decline of purchasing power of about 1 percent per year. People are earning a little more each year, but each year it buys a little less.

The growth in the economy in the last few years has been accomplished not by higher wages for workers but rather by a significant increase in the *number* of workers (mostly young mothers), so that each worker gets a little smaller piece of a much larger pie. On the graph, you can see that in the last two years, there have been small increases, but not nearly enough to recover earlier losses. The recent gains occurred during a time when the overall economy ex-

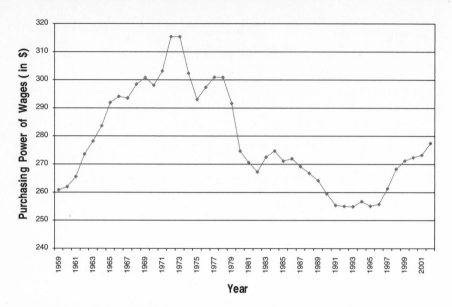

FIGURE 2.1   Average American Wages, Adjusted for Inflation

Source: Council of Economic Advisors, Report to the President 1993, 1996, and 1998 (Washington, DC: U.S. Government Printing Office, various dates).

perienced previously unknown peacetime growth rates, which most economists consider to be unsustainable.

Just because the purchasing power of the average income is decreasing doesn't mean that you are required to participate in this trend. In the next chapter you will learn the importance of the globalization of the world economy. Later chapters explain skills you can learn and steps you can take to ensure that your income does not follow this decreasing trend.

The decline of incomes in America is rarely discussed publicly. Politicians don't address it lest they be asked for a solution. Corporate leaders don't address this topic because lower wages increase their bottom line. Labor leaders, usually the champions of increased income for all workers, don't address the decline in income lest their powerlessness to prevent it in the first place becomes evident. Income decline, although experienced by many, is discussed by almost no one.

One clear response to the wage decline has been a larger percentage of women with young children entering the workforce. (See Table 2.1.)

Clearly, everyone benefits from equal employment opportunities for women. Freedom for women to enter the workforce in greater numbers and earn greater incomes than ever before must be a sign of economic vitality. That many dual-income couples find it *necessary* for both people to work just to make ends meet can hardly be a sign of economic well-being.

The Economy and the Media

The economy always has been a prominent topic in the news media. In contrast to the media practice of focusing on bad news such as wars, natural disasters, and accidents, the focus is different when it comes to economic news. Positive economic news gets more coverage than negative. For example, here is an article from the Associated Press reprinted in its entirety.

FED THINKS JOB MARKET MAY NOT RECOVER TILL '05
Washington—The Federal Reserve policymakers expressed concern at their October meeting that the battered job market might not fully recover until at least 2005 even if the economic recovery grew stronger, according to minutes released Thursday of the discussion. That concern was one reason Fed Chairman Alan Greenspan and his colleagues who set U.S. interest rate policy held a main short-term rate at a 45 year low of 1 percent and suggested rates might stay in that range for a "considerable period."

"Members generally anticipated that an economic

TABLE 2.1   Percentage of Women with Child
under Six Years Old in the Labor Force

Year	%
1960	18.6
1970	30.3
1980	45.1
1993	59.6
2003	70.0

Source: U.S. Congressional Children's Caucus.

performance in line with their expectations would not entirely eliminate currently large margins of unemployed labor and other resources until perhaps the latter part of 2005 or even later," according to minutes of the Federal Open Market Committee's Oct. 28 meeting.
Copyright © 2003 by Associated Press. *Reprinted with permission of the Associated Press*

This article appeared on page 3 of the Business Section of the *Charlotte Observer* on December 12, 2003. That same day the front page carried a much longer article about the positive outlook for North Carolina furniture companies in 2004.

The U.S. Stock Market—Psychology and Prognosis

Starting in the mid-1980s, a combination of events contributed to a pronounced and sustained increase in the value of equity shares traded in the U.S. stock market. (See Figure 2.2.) Figure 2.2 shows the monthly closing price of the Dow Jones Industrial Average (DJIA) from 1965 to 2003.

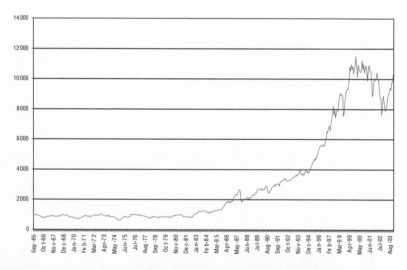

FIGURE 2.2   Dow Jones Industrial Average 1965 to 2003
Source: Adapted from data from Yahoo.com.

Major companies began phasing out defined benefit pension plans in the mid-1980s. Under a defined benefit pension plan, an employee of a company is guaranteed a defined lifetime pension, calculated on his or her years of service and salary earned. The companies, as guarantors of these pension payouts, deposited cash with a life insurance company or other financial institution that served to manage these pension funds. These institutions invested the funds and paid the retirees. Each year the companies calculated how much they must contribute to the pension plan based on the rate of inflation and the demographics and retention rate within its workforce.

Some major companies are behind in their contributions to their pension plans to this day. You can determine this amount for any company by looking at the unfunded pension liability on their balance sheets. The pension funds were strictly regulated in regard to what investments they could make with the funds they held in trust for the future retirees. Most had to be invested in bonds or other fixed-income securities, and only a small portion could be placed in the stock market—and then, typically, only in blue-chip stocks.

Seeking ways to reduce this pension expense, most large companies shifted from defined benefit pensions to defined contribution pensions, which are the schemes most prevalent today in the private sector, with the ubiquitous 401(k) plan. This shift resulted in a big increase to the amount of money flowing into the stock market. The money held in the pension funds is now managed by the employees themselves, who hold it in trust for themselves until retirement. With the restrictions that prevented retirement savings from being invested in the stock market gone, 401(k) money poured into the stock market. Buoyed by a booming economy, the dot-com craze, and this new and enduring influx of cash from retirement savings, that had traditionally gone to the bond market, the stock market as characterized by the Dow Jones Industrial Average (DJIA) more than tripled. Employees put their retirement savings into mutual funds that invested primarily in the stock market and forgot about them, except to watch the growth in portfolio value each quarter. "Buy and hold" became an investment strategy that anyone could win with. Many new investors realized unprecedented gains with little or no understanding of the market, business, or accounting. Stock market success seemed deceptively easy.

In 1999 the dot-com bubble broke. In 2001 the war on terror

began (more on this later), as did accounting scandals in a score of major U.S. industrial companies. The Dow Jones Industrial Average lost 25 percent of its value from 2000 to 2002. The technology-laden Nasdaq Composite average lost more than 50 percent.

Conflicts of interest in brokerage firms were revealed in 2002, calling into question the validity of professional market research. Although these conflicts of interest came as a surprise to some, they are nothing new. They were first exposed to the public in a book that is a must-read for anyone even considering the stock market. *Where Are All the Customers' Yachts?* by Fred Schwed, published in 1940, explains that the basic conflict in a brokerage company is between its investment banking arm and its research arm. This conflict results in research recommendations to the public to advance the interest of the investment banking arm—known in Wall Street vernacular as "talking the book."

It is unwise to count on a broad stock market comeback with sustained double-digit annual growth anytime in the next 5 to 10 years. The war on terror has placed a significant and long-term cloud of uncertainty on the economy.

Prolonged Low-Intensity War—Not Favorable to Stock Market

Surely no one expects the war on terror to be anything like the Gulf War. It will be much more similar to the Vietnam War, except tougher. "Find the enemy" has forever been the first essential to military victory. It is impossible to win any armed conflict if the enemy cannot be found. Our inability to precisely locate the enemy in Vietnam caused the war to drag on for almost 10 years of frustration that deeply divided America. During this period (1965 to 1973), the Dow Jones Industrial Average showed no growth. (See Figure 2.3.)

This economic result, combined with the political result of the Vietnam War, leads to the conclusion that Lyndon Johnson's guns-and-butter strategy failed to produce sufficient quantities of either.

Characterizing the War on Terror

The war or terror can be characterized more accurately as a war on *Muslim* terror. Such a characterization may not be politically correct, but you can be pretty sure that the FBI and other intelligence agencies are not busy looking for Presbyterian terrorists or Amish

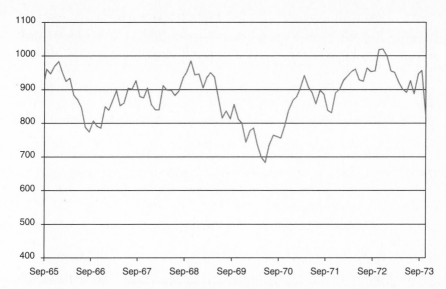

FIGURE 2.3 Dow Jones Industrial Average during the Vietnam War
Source: Adapted from data from Yahoo.com.

terrorists. Islam is the world's fastest-growing and second-ranked religion; the Muslim world represents a vast sea of people for terrorists to hide in.

In the Vietnam War the challenge was to find the enemy among a population of 70 million in an area the size of New Mexico. Compare that with searching for a small number of extremists among a population of more than a billion people stretching across eight time zones, from Indonesia to Morocco.

The war in Iraq is only an early skirmish in the war on terror. Even if an ideal outcome results in a democratic government there, remember that Iraq contains only about 2 percent of the world's Muslims. Clearly Iraq is a better place following the war. But this is not saying much. Any country would be improved by the elimination of widespread murder of its citizens, not to mention systematic torture and rape as expressions of government policy. Whether this improvement wins over the hearts and minds of a significant number of the world's billion Muslims remains an open question.

Public awareness that the war on terror will be both difficult and prolonged has only just dawned. This lack of recognition is reflected in forecasts of broad-based improvement in stock prices in the near future.

The stock market will continue to present attractive opportunities for the investor with a sharp pencil and a strong stomach. However, the days of broad-based, double-digit annual gains experienced in the final decade of the twentieth century are over. To profit in the stock market over the next 10 years, very different skills are required from those that grew portfolios earlier. Buy and hold won't work anymore. You must be prepared to buck the trend, to do your own research on individual stocks, to pay careful attention to timing, and to admit errors quickly. Most people are not interested in going to all this trouble and expenditure of time; for them, their own business will be a far more reliable and satisfying producer of wealth than the stock market.

CHAPTER 3

WHAT THE
GLOBAL ECONOMY
MEANS TO YOU

*Today events on the other side of the world affect your paycheck
and your prospects. The globalization of the economy has created
a single worldwide standard for industrial productivity. Freer
movement of goods and services across national borders places
all American workers in competition with wage earners in very-
low-income areas. An overall increase in income from American
jobs is very unlikely any time during this generation because capital and technology are far more portable than labor.*

The press started talking about the global economy in the late
1980s as if it were a recent invention. Yet Marco Polo returned from
China with silks and spices in 1275; Spanish gold doubloons circu-
lated freely in China in the 1500s; French champagne has been
served at stylish American weddings for centuries; we have been
drinking imported coffee, tea, and liquor since before anyone can
remember. Nevertheless, the American economy has become much
more global since the 1970s.

Figure 3.1 shows how the reduction in American tariffs has resulted in significant increases in international trade as a percentage
of the total American economy. Globalization became much more
prominent in the mid-1970s, about the same time as the purchasing
power of wages of Americans began to decline.

With the exception of the World War II years, trade has represented slightly more than 10 percent of the U.S. economy since
the 1930s. This trend continued until the 1970s, when trade as a

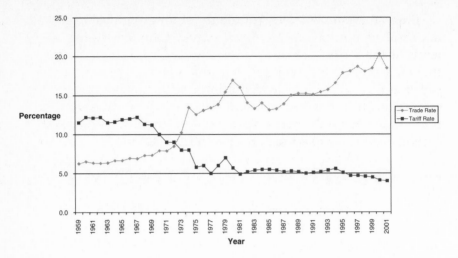

FIGURE 3.1   Globalization of the U.S. Economy since 1959

Source: Statistical Abstract of the United States and *Historical Statistics of the United States* (Washington, DC: U.S. Government Printing Office).

percentage of the national economy began a gradual increase to beyond 20 percent.

An important consequence of economic globalization is the creation of a worldwide competitive standard. In the 1960s the benchmark for General Motors was staying as competitive as Chrysler or Ford Motor Co. Today that is not good enough. Globalization has raised the standards across the board. American industries that measure up to the new higher standard, such as entertainment and computer software, prosper greatly. The rest struggle to hang on to their market share by merging with each other. On average, this consolidation has resulted in the gradual decline in purchasing power for the wage earner discussed in Chapter 2.

The move from the National Finals to the World Business Olympics is much more than simply an enlargement in scope. Capital and most products (and some services) are portable. Labor is less portable. Although the desire of Third World residents to work in the West is substantial, there seems to be no reciprocal desire on the part of North Americans or Western Europeans to relocate to the Third World. Thus, we see textile plants closing in the South, computer help desks closing in Silicon Valley, while downtown Detroit is an urban wasteland.

Even an eventual reversal of the trend toward globalization will not result in a return of American wages to the purchasing power levels of the 1970s. There are two reasons for this. One is that although sentiment for political, and to a greater degree economic, isolation is never very far beneath the surface in America, isolation movements historically generate more noise than widespread support. That freer trade contributes to the prosperity of everyone is accepted as fact in political and economic circles today.

The second reason is that there are many places in the world where wage rates are a lot lower than in the United States and the European Union. Although there have been recent increases in the purchasing power of American wages, a long and continued upward trend in wage rates is very unlikely simply because there are so many places where wages are lower. (See Table 3.1.)

In Western Europe, a general sustained upturn in the purchasing power of wages (except possibly in Britain) is unlikely. Throughout the rest of Europe, persistent unemployment rates exceeding 10 percent almost everywhere will stand in the way of widespread wage increases.

TABLE 3.1   Manufacturing Wages 1996

Index USA = 100	
Belgium	147
Denmark	137
Europe	125
Japan	119
Italy	102
United States	100
Canada	94
Australia	93
United Kingdom	80
Ireland	80
Spain	75
Singapore	47
South Korea	46
Taiwan	33
Mexico	8

Source: Statistical Abstract of the United States 1998 (Washington, DC: U.S. Government Printing Office).

There are no reliable data about the wages in Communist China. However, a visit to your local discount store will turn up silk shirts for $25 and AM/FM portable radios, with headphones (batteries not included), that work quite well for $5, both made in China. It is probably impossible to determine the wages of the people who made these things. Common sense says they can't be very much, perhaps slave level.

To a significant extent, the cause of the decline in income in the United States is irrelevant. Whether the statistics accurately describe reality is somewhat irrelevant, too. For many people the freedom and joy of self-determination and self-expression that they reap from their own business far exceeds the value of even a lot more money from a job.

The remainder of this book is designed to equip you to meet the economic challenges that are the legacy of the economic developments just described.

Entrepreneurial skills will aid you in your job search, should you choose to continue as a wage earner in the unstable job market, because you will be more competent and confident selling yourself. Obviously, the skills you are about to learn also will aid you greatly if you choose to start a side business to augment your current income from wages or to launch your own business full time.

CHAPTER 4

THE EMOTIONAL
DYNAMICS OF CHANGE

Taking responsibility is the first step to personal empowerment. Get yourself ready for change by learning to use the Optimal Learning State and the Five Essential Principles for success. Understand the emotional dynamics of change that we all experience, why change is always at least a little uncomfortable, and why humility and patience are essential when making changes. Change is always scary, producing fear of the unknown. Misperceptions of risk can make you feel trapped. How do you motivate yourself? Even if your answer may be "not very well," you'll discover you don't need more *motivation, but rather different motivation.*

Cause and Effect

In order to truly achieve all the success that you desire, you must take complete responsibility for every result you get. This is a far more attractive proposition than it may seem at first. Look at Figure 4.1.

The expression states that cause is greater than effect. What does this really mean? When living our lives on the effect side of the equation, we are not taking responsibility for our results. We tend to blame others, our environment, and the circumstances around us for the results we achieved. In essence we are giving away our personal power. Conversely, when we live on the cause side of the equation, we accept full responsibility for every result we get. Whether the result was good or bad, we accept that we created that result. This is personal power. Our personal power is taking full responsibility for the results we produce instead of making excuses for what happened.

Empowerment   Victim

Taking Personal
Responsibility
for Every Result
You Get

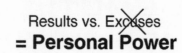

Blaming Others,
Circumstances, or
Your Environment
for Your Current
Results

Results vs. Excuses
= **Personal Power**

FIGURE 4.1   Cause and Effect

Source: Adapted from the work of Tad James, *Advanced Neuro Dynamics, The Accelerated NLP Practitioner Certification Training Manual,* Copyright © 1987–2000, Tad James, & Advanced Neuro Dynamics. *Reprinted by permission.*

If the benefits of taking responsibility for one's life were in short supply, you would expect to see people lined up around the block to get them. Well, there really is no shortage. Whatever your current circumstances, they are the result of goals you established, consciously or unconsciously, in the past. Clearly the circumstances you don't like are the result of unconscious intentions. Responsibility has nothing to do with blame or fault. Blame and fault are best thought of as legal concepts of great importance in courtrooms, but detrimental to successful accomplishment. Responsibility gives us the power to change ourselves, which is all we control anyway. Responsibility promises freedom from the pain that comes from allowing your well-being to depend on factors you do not control. Additionally, responsibility exposes compulsive complainers for the irresponsible people they are.

If you use blame or fault to justify your shortcomings and, in particular, your financial lack, then, by the dynamic and highly cooperative creative power of your mind, you are bound to create more of the same. "Are you telling us that my overdue credit card bills or (the boss who won't give me a raise) or (the stagnant post 9-11 economy) or (my low self-esteem) or (feelings of depression) are my fault?" you may ask. No, these things are not your fault. But by taking responsibility for these conditions, you empower yourself to change how they affect you. Responsibility frees you from the inevitable pain that results from allowing your well-being to be determined by things you do not control. Taking responsibility is not arrogant, either. It won't make you better than people who remain stuck in blame and fault. They can take responsibility, too, if they are willing. But taking responsibility certainly will make you far happier and more resourceful.

People who blame their financial lack on outside circumstances find progress difficult or impossible. If you believe your lack is caused by factors beyond your control—age, sex, upbringing, height, or race—then it could be that you are "right." If you blame your financial lack on past choices you have made, such as your spouse, ex-spouse, weight, or credit card debt, then you may be "right" again. Would you rather be rich, or would you rather be right?

What Does This Mean to You?

It is almost impossible to solve a problem with the same mind-set that created it. For this reason, most effective solutions occur after you shift your thinking. Responsibility is the perspective that you are the creator of events and circumstances. So, in order to improve external events, results, and circumstances, the first step is to change the emotional and psychological dynamics that created them. If you keep thinking the same way, then you will keep getting the same results.

In this book you will be learning a wide variety of methods to change your internal ways of thinking about, feeling about, and perceiving yourself and the world. These methods and tools, used daily, will take you far beyond the momentary jolt a motivational speech provides.

Perhaps you are not completely convinced that you are the cause of the internal and external circumstances in your life. "You guys just don't understand," you might be thinking, "I've got some real problems." We authors know about the real problems. We have seen the lines at the unemployment office and people having their vehicles repossessed.

You already control your results, whether you take responsibility or not. So why not take the position that you are responsible for how things turn out and start shaping your life the way you prefer?

Responsibility is not about blame. Taking responsibility is not necessarily the truth, either. Instead, it is a perspective that empowers us. True winners in life live on the cause side of the equation. They take full responsibility for everything that happens to them. Even if someone cuts them off on the expressway, they take responsibility for that. Winners say they could have been more aware of what was going on around them. They may say that the other driver must be in a hurry because their spouse or child is in the hospital. They believe that they have attracted the situation to them through their thoughts. They do not make excuses and blame the other person for cutting them off. This is true personal power. Which side of the equation do you live on now? Have you ever blamed your environment or circumstances for where you are today? Which side of the equation do you believe is more empowering?

The key to self-empowerment is to move from the effect side of the equation to the cause side to become empowered and produce the results desired. It doesn't matter where you are now. It only matters where you are going. What new actions are you going to take to succeed? Make the commitment now to move yourself over to the cause side of the equation. Living there is much more fulfilling and rewarding. Don't be surprised, though, if your friends and family don't follow you there. Living on the cause side of the equation puts you in the top 10 percent of achievers.

Throughout this book we will show you how to move yourself to the cause side of the equation. Will you take the action necessary to move there? Only you can answer this question. Continue reading, and learn to run your mind in such a way that operating from the cause side of the equation becomes a daily experience, not just an intellectual concept. Take responsibility for everything that happens in your life today. Notice what a difference doing so makes inside you.

How to Reliably Produce Results You Do *Not* Want

Knowing how to create results you do not want is much more useful than it appears at first, because conscious awareness of the process that produces such results enables you to avoid the behaviors that create them. If you have results that you don't like, if you are broke, depressed, and upset, knowing what you do to create this result could be an important step in changing things. Obviously, the strategy described next is *not* a resourceful way to run your mind. It illustrates the unlimited creative power you are using to create and maintain these unpleasant conditions.

Most of us experience periods of lack, depression, and upset. For some, these periods last a few minutes; for others, decades. There is a definite strategy that produces these unfavorable results. This counterproductive strategy is described in general terms, so that you can choose a different course and different results. Gaining awareness of the precise nature of your personal unconscious negative thinking is an extremely valuable resource because you can change what you know about and cannot change what you don't know about.

The strategy for poverty, depression, and upset is easy to remember because each component begins with the letter *p*. In summary, take everything that happens personally and then consider it to be pervasive and permanent.

TAKE IT PERSONALLY

Take everything that happens personally. At the extreme, conclude that everything happens is an indictment of you. Assume that people who reject you have it in for you. See the world and the people in it as hostile or, at least, uncaring. Blame your condition on external circumstances. Blame puts you at effect of external circumstances and renders you helpless. Compare yourself to others frequently and unfavorably. Complain about the people around you to anyone who listens and to some who don't. Rely on this complaining as a temporary respite from misery and as an opportunity to justify unhappiness or lack of accomplishment. Stay with work you don't like and expect the money to make up for the dissatisfaction. Assume it is your responsibility to fix things that are beyond your control, including the feelings of others. Avoid asking for what you want.

CONSIDER IT PERVASIVE

Allow the negative attitude created by taking things personally to pervade other areas of your life. For example, allow setbacks at work to affect your close relationships and allow upsets in your family to detract from your performance at work. Increase the pervasiveness even more by listening to country western music or rap, so that your negative thinking gains rhythm and melody, thus becoming easier to remember. Then seek to reenforce this thinking by associating with like-minded individuals who drain your energy and complain to you about their plight.

Use the words "always" and "never" frequently in your conversation and in your own internal dialogue.

CONSIDER IT PERMANENT

Make all of this permanent by thinking it will never change—or by thinking you are too old to change or you will change after you have more education, a better job, get married, get divorced, have children, move to California, or the children grow up. In your relationships, refuse to give other people what you know they want until you get what you want from them.

These three *p*'s are an excellent strategy to follow *if* you want to become broke, depressed, and upset. Surely all of us engage in the three *p*'s some of the time. Now that you understand the *p*'s you can catch yourself engaging in these behaviors more quickly than before.

Learning More Effectively—The Optimal Learning State

Being a good learner is far more valuable than being a good student. A good student can repeat back on the exam paper what he or she has been taught. A good learner applies lessons in life for maximum benefit. Become the best learner possible before going any further.

The Optimal Learning State increases your awareness of everything that is going on around you while you are learning. This very useful strategy takes advantage of the photographic memory that you may not realize you have. The Optimal Learning State uses both the conscious mind and the unconscious mind. Learning occurs when new information enters the mind through our five senses. Then we contrast and compare the new information to information already stored in the unconscious mind and add the new information. Optimizing your learning state increases the access that your conscious mind has to your unconscious mind. Doing this produces two highly valuable results:

1. Your retention is greatly increased.
2. Your mind naturally absorbs more because your senses are keener.

The conscious mind is the part of your mind that reasons and thinks logically. The unconscious mind is where everything is stored and is the real horsepower. Think of your unconscious mind as your supercomputer. Right now this supercomputer is processing more than a billion instructions every second. Your unconscious mind records everything: what you see, hear, feel, smell, and taste during all your waking moments. The amount of information stored is phenomenal, and we can have access to all of it.

Our minds do not come with instruction manuals at birth. Use the Optimal Learning State each and every time you are ready to learn something new. For example, if you are in school, go into the learning state at the start of each class. When you are working with this book, go into the learning state before you start reading or performing any method. Doing so ensures that you retain and comprehend the material optimally. Your unconscious mind will organize it for easy and effortless retrieval later.

 Take the time and do the method now. Don't put it off!

Entering the Optimal Learning State

Find a comfortable chair. Sit up straight in the chair, and make sure your head and eyes are pointed forward, looking at the wall. Now, pick a spot on the wall about 45 degrees above eye level. Move your eyes only to the spot 45 degrees above the horizontal. Do not tilt your head back. (For most people, 45 degrees above the horizontal is as far up as they can see without moving their head.) Focus on the spot you picked for one to two minutes. Soon you will notice you become more and more aware of your peripheral vision. Continue to stare at the spot until you can see approximately 180 degrees using your peripheral vision. To check this, place your hands at eye level, about one foot from the side of your head. Now, move your hands slowly forward from behind your ears, keeping them a foot from your head. Notice where your hands come into view. The Optimal Learning State increases the range of your peripheral vision and in general raises sensory awareness. When you can see approximately 180 degrees in your peripheral vision, you are in the Optimal Learning State. (See Figure 4.2.)

When I (AF) use the Optimal Learning State, it is much easier for me to remember what I learned. I have even used the Optimal Learning State before driving. To my amazement, I was much more aware of what was going on around me and was able to anticipate

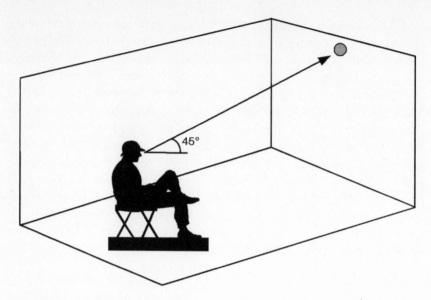

FIGURE 4.2 Optimal Learning State

potential hazards. The awareness of my surroundings made driving much safer for me. I could detect vehicles coming up on the side without having to look in the mirrors or out the windows. This is very useful on busy freeways.

This is also a great technique to teach your kids. Their grades will go up by at least one grade point. I must caution you, though— their teachers may think that they are not paying attention when they are in the learning state. If you get complaints from teachers, just tell them that this is the way your child learns best and everything will be fine.

Four Steps to Mastering Anything

This book does not offer a magical, get-rich-quick solution. Learning the skills to be a wealthy entrepreneur is a process, much like other skills you have already mastered and now take for granted, such as walking, talking, driving, and proper use of knife and fork. No one was born knowing these things.

Understanding the learning process is essential to gaining mastery in any area. If you are not currently earning the income you want from satisfying work, then this is a skill you can master, just as you learned the use of knife and fork.

What actions are required to move from being a rookie to being a master in any area, so that the thinking and actions required to produce the results you desire become automatic and instinctive?

Let's examine the four-step learning diagram in Figure 4.3.

Mastery Level 1 is called Unconscious Incompetence. At this point the individual does not acknowledge that he or she lacks the necessary knowledge. Perhaps many of the people you know are at this point regarding knowledge about creating financial security. They are relying on a job and still believe it to be an adequate pathway to financial security. In some cases they may even vehemently deny the current job situation and almost always strongly rely on hope. Other people may think they know it all and would not consider doing something new until the circumstances become so severe that there is no choice.

Awareness is all that is required to move from Mastery Level 1 to Mastery Level 2. Thus, the awareness that you don't know (referred to as Mastery Level 2, Conscious Incompetence) is a powerful position and the doorway to mastery. At this point you are aware that you don't know yet. If you are reading this book, you have most certainly arrived at Mastery Level 2. Learning the material in this book takes you to Mastery Level 3.

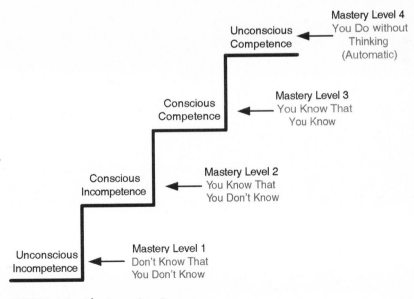

FIGURE 4.3   The Learning Process

Information takes the learner from Mastery Level 2 to Mastery Level 3 (Conscious Competence). Remember driver's education class in school? You learned the rules of the road and the mechanics of operating a car. Most people can remember how nervous they were their first time driving on the road. Back then you needed 100 percent of your attention to operate the car safely. This is Mastery Level 3. You were able to do it, but you needed to use most of your conscious awareness.

Practice takes the learner from Mastery Level 3 to Mastery Level 4 (Unconscious Competence). Continuing with the driving example, after years of driving, most people have so much practice at it that they can (perhaps regrettably) drive and simultaneously eat lunch, talk on the phone, and apply makeup. The skill of driving has been so installed in the unconscious mind that 100 percent of awareness is no longer required to do it. Using the material and methods in this book takes you to Mastery Level 4.

Five Principles for Achieving Success

In order to achieve true success, you must understand the following five key principles. If you are missing any one of them, your chances of success are greatly reduced. All great achievers have used these principles to achieve the outcomes they desired, and so can you, too. The five principles for achieving success are:

1. Know your outcome.
2. Develop sensory acuity.
3. Develop mental and behavioral flexibility.
4. Operate from a physiology and psychology of excellence.
5. Take massive action.

KNOW YOUR OUTCOME

If you don't know what you want, then how will you know whether you have it or not? Because of childhood conditioning, some people have greater awareness of what they don't want and can identify only with difficulty what they do want. We motivate ourselves all the time in two ways: by moving toward pleasure and moving away from pain. If your motivation is based solely on moving away from what you don't want, you tend to be primarily reactive to outside conditions, rather than motivated to take the initiative that would produce your internal desires. Chapter 8 explains how to formulate goals that serve your purpose so you motivate yourself to move toward what you want rather than react to circumstances.

DEVELOP SENSORY ACUITY

Developing sensory acuity means paying attention to what is going on around you. When challenges or obstacles surface, you must be in tune with your senses to determine your next course of action. The obstacles come up not to stop you from achieving success, but to show you that you must think in a different way to move ahead. If you view challenges as learning experiences, rather than getting frustrated and upset by them, you will achieve success much more quickly and easily. Become aware of what people say, how they say it, and of every result you get. They are all clues for you to use.

Notice what you are thinking, saying, and feeling. A simple but effective description of our mind is to say that it consists of two parts, the Thinker and the Prover. The Thinker thinks and the Prover proves whatever the Thinker thinks to be true. Now, the Prover does not care what the Thinker thinks. The Prover will prove positive thoughts just as happily as negative thoughts. The only thing the Prover can do is prove the truth of what the Thinker thinks, and it does just that 24 hours per day, 7 days per week, as reliably as gravity. Keep in mind that whatever you say comes out of your mouth and into your ear. The Thinker hears it, and the Prover immediately goes to work proving it to be true.

By using the skills in Chapter 13, you will be able to interpret what people actually mean by their communication and will learn how to design your own communication to make rapid connections with others.

DEVELOP MENTAL AND BEHAVIORAL FLEXIBILITY

When you notice that things are not going the way you intended, you must have the behavioral flexibility to achieve your outcome. Behavioral flexibility is all about changing what you are doing currently to produce a different result. Some people think that by doing the same thing over and over again they will produce different results. This is one definition of insanity. To achieve different results, you must change your strategy and behaviors to produce the results you desire. You are about to learn a method that will build a "moving-toward" motivation into your neurology and take you beyond survival to peak performance and contribution.

Physiology and Psychology of Excellence

To achieve our desired results, we must run our minds and bodies in a peak state. If you are depressed or lethargic, you will not achieve your goals unless, of course, your goals are minuscule. Your goals should be big and worth pursuing. Since your goals are big, you must be in a peak mental and physical state in order to produce the desired results.

Thomas Edison was a person who knew and used the five principles for achieving success. Known as the Wizard of Menlo Park, he set the record with 1,300 patents registered in his name. He was an entrepreneur. While in his 20s, he set up a laboratory employing 50 engineers. His best-known inventions include the phonograph, an automatic telegraphy machine, the stock ticker machine, the kinetoscope motion picture machine, and the incandescent light bulb, all of which owed their success to his work in the storage and transfer of electricity.

The invention of the light bulb was definitely Edison's greatest achievement. It also had the most obstacles to overcome. Edison made over 10,000 attempts to invent the light bulb before he succeeded. Can you imagine doing anything over 10,000 times to produce the desired result? Most people would have given up long before, but not Edison. After Edison completed his 9,999th attempt to invent the light bulb, a reporter asked him if he was going to try again and possibly fail a 10,000th time. Edison replied, "Son, I have not failed. I have figured out 9,999 ways not to invent the light bulb." He used his failures as feedback to learn from. He used laser-sharp focus and was always positive.

Edison was very clear on the outcomes he wanted to achieve. He took constant massive action to achieve his outcomes; otherwise he never would have won 1,300 patents and changed the world. Edison had great sensory acuity, always observing what his results were. No matter what they were, he recorded them in his journal for future use. Then he used his behavioral flexibility to make the changes necessary. He kept changing until he achieved the outcome he desired. And last, he operated from a physiology and psychology of excellence. If he didn't, he would have given up long before he ever achieved his greatest success, the light bulb. Imagine what life would be like had he given up. How different would your world be if you use these principles as Thomas Edison did?

THE STATE OF EXCELLENCE

Figure 4.4 locates the state of excellence.

The left side, or bottom 10 percent, is where the losers of the world live. They expect handouts and are not willing to do anything for themselves. They expect that everything should be given to them just because they exist. The middle section, or middle 80 percent is where most people are—the middle of the road, just existing but not feeling satisfied. On the far right side, or top 10 percent, is where the winners of the world live. They always strive to achieve at the 100 percent level. They believe, "If it's going to be, it's up to me." They do not look for handouts or charity. They work hard and strive to be the best. They continually improve themselves in order to achieve what they desire in life. This attitude is the difference between the winners and the whiners, the champs and the chumps. Ask yourself where you live on this graph. More important, ask yourself where do want to place yourself. Since you are reading this book, you are already on your way to the state of excellence. But remember, simply reading this book will do you no good unless you take massive action.

We can achieve the state of excellence through either physiology or psychology. Let's start with physiology. The state of excellence through physiology is how you sit, how you stand, how you breathe, how you hold your head, and where you focus your eyes.

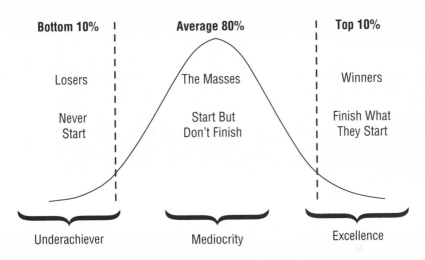

FIGURE 4.4 State of Excellence

We can produce the state of excellence anytime we wish. We are in control of our bodies and, therefore, our state.

For example, say you are about to enter an important meeting or you have an important phone call to make. You're feeling anxious and upset or maybe even depressed. You already know how to produce this state. Let's go through this method consciously so you can see what you do now to produce this nonresourceful state. Then later, you'll see how to change it.

PHYSIOLOGY OF EXCELLENCE METHOD

R℞   Do the following method now. Do not skip ahead until you understand what you are doing now.

Find a comfortable place to sit. Find a chair that does not recline. Just relax and take a few deep breaths. Now, slump your shoulders and body forward. Hold your head down and look at the floor. Breathe hard and sigh several times. How do you feel? Probably not so well right now. Maybe you're even a bit depressed. You're probably thinking: "That's great; now you've got me all depressed. Thanks a lot." This state is a result of what you are doing with your body. Become consciously aware of how you use your body and how you feel. This is part of sensory acuity.

Enough of that state. Now let's adopt the physiology of excellence. Sit up straight in your chair. Put your shoulders all the way back and hold your head up. Look up toward the ceiling, smile and take a deep breath. Now, how did that feel? You probably are feeling much more resourceful and ready to take action. Did you experience both states? Which state did you prefer? Remember, you can change your internal state of being at any time by changing your physiology. From here on, use your physiology to be in a peak state. Imagine how much better life will be when you feel good all the time.

R℞   Let's do one more method to help you understand the importance of using your physiology. First, stand up straight with your shoulders back. Now look up at the ceiling, tilting your head all the way back. Stare at the ceiling. Now try to be depressed. What did you experience? Most people will start to smile or even laugh. Did that happen to you? In this state, it is impossible to become depressed.

You have experienced how you can change your state instantly through your physiology. Which state felt more resourceful to you? Which state do you believe will produce better results for you? Use your physiology to produce the state that will assist you in achieving the outcomes you desire and deserve.

Take Massive Action

It's great to have goals. However, if you do not take action to achieve them, they are merely dreams. So action is an integral part of your success. We authors like to use the phrase "massive action," which is eloquently promoted by author and trainer, Tony Robbins. It means doing more than is required and getting rid of the mentality of just doing enough to get by. Massive action means being focused and continually taking action no matter what happens. Challenges and obstacles always will get in your way. Use them as learning experiences. Thus, there is no failure except failure to learn. Many people give up just before they achieve success. Then someone else goes a little further and gets the rewards. That is why you must continually take massive action to achieve the success you desire.

Herein lies the importance of loving the work you do. Massive action will feel like drudgery if you don't like your work or barely tolerate it. For people who love their work, massive action is a delightful challenge.

This book stresses the importance of goals repeatedly for good reason. As soon as you commit to a goal that will make you stretch, two very important things happen to facilitate your accomplishment of that goal.

1. Your mind begins to attract to you and also causes you to notice the resources required for accomplishment.
2. Your mind promptly brings to your attention the thoughts it has been thinking in the past that will prevent you from achieving your goal.

Let's say you are accustomed to earning $7,500 per month and, as a result of reading this book, you decide you can do better for yourself and your family, so you commit to your new goal of earning $12,000 per month within 18 months. As soon as you do this, your mind will report to you those thoughts that stand in the way of accomplishing this goal. For example, you may hear your mind saying, "My parents told me to take what I was given and not ask for more" or "What do I need this for? I will only have twice as many worries." This is highly valuable information. Your mind is reporting to you what it has thought in the past that needs to be changed so you can accomplish this goal. Just because limiting thoughts like these spontaneously bubble up in response to your new goal does not mean that you cannot accomplish it. Instead, realize that your mind is simply doing its job and reporting to you the thoughts you must change to accomplish your goal.

Changing Your Motivation—From Inconsistent to Unstoppable

The human nervous system is wired to motivate us at a very basic level: to move toward pleasure and away from pain. Your nervous system is already doing this 24 hours per day, whether you think about it or not. Such motivation comes without effort or intention. Imagine if you use this essential unconscious motivation to obtain and achieve your consciously intended goals.

The moving-toward and moving-away motivation are instinctive and unconscious. You don't have to do anything to get them. Thus, everyone can use these motivations. You will be using motivation that circumvents the conscious mind and its intellectual, sometimes conflicting, messages. You won't need willpower anymore, nor will you have to talk yourself into doing the things you don't want to. Even animals use such motivation. Next, you'll be learning to use your natural instinctive resources to move yourself toward whatever you desire. This way of motivating ourselves originates in our unconscious mind, the same source of commands that causes our heart to beat 100,000 times per day, reliably, day after day without thinking about it.

The other day I (PL) watched a squirrel in my backyard. It spotted an acorn and bounded toward it (moving-toward-pleasure motivation). Before it got to the acorn, it spotted the neighborhood cat lurking behind a fence. Immediately it changed direction and scurried up the nearby oak tree (moving-away-from-pain motivation). We humans possess these same resources to motivate ourselves.

LIMITATIONS OF RELYING SOLELY ON MOVING AWAY MOTIVATION

We all use moving-away motivation. It helps us avoid danger, unpleasant people, and a wide variety of things that are not good for us. But the moving-away motivation has some very serious limitations. It ensures survival—you run much faster when a bear is chasing you than when you chase a bear—but you desire far more from life than mere survival. To be a peak performer, a person who makes a contribution to the world based on his or her personal values must use moving-toward motivation.

If you are motivated only by the bear chasing you, then once you have evaded the bear (perhaps it got tired or found something else easier to catch), your motivation is gone, so you slow down. For most people, this reliance on moving-away motivation represents the underlying cause of inconsistency. If you experience roller-coaster finances or are just getting by, some introspection may reveal that these ups and downs are caused by relying primarily on moving-away motivation. In extreme cases, relying on this motivation produces behavior that avoids any sort of action that would improve your situation until things become unmanageable. People familiar with 12-step programs call this concept "hitting bottom." Most addictions are the result of moving-away motivation. The addictive substance moves addicts away from pain, causing them to accept the obvious painful side effects, which are at least temporarily less painful than the pain they are trying to suppress with the addictive substance. When the pain from the side effects gets bad enough, addicts become willing to give up their addiction, exactly when things get bad enough in an individual decision. Some people never make it.

Some people began relying on moving-away-from-pain motivation in childhood as a way to escape abusive situations at home. In some cases reliance on this motivation was reinforced by punitive educational systems, where the intensity of pain associated with punishment for mistakes and infractions was far higher than the intensity of pleasure associated with rewards for excellence and achievement.

Moving-away motivation requires an external crisis, or at least impending danger, to produce action. For this reason, the action that results typically lacks the consistency required to produce excellent results. Once the external crisis or danger has passed, the motivation to act disappears. By comparison, moving-toward motivation produces the consistent behavior required for excellence, because it is generated from internal desires, which you control.

EMOTIONAL MOTIVATION STRATEGY

Change requires conscious intention and purpose-driven mental energy. For example, if you drive to work every day on the same route, you don't need to think about it anymore. You can get into your car in the morning and daydream about your upcoming vacation all the way to work and you will get there with very little conscious effort. You have imprinted the usual route into your neurology by the many times you have used it in the past. If you decide to use a different route, this will require greater conscious effort—at least until *it* is imprinted into your neurology.

How do you really motivate yourself at the emotional level? Do you let your emotional dynamics stop you from achieving success? You can change your programming by changing your way of motivating yourself.

There are two sources of motivation: external motivation and self-motivation. External moving-toward motivation occurs, for example, when you listen to a motivational speaker; you might get the idea that you'd be better off with *more* motivation. Unfortunately, the boost from such talks usually lasts until you get to the parking lot. Such an experience leads us to conclude that more motivation is not the answer; *different* motivation is.

External moving-away motivation occurs when your boss tells you to produce better results or you will be dismissed. Threats based on moving-away motivation tend to produce temporary improvements, which is why the threats must be repeated in order to be effective.

Relying on motivation that moves you away from pain can produce good results for people working in organizations. The hierarchical structure ensures everyone has a boss to set standards and enforce rules. Military organizations provide the most graphic example of the use of moving-away motivation. This management style is appropriate for the situation, which requires that people follow orders, even under combat conditions, where survival instinct would normally act toward self-preservation rather than following orders that conflict with it.

I (PL) had the honor and privilege to serve as commanding officer of two Coast Guard patrol boats, one on Cape Cod and the other in Vietnam. Traditionally, the captain has ultimate responsibility for everything that happens on the ship and therefore is granted considerable latitude in exercising this responsibility. The reward and punishment system in the Coast Guard relies primarily on moving-away motivation. People have been going to sea for centuries, resulting in unwritten rules that often are stronger than the written ones. These unwritten rules say that the three mistakes the captain must avoid are collision at sea, running aground, and disorder of the money allotted for the crew's mess. Any of these mistakes usually results in severe punishment, most likely court-martial.

In contrast, rewards for stellar performance are far less than the potential intensity of court-martial and consist primarily of congratulatory letters in your service jacket and brightly colored ribbons to wear on your chest.

Now, a moving-away-from-pain motivation system such as this tends to work satisfactorily in the military or a large corporate organization, where there are lots of authority figures to enforce the rules. However, for entrepreneurs, there is little outside authority. Thus, it is essential for you to play baseball to develop internally generated motivation that moves you consistently toward pleasurable goals.

Self-motivation is when you are motivated without any outside influence or stimulation. It occurs when you are emotionally attached to achieving a goal—for example, going on vacation. That is self-motivation. So how can you become self-motivated to accomplish tasks you are not as emotionally attached to?

Here is how I (PL) changed my way of self-motivation. When I first became interested in the possibility of improving my motivation, I listened to pep talks by several motivational speakers. Although I felt pumped up and inspired during and shortly after their presentations, there was no permanent effect. This experience showed me that *more* motivation was not the answer. I began to explore the possibility of *different* motivation.

First, I realized that it would be important for me to understand how I had been motivating myself. I reviewed how I had motivated myself to complete projects that had been successful in the past as well as some that were not. Many people have since told me that their own motivation strategy is similar to what I had originally used.

I'll describe first my original unconsciously developed motivation strategy and then the new one I now use.

When I got started on any new goal, I was excited and began moving forward. Soon after the fear of failure set in, but somehow I got over that. Then after a little while I bumped into obstacles and got frustrated and angry. Still, somehow I got through them. Next, as I continued to move forward, lots of distractions appeared. Somehow I moved past those. Then a combination of fear of success and the concern that the results would not be as good as I originally thought came to my awareness. Yet somehow I got over them and completed the project. I've charted this original motivation strategy in Figure 4.5.

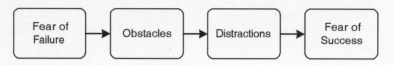

FIGURE 4.5   Old Motivation Strategy

Perhaps you have the same or a similar motivation strategy. Although this way of motivation worked, I wanted a better, easier way.

BASEBALL DIAMOND METHOD

Do this now! Don't put it off. You'll be surprised how quickly things change. Use this method to regroove your neurology. The actual movement of walking in the method is very important, because motivation is a physical, rather than intellectual, experience. If you simply read about this method, you will gain about what you paid for the book. Getting up and actually doing it produces results worth thousands of times greater. By mentally and physically moving yourself through the phases of accomplishment and instilling these new motivation factors, you will notice that your behavior related to goals will shift rapidly.

Take four blank sheets of paper. Write the word(s) PATIENCE on the first, OK on the second, FOCUS ON INTERNAL DESIRE on the third, and APPRECIATE THE RESULTS on the last. Place these sheets of paper on the floor, in the corners of the largest room in your house, as shown in Figure 4.6.

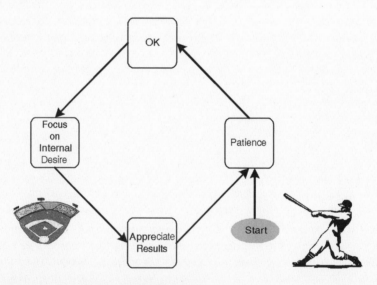

FIGURE 4.6   Developing Self-Motivation

Imagine the sheets of paper are a baseball diamond and you are going around the bases. Now think of a goal that you want to achieve. See yourself working on your goal through your own eyes. See the pictures, hear the sounds, and feel the feelings associated with achieving your goal.

Now move through your mental image of achieving your goal. It is only natural that you experience some fear of failure. If you don't, then either your goal is trivial or you are denying your feelings. Consider a larger goal that offers a bigger challenge or slow down so you can focus your awareness more carefully on your current feelings, whichever is appropriate. Now stand on first base (PATIENCE). Notice that the goal is not accomplished yet. While you are there, be patient. Really experience being patient and relax. Allow patience to pervade every part of your consciousness and all the cells in your body.

Once you have done that, move forward in your mind again to achieving your goal. Physically walk to second base (OK). Allow yourself to notice any obstacles that could stop or slow your progress toward your goal. On second base, just imagine that everything is OK. No matter what happened or what obstacles have come up, let all of them be OK. You see, OK is the most resourceful reaction you can have to any obstacle. It is more resourceful than fighting with obstacles, denying they exist, wishing they would go away, or engaging in nonproductive thinking that typically begins with the phrase "If only. . . ." These nonproductive reactions assign the power to the obstacle and take power away from you. On second base, allow the experience of OK to pervade every part of your consciousness and all the cells in your body.

Start moving forward again toward achieving your goal. Walk to third base (FOCUS ON INTERNAL DESIRE). It is only natural for distractions to come to awareness as you progress toward any goal. The football game on TV, the person who interrupts you, or the pie in the refrigerator can prevent your accomplishment if you allow them to. Fighting with these distractions or using willpower to overcome them can consume more energy than productive work toward your goal. Instead, return your awareness to your original desire—why did you want this goal in the first place? On third base, focus on the internal desires you have about achieving your goal. Make sure to enhance the image of your goal now by changing the details of your image. Make sure your image is large, bright, and colorful, and don't forget to add sounds, feelings, smells, and tastes. Let yourself enjoy the image you have now when your goal is achieved.

Move forward again. Stand on home plate (APPRECIATE THE RESULTS). Once there, appreciate what you have achieved already. Look back at the progress you have made and notice how far you have come. Now really appreciate all that you have gained in the process, no matter how large or small. It is appreciation that continues to move you forward in achieving the success you deserve and desire.

In a real baseball game, after you run around the bases, you must sit down for a while and wait your next time at bat. Not so here. In this game you can go around the bases again right away, if you don't yet feel the passion you want after your first circuit.

How do you feel now? Do you feel more motivated to achieve your goal? Are you emotionally involved in attaining it? Can you truly appreciate where you will be when you achieve your goal? Now keep going. Don't stop here.

What We Control

The impossible struggle to control those things we have no control over represents a significant waste of energy. Therefore, a brief discussion about the things that we do control seems in order, even if it is elementary for some.

We control our major body movements: walking, writing, and the like. Minor body movements such as blinking, digestion, and perspiration are beyond our control. We control our thoughts. Regardless of the situation, we have the freedom to think whatever we like. An offensive person may be behaving badly to make you upset; or she could just have learned that her husband has a terminal disease. Not only may you never know the cause of the offensive behavior, you are completely free to come to any conclusion about its cause. Even in the midst of your worst obsessive thinking, you can catch yourself doing it and *decide* to think about something different.

We control what we put into our mouths. Judging by the number of diet books for sale, the exercise of this choice troubles many people. We control what comes out of our mouths (and what does not). This means we are responsible for what we say and for keeping our word. Errors of omission matter, also. We are responsible for the times that we neglected to speak up to ask for what we want, failed to point out injustice, or failed to say no when we would have been better off doing so.

We also control how we interpret our feelings. We don't control the feelings themselves, because they are stored and generated by our unconscious mind. That we feel sad related to loss, afraid related to danger, and angry related to unfulfilled expectations is part of the human condition. However, each of us has a personal choice about how we interpret the energy of feelings and then, based on that interpretation, how we respond.

Although it appears that many humans would wish it different, we have no control over the behavior of others, the desires of others, or the weather, just to name a few things we complain about the most.

Our State of Being and How We Can Change It

Our state of being (or state, for short) relates to how we feel or our internal condition. It refers to our way of being in the moment or mood. For example, we can be in a happy state, sad state, motivated state, or depressed state. There are positive and negative states. Our state determines every result we get. The results we achieve depend on which state we focus on. We also can change our state anytime we want. Each of us is in total control of our state, whether we know it consciously or not. Think about these questions: Who is in control of your thoughts? Who is in control of how you feel? Who is in control of your behaviors? Do you allow someone else to control your thoughts, feelings, and behaviors? Who is at the controls? Who is flying your airplane anyway?

If you are not in control of your thoughts, feelings, and behaviors, then who is? Viktor Frankl, who wrote a book entitled *Man's Search for Meaning*, sums this question up nicely. Frankl was a Jewish psychiatrist put into a German concentration camp during World War II. He noticed that most of his comrades gave up hope and died. Frankl chose to hold on to his dream of being free once more and to be able to tell others about this atrocity so that it could never happen again. He was freed after many years of suffering and physical torture. The empowered state he chose kept him alive. He made a decision to live to tell his story to others. This commitment kept him in an empowered state throughout his ordeal. He lived on the cause side of the equation and took full responsibility for every result he got. He took control of his thoughts, feelings, and behaviors in appalling conditions and lived to tell the tale; others who blamed their environment died.

I (AF) had a client named Joe who lived on the effect side of the equation. Joe was a writer and had difficulty writing a manuscript. For eight months he had an extreme case of writer's block. He blamed the economy, the people around him, and his roommate for his lack of achievement. Joe felt absolutely miserable. He was in a downward spiral. The longer he didn't write, the worse he felt. Any sort of productive action was impossible in his depressed state. After I explained to him that living on the effect side of the equation was nothing more than living in excuses, he took notice. When he realized that he was in charge of how he felt and that what he thought about was up to him, he felt empowered. Joe dwelled on this concept for a few days and completely changed his actions. He placed himself in an excited and motivated state and took control of his destiny. In the next three weeks Joe produced two first draft manuscripts and had ideas for a third. He was now flying his own plane.

Why is taking responsibility so important? In order to succeed, we must live on the cause side of the equation and take responsibility for our state. When you changed your state through physiology, you may have noticed that you had control of your state. You also may have noticed that you can change your state at will in seconds. It is completely up to you. Right now, you may be generating your state unconsciously.

Our Internal Sensory Representations

In the physiology of excellence method, you learned that physiology determines your state of being and how to get and keep yourself in a state of excellence. Figure 4.7 takes this idea a step further and shows that our state is determined not only by our physiology but also by what we focus on mentally. The box labeled "Internal Sensory Representation" refers to your internal mental reality, not just your abstract thoughts. As mentioned, our minds function, respond to, and react to information delivered to them by the five senses: seeing, hearing, feeling, tasting, and smelling. Additionally, we store and process information using these senses. Different people rely on one sense or another more so than other people. If someone asked you to describe your experience in third grade, you probably would describe your visual memory of the room, furniture, and occupants, your auditory memory of the teacher's voice and other sounds, the feeling or kinesthetic memory of what the chair felt like, and perhaps the smell of the room on a winter day as everyone's woolen coats dried out; perhaps you could even remember some tastes from the third grade. Thus, your memory of the third grade is represented to you by your senses. Now all you have left are these internal sensory representations.

Figure 4.7 presents a great deal of important information in a small area. Study this information and how it relates to you. The three boxes at the left refer to your *internal* reality—how your body feels and what is happening in your mind. The vertical dashed line

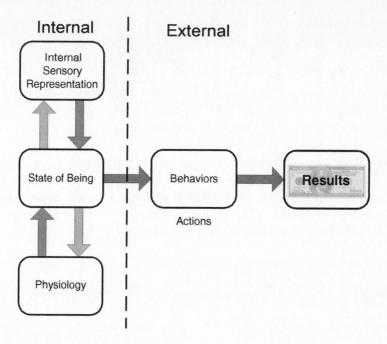

FIGURE 4.7   Producing Your Results

Source: Adapted from the work of Tad James and David Shepard, *Presenting Magically, Transforming Your Stage Presence with NLP,* Copyright © 2001. *Reprinted by permission.*

indicates the boundary between your internal and your external reality. The diagram takes into account that your mind and body are part of the same system. Change your body and your mind changes, and vice versa. The two right-hand boxes refer to your *external* reality. We have direct control of our internal reality and no direct control of external reality, particularly the behavior and opinions of other people.

The arrows on the diagram indicate the direction of causation, so you can see what is cause and what is effect.

Direct your attention to the vertical arrows at the left. Notice that there are both darkly and lightly tinted arrows, pointing in opposite directions. What does this mean?

A two-way relationship exists between our state of being and our physiology and thinking. When our internal state is sufficiently intense, it takes control. The lightly tinted arrows represent this situation. In these instances, our state of being controls thinking and physiology without conscious intention. Whether this is a bad thing or not depends on the results produced. If all of your behavior is consciously intended, you will have a life devoid of spontaneity. In order to appreciate humor or sex, for example, you must let go of conscious intention and allow instinct to control your physiology and thinking. All of us have heard stories of mothers lifting cars to free a child trapped underneath. These mothers could not have accomplished such feats through conscious intention.

However, if you allow your state of being or mood to govern your entire behavior, you are likely to experience inconsistent accomplishment and even meaningless indulgence of your latest whim. Allowing your state to control your internal reality is the source of bad habits. Rage-aholics, for example, experience such an intense emotional state of rage that, at least temporarily, it controls their thinking and physiology, producing behavior that they later deeply regret or struggle to justify.

Allowing an unchosen, intense state of being to control your physiology and thinking may be appropriate in some instances. People who do so consistently, however, often become depressed, behave like a rage-aholic, or do not accomplish much.

When you were a child in school, at times you probably felt depressed, anxious, or upset when an assignment or a work project was due. This unresourceful state served as a distraction from the work at hand and encouraged you to do just enough to get by to complete the project. You may have felt relief that it was over, but you knew that it was not your best work. You knew that you could have done much better. What could you have done differently? How could you have changed your state right then to produce results you would have been proud of?

Consciously choosing your internal state of being by choosing particular physiology and particular thinking to provide yourself with the most resourceful state possible moves you ahead in a natural way. No willpower is required here. Why struggle to control your external reality from a less than resourceful state, when you can control it far more easily by moving to a state that is most resourceful? Earlier in this chapter you learned how to use physiology to bring yourself to a resourceful state. Chapter 8 will teach you how to do so using your mind.

The Power of Our Perceptions

Our perceptions are our own reality. Thus, reality is different for everyone. We see the world not as it is, but as *we* are. Our reality may not be the truth. Our filters and past experiences make us think and believe that our perception is the truth. Have you ever seen a movie of a crime investigation? The detective talks to numerous people who saw the same incident, yet they all have different stories. The detective puts together the various perceptions to gain the truth of the incident. There are never two stories exactly alike.

Because we all perceive things differently, each of us has different experiences even if we are experiencing the same event. We filter information selectively and differently from each other. That's what makes us all different and why we experience things differently. We each uniquely code the experiences that pass into our brains. These codings are the internal sensory representations mentioned earlier.

Why are perceptions or internal sensory representations important to us? Our perceptions determine our state. We can be in a state of depression or a state of excellence. How we filter information determines how we represent each experience and therefore our state. Our state determines how we feel about the experience. Think back on how you were affected through the physiology method. How did that affect your state?

To illustrate this point, refer to Figure 4.8. It shows that 2 million bits or pieces of information (2 million bits per second) are coming into our minds every second. This information comes in from our five senses. Each experience we have uses all five senses.

After the information comes into our minds, it gets filtered. The

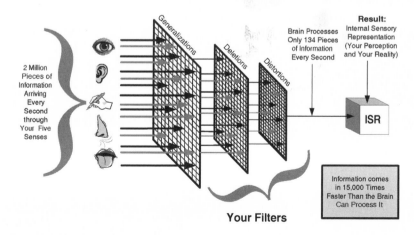

FIGURE 4.8   Your Mind in Action

filtering generalizes, deletes, and distorts the information because the brain can process only 134 bits of information per second. Information comes into our minds 15,000 times faster than our brains can process it. If we did not filter our experiences by generalizing, deleting, or distorting our experiences, we would go insane.

Consider, for example, how difficult it might be to focus on work if your brain did not automatically delete your memory of each car you saw on the way to work. Some of the filters you currently have serve you, and others may not.

Awareness of your own generalizations, distortions, and deletions provides the power to take control of your mind.

GENERALIZATIONS

Pay attention to your internal self-talk. Phrases and sentences that contain the word "never" or "always" are surely generalizations. Racial prejudice is an area where generalizations produce harmful results for many people. We authors believe that white people, black people, yellow people and red people are mostly the same, at least in the internal qualities that matter most. Some of them are delightful individuals, and some of them are jerks. However, such a judgment can be made only after getting to know them a little. The appearance of the external few millimeters of a person's body does nothing to determine his or her inner qualities. Do you find your mind making generalizations based on irrelevant information?

DELETIONS

Our minds tend to ignore or minimize the importance of information it has been conditioned to consider irrelevant. Almost everyone has had an experience like this. You purchase a make of automobile that you have never owned before. All of a sudden there seem to be three to five times as many cars of that kind on the road than you ever noticed. Actually, the number of cars on the road of your make has increased by only one. Your mind deleted as unimportant your past sightings of such cars.

DISTORTIONS

The most damaging distortions stem from denial or avoiding the truth, usually for the purpose of being right. The major financial distortion in the developed West today stems from the belief that a good job is the foundation of long-term financial security. If you have always had a job, your mind may be uncomfortable considering the risks of a job—of having all of your eggs in one basket. With a job you could lose 100 percent of your income at any time. Without a plan and without entrepreneurial skills, job loss is emotionally and financially devastating. This book is dedicated to eliminating the job distortion from your mind.

Addictions and Prosperity

There is nothing so expensive as a bad habit. The trouble with addictions is that they take over your life—sooner or later your life's purpose becomes the maintenance of the addiction. Moneymaking efforts, relationships, and, most of all, self-respect are sacrificed to the addiction without a second thought. Bad habits cost the victim twice. This is because an impenetrable curtain of denial prevents addicts from seeing the truth about their addiction and its resulting devastation.

The trouble with an addiction is that it provides only temporary relief from those feelings we are unwilling to acknowledge. At first the addiction suppresses uncomfortable feelings, but as a tolerance is built up, eventually the feelings we were trying to avoid return stronger than before.

Addictions are caused by a perceived lack of power. After a while, they result in a specific lack of power over the addictive substance or activity. If you had the power to quit, you would have done so already, right?

Since the power addicts lack comes neither from inside them nor from other people, classical therapy methods are less than effective in treating addictions. Because addictions are caused neither by low self-esteem nor by an abusive childhood, popular psychology is less than useful for dealing with them. You can save time, money, and misery by phoning the local 12-step program for help in dealing with any addictions you may have.

An essential element of making any change is the acknowledgment that your current situation could be improved. Room for improvement is the largest room in the world. If you are unwilling to recognize this, you will think that the desire for improvement only means that there is something wrong. Such perfectionism can keep you miserable. People with this way of thinking don't make changes until the situation becomes agony. In the next chapter you will learn to accept things as they are (which is actually empowering) and seek improvement rather than perfection.

THREE INGREDIENTS TO EFFECTIVE CHANGE: AWARENESS, ACCEPTANCE, AND ACTION

Change is inevitable. The question is, are you making the changes you want, or does change happen to you? Learn to use awareness, acceptance, and action so that changes are both favorable and the ones you choose. You will learn from the examples of people who effectively used these ingredients.

Structure of Your Mind

To put it simply, the mind is divided into two parts, the conscious and the unconscious. The conscious mind contains the thoughts you are aware of, and the unconscious mind contains those you are not aware of.

Right now your conscious mind is focused on the words on this page. But your unconscious mind is busy, too, taking the shapes of the letters that you see and translating them into what they mean. You programmed your unconscious mind to do this during the process of learning to read. As you can see, the unconscious mind is a great convenience. Without it, you would have to consciously think about the definition of thousands of words all the time. But your unconscious mind makes it possible to just think about the definition once or twice, until you learn it, and then store it away until that particular word appears.

The unconscious mind is divided into two parts. One part is, in fact, accessible. The accessible part of your unconscious mind contains the definitions of words that are *not* on this page and much more. Additionally, the accessible part of your unconscious mind contains some thoughts that you unintentionally repress because of denial, arrogance, or unresolved past trauma. We are not picking on you here. All of us repress information in our unconscious mind. Everyone has experienced "ah-ha" moments, where the unconscious cause of some past event becomes suddenly crystal clear. "Ah-ha," you say, "Now I understand why that happened.

Our fear of being upset by its insane contents may be why the temporarily inaccessible portion remains so. Increased awareness is quite likely to put you in touch with more parts of yourself. Some of these parts will be previously unnoticed resources and qualities that you are delighted to have. Others you may not like very much. Awareness eliminates denial.

The permanently inaccessible portion of the unconscious mind is the part that controls autonomic functions, such as breathing, digestion, and perspiration.

Awareness

It is virtually impossible to change what you don't know about. For example, at the outset of consultations with us, many clients are unaware that their fear of earning an income greater than that of their parents limited their moneymaking activities. Their pattern of income and net worth ostensibly looked like a roller coaster. There are usually valid reasons for each descent. These valid reasons block awareness of the underlying fear of exceeding their parents' income.

It does not take a great deal of awareness to see how your financial life is affected by your thinking. The decisions you have made and those you haven't, along with your attitudes, persistence, consistency, and emotions about money, all originate in your mind. Just as you can find your way around the darkest room with just one candle, a bit of willingness to give up denial serves to open a path for you to recognize the unconscious psychological dynamics that act to limit your success.

Sean sells high-ticket business services to people looking for franchise opportunities. Even though each completed business transaction provides him a commission of $15,000 to $20,000, his business had limped along, producing an income that left him scrambling to pay the bills.

I (PL) asked him about the promotional activities in his business. From his response, it was quite evident that, although he was doing some things very well, he was compulsively avoiding use of the telephone. I suggested that he was suffering from phone phobia and offered to aid him in changing this. He responded with a lengthy, well-reasoned denial about the phone phobia, including his assertion that the phone was not important, that he would be disturbing people, that there are better ways to contact people, how he sometimes intended to make calls but then got too busy to do so, and concluding with his hope that his business would turn around soon. I asked him to consider the possibility that he had created well-reasoned denial to avoid the uncomfortable awareness of his phone phobia.

He acknowledged that his hope for a business turn-around was not a feasible plan and that he was willing to change his perceptions about the phone from dread and avoidance to excitement. In subsequent sessions, I taught him to change his perceptions about using the phone with the methods presented in Chapters 8 and 9. Within a few weeks he reported that he actually felt enthusiastic about using the phone. Soon his monthly income equaled his previous yearly income.

At the outset, Sean had only a glimmer of awareness that phone phobia was his major obstacle. Perfect clarity of awareness is not necessary here. He did have enough awareness to see the possibility that phone phobia was the issue and the willingness to work on this.

Acceptance

Acceptance of anything doesn't mean you like it, it doesn't mean you would consciously choose it, it doesn't mean you would order it in a restaurant. It just means it is OK. The alternative to acceptance is condemning it and then trying to change it from that position of condemnation. The primary disadvantage of such condemnation is that your mind's desire to be right creates situations to justify your condemnation. Additionally, such condemnation wastes energy.

Perhaps a good way to describe what we mean by acceptance is to describe some examples of lack of acceptance. If you do not accept yourself as you are, you may tend to gain temporary self-acceptance by destructive means such as addictions, people pleasing, workaholism, or trying to control things over which you have no control.

You may know some people with a very high degree of awareness about how their thinking, attitudes, and personal history affect them, but who allow themselves to be victimized by their past so that each setback or disaster serves only to confirm their thinking that they are hopeless. (This may be an exaggeration, but we are doing it to make the point.)

If you do not accept your feelings, you tend to allow your fears, past resentments, or guilt feelings to hold you back from your desires. Feelings are energy. Feelings are your passion. Your body naturally provides you with this energy to deal with the challenges you face.

Acceptance includes accepting responsibility—responsibility for your income, success, and satisfaction, without reliance on outside sources. Responsibility is not about blame. Accepting responsibility empowers you to change. The acceptance of situations that are intolerable empowers you to change them, if in no other way than removing yourself. Fighting against them and struggling to change others usually is fruitless. Instead, accept them as they are, recognize that it is unlikely that they will change, and move on.

Acceptance does not mean you don't care. It means that you acknowledge that there are things you cannot change. From acceptance you can exercise preference.

Disapproval and desire for revenge are perhaps the two most important psychological factors that stand in the way of acceptance. If you did something your parents didn't like, they disapproved. Expressing this disapproval became a convenient way for them to motivate you not to do it anymore. Some people fear that if they accept themselves and stop disapproving of themselves, they will have no motivation whatsoever. Motivation comes naturally from a person's values. Everyone is naturally motivated to express those values, whether the values are consciously chosen or unconsciously adopted due to past conditioning. Do not worry that you will have no motivation if you accept yourself.

Wanting revenge for past hurts and upsets also holds people back. If you had abusive childhood or adult relationships, likely you still experience a degree of justified resentment about the events or the people involved. Unconscious failing to get even is a common example of this. In the failing to get even syndrome, a person fails as an adult in order to unconsciously keep himself in a position where his parents must continue to support him or else feel guilty for not doing so. Unfortunately, this resentment can be carried for decades, not only robbing people of enjoyment of life but also preventing them from achieving their desires.

Forgiveness is the path out of the lack caused by resentment. Forgiveness means giving up the right to administer punishment—whether the punishment is directed toward yourself or toward another person. Forgiveness frees you from the grasp of the resentment, which keeps you dragging along the unpleasant aspects of your past in your current life.

Nancy was a struggling real estate agent. When she started working with me (PL), her credit card debt was out of control. She had a recurring pattern of real estate deals falling through at the last moment, which resulted in an income that fell short of her bills.

When we discussed this, I discovered that whenever she got a commissionable listing contract, she tended to cease prospecting efforts to find new clients until the deal in process was either completed or fell through. She told me that the deals usually fell through for rather bizarre reasons that weren't mentioned in the contracts. When either the buyer or the seller pulled out of the deal, there were usually threats of lawsuits and bitter words.

When we discussed this, Nancy realized that she had unconsciously re-created her childhood relationship with her father in her real estate clients. She also saw that her natural childhood tendency to rely on her father as her sole source of financial support caused her to cease prospecting efforts as soon as she had attained one commissionable contract. Her father is a wealthy investor who uses money to control his daughter. Over the years, Nancy often asked him to rescue her from the financial jams she created. Strings were always attached to the help he offered. Nancy told me that, as any past discussion with him about him giving her money progressed, he would keep adding conditions to the "gift."

Sometimes she accepted the "gift" and its conditions, but in most cases she had declined his offers of help. In these cases her father would become angry, making dire predictions about her financial future and abilities and threatening her with disinheritance.

I asked her whether she was willing to accept the fact that he would never help her in any reasonable adult manner. By forgiving her father, she was able to disconnect her emotions from his behavior and realize that he would have treated anyone as he had treated her. She realized that her dependence had given him more power than he was due, and she was able to stop taking his attempts at manipulation personally. Accepting that her father was, in fact, her least likely source of reliable financial support was a tearful experience, but it was surely less painful than the prospect of continued reliance on him.

Using the methods described in this book, Nancy was able to see that she had a choice about how to perceive her father's behavior. She was able to accept the reality that she could not count on him and able to accept the challenge of becoming the generator of her own abundant income.

Action

By "action" we refer to consistent, effective behavior that moves you toward your goal. To learn the proper steps to take, you can seek out advice from people who have done it before, or you can figure it out yourself. Procrastination and struggle are energy drainers and time wasters that will distract you from taking effective action. Procrastination is caused by fear. It doesn't matter what the fear is exactly, but accepting the fear will relieve you of procrastination.

When we talk about action, many times people leap to the conclusion that we are suggesting additional action. You may be thinking "I don't have time for any additional action." As the next example shows, we don't necessarily mean *more* action, but rather *different* action. Doing more of what is not working for you is foolishness.

Dorothy is a dedicated sales representative for a telephone service provider. She worked part-time in her business several nights per week to fit it into her schedule of a full-time job and family responsibilities. She was diligent about making her prospecting calls during the time she scheduled for them, but the results were disappointing. When I (PL) suggested that she change her action, she immediately insisted that she didn't have enough time due to her full schedule. I pointed out that I thought she would benefit not from more action, but from *different* action.

Instead of the two hours of prospecting phoning she had been doing, I suggested she divide her scheduled work time in her part-time business into two sections. In the first section, of 15 minutes, she would use the affirmations and visualization methods that I had taught her. The second section, to be one and three-quarter hours of prospecting as she had already been doing. The same amount of time, just slightly different action. The results were different, too. "All of a sudden, people are signing up," she told me.

The Hollowness of Being Right

Righteousness is a poor standard for producing success. Everyone's experience of money is his or her own creation. This is good news for those with the knowledge and willingness to examine their unconscious beliefs and attitudes about themselves and about money that are the causative factors in their experience of money. A lean purse is more easily cured than endured. For example, if you think rich people are evil, then you are right. But there is more to it than that. Loyalty to this belief attracts to you evidence that proves it true and filters out contradictory evidence. The same is true if you believe that money is hard to come by, scarce, or will corrupt you.

This self-confirming dynamic also works for your opinions about yourself. If you believe you are lazy and worthless, for example, then you will tend to waste your time watching television, an activity that serves to confirm the belief that motivated it. Every act is a self-defining act. The impulse to improve is built into all of us; wanting to change doesn't mean there is anything wrong with you. Would you rather be right, or would you rather be rich?

What you focus on is what you get more of in your life. When you focus on the negative aspects, you attract more of that negative. The good news is then when you focus on the positive, you receive more positive. For example, when we view ourselves in a more positive manner, we become more positive. Others will notice and respond more positively. Have you ever noticed that when you smile at someone, the person usually smiles back? Conversely, when you sneer at someone, you tend to get a negative reaction from that person. What are you focused on the majority of the time? Are you focused on the positive or the negative? Pay attention to your focus.

I (AF) worked with a client named Jim whose mind was strongly focused on the massive debt he had accumulated. Jim had more than $60,000 in credit card debt, an amount that was steadily increasing. When I spoke with him about his finances, the primary focus of his mind was evident. He constantly talked about his debt as if it had been a puppy that he watched grow into a full-grown dog. Jim was so intensely focused on the growth rate of the debt that he lost sight of the income opportunities right in front of him. He procrastinated and became a recluse. He knew he had to change but didn't know how.

After two hours of consulting, Jim started to focus on income-producing activities in his business. He discovered that he felt much more empowered when focusing on what he wanted, and therefore he increased his income very quickly. This took the pressure off him, and he was able to eliminate the mountain of debt and produce positive cash flow.

Remember: *What you focus on in your mind is what grows in your life.* Are you focusing your attention on what you want or what you don't want? The choice is yours.

Values Motivate Us All

Each of us is motivated differently. What drives us to do what we do? There are six reasons for everything people do:

1. Certainty
2. Uncertainty or variety
3. Significance
4. Love or connection
5. Growth
6. Contribution

You must have a level of certainty to accomplish anything. If you had no certainty, you would be too afraid to start anything. Conversely, you also must have uncertainty or variety in your life; otherwise you would be very bored.

All of us are more motivated to do tasks or achieve goals when we feel significant. Typically, we get a feeling of significance either through work or from friends and family. If we feel worthy about what we do, then we do what must be done. In addition to feeling significant, we must feel a connection or love to the people we are dealing with. For example, if we felt no connection to our significant other, would we be motivated to do things for him or her? Probably not! Because we do feel a connection with and love from our significant other, we will be motivated to do things to make him or her happy that we may not normally do for ourselves.

To be motivated, we must be growing and learning all the time. If we are not growing, we are stagnant. When we stagnate, we actually move backward. Moving backward does not feel good, and we may even become depressed. That is why we continually stretch ourselves and grow. We also must feel that we are contributing not only to ourselves but also to others. When we contribute beyond ourselves, we are fulfilling our spiritual need.

Change is inevitable in today's turbulent economy. Companies go into and out of business constantly. This book is teaching you the skills to make the decisions about which changes take place. No more will you allow change to happen to you.

CHAPTER

YOUR RECOVERY FROM
A GOOD UPBRINGING

Blamelessness is essential if you are going to get over the limited thinking about money you learned from your family. Decide how you wish to associate with the people you grew up with. A family is a dynamic system of rules and roles, boundaries and bonds. Discover how this system affects your financial life. Many people report that no matter their success, visiting their parents makes them feel 10 years old again. You must uncover, declare, and develop an adult relationship with your parents in order to begin to live your true purpose. Are your desires OK with you? Learn to become the source of your own permission. Upgrade your money vocabulary.

From teaching our Trainings and from our consulting work, we are accustomed to people being skeptical about the effect that family conditioning and upbringing have on their financial results. Some of this skepticism stems from examples of people with unfavorable family conditioning who became millionaires, as compared to others from so-called better backgrounds who never seem to get money right. As you will learn in this chapter, the important issue is not really your childhood experience itself, but rather the conclusions and decisions that you have carried forward from it and that still operate in your life today.

Your parents didn't give you useful information about money. It's no one's fault. If we could do so and still maintain a degree of literary flow, we would repeat that sentence constantly throughout this chapter: *It's no one's fault.* Your parents gave you everything they had. They could not give you something that they themselves were never taught. Keep in mind that the most important aspect of the past is not what actually happened but how it affects you today. Money comes from other people, so your ability to get more of it depends a great deal on how well you discuss money with others.

Just like most of us, you were brought up to believe certain things and to believe *in* certain things. You are grown up now. Use the information in this chapter to reevaluate the beliefs you adopted in childhood. Most people discover there are some beliefs they wish to keep and others they would be far better off without.

Take a moment to recall your parents' discussions about money. Probably their discussions were nonexistent, negative, or very negative. If your parents avoided discussing money issues, it is most likely that you concluded that money is something impolite to discuss or mysterious.

In many families, discussions about money are negative only and deal with shortage, limitation, and complaints about the items that cannot be afforded. In extreme cases, the discussions about money are so negative as to be loud arguments. If your parents argued about money, it is likely you have financial problems as an adult, and will do so at least until you resolve this issue and the associated uncomfortable feelings. You may have concluded that money causes arguments. Therefore, the way to have peace is to have as little money as possible. The person with such a childhood experience would avoid discussions about money.

Whatever your parents taught you about money, it has been so deeply ingrained during your 20,000 meals with them that the information may inhabit your consciousness as unnoticed, unquestioned truth. Recalling your parents' discussions about money is likely to bring to mind some of the vocabulary you commonly use when talking about money.

Cleaning Up Your Money Vocabulary

Are you the victim of fuzzy thinking? Do debilitating unconsciously held rules about money stand in the way of your wealth? Be careful about what you say. Remember that everything you say goes out of your mouth into your own ears and into the Thinker part of your mind. Then the Prover part of your mind goes to work to prove that whatever you just said is true. The use of one or more of these words often expresses fuzzy thinking and debilitating rules about money:

Afford
Can't
Charge
Deserve
Fair
Need
Try

We consider these meaningless words because the interpretation of them is so emotionally charged for many people that the dictionary definition is meaningless. The definition of each word according to the *Oxford American Dictionary* is shown for reference purposes. However, what you think these words really mean determines how they affect you.

Afford: To have enough money means or time for a specified purpose

To demonstrate the fuzzy thinking about this word, at Trainings, we ask the participants to raise a hand if they can afford a Rolls-Royce. Usually no hands go up. Then we ask for hands of people who can afford a nice place to live. This time most hands go up. Now, if you were to move out of your house and use the money you had been paying for rent or mortgage payment toward payments on the car, you could pay for the Rolls and live in your car. Additionally, in nice neighborhoods, it would be easy to find someone who would offer you a room just to have a Rolls parked in the driveway. Perhaps you do not own a Rolls-Royce, either, but if you don't, consider that it is not because you can't afford one.

Can't: An expression of inability or helplessness

Clearly there are things you can't do. You cannot fly to the moon by flapping your arms. Most people cannot swim the English Channel or climb Mount Everest. Notice carefully the things you say you cannot do or the things you say cannot happen. Many of the things you now say you can't do may actually be within your current capability or within capabilities you could easily acquire. Some examples might be "I can't sell" or "I can't get over that divorce" or "I can't get over being fired."

Charge: The price asked for goods and services

Typically, there is a resentful tone associated with the use of this word. The resentment stems from the helplessness people experience about spending money because they are unaware of the choices available. "That store charges too much" is one example. To determine whether this resentful tone applies to you, write down four or five sentences that come to mind that contain the word "charge." The dictionary defines it accurately as the price asked. In any free market economy, people have a wide variety of possibilities in obtaining products and services. Only the government tax collectors take your money by force.

Deserve: To be worthy or entitled to (a thing) because of actions or qualities

The important question here is what qualities you have and what actions you take that cause you to be entitled to what you want. Regarding money, many people have an unconscious formula that determines the income they receive; they believe that a certain amount of work produces a certain amount of income, and any income beyond that would require even more work. Such an unconscious formula, for a person working full time, earning $40,000 per year would produce a feeling of helplessness if that person were to consider what it would take to earn $80,000 or $100,000 per year. The unconscious formula would cause the person to believe the two full-time jobs would be necessary to earn such an amount. Using the methods in this book cultivates the qualities of initiative, resourcefulness, and willingness to serve others, as well as to learn to take effective action so that you are worthy and deserving of more of what you desire.

Fair: Just, unbiased, in accordance with the rules

Related to money, "fair" is most often used when referring to the rate at which goods and services are exchanged—fair prices or fair wages. A free market requires the agreement of two or more parties for a transaction to occur. There is no reason for you tolerate what you consider to be unfair treatment (at least in the long term) from anyone you buy from or sell to.

In the former Soviet Union, manufactured goods were, by law, permanently stamped with their government-mandated sales price. Such a system certainly qualifies as fair. Or does it? The goods had to be sold at the same price across the nine time zones in the Soviet Union. Purchasers of goods produced nearby were compelled to subsidize the consumers located far from the factory. If you ever visited the Soviet Union, then you know that such so-called fairness criminalized the normal entrepreneurial activity that occurs here everyday as manufacturers and retailers juggle prices to maximize their sales and profits in the face of changing demand for and supply of their products. What all of us in the West consider normal entrepreneurial activity was characterized as illegal and subversive black marketing in the Soviet Union.

Need: A requirement, a thing necessary for life

If you carefully consider the things you really need to live, they are quite limited. You can survive without air for five minutes or so, without water for five days or so, and without food for five weeks or so. Not that you would intentionally create any of these situations. In terms of money, none of these needs is very expensive to meet. Regarding money, if you give yourself only what you need, then you won't have very much. People who think that money is primarily for survival are already as rich as that sort of thinking will ever get them.

For most people, need has already created a "must" motivation. To render more effective the internal motivation you already have about need, increase the scope of the items you must have and the things you must do. Hitherto unnoticed resources come to awareness when you think or say "I must do this" or "I must have that."

Try: To attempt, to make an effort to do something

In most grade schools, students are graded on effort. Although this may serve to motivate some, trying really accomplishes nothing. Right now, try to stand up. Try even harder. You'll notice that you accomplished nothing. Trying can never be enough. It is only a start. At the emotional level, which is what really matters, "trying" refers to failure with honor.

Parental Teaching about Money

Regardless of the particular information we absorbed about money as children, it was most likely distorted by the fact that we learned much more about spending from our parents than about earning. Most of the time children observe their parents spending but do not accompany them to work, where the earning occurs. This gives spending an erroneous emphasis. Compare the number of times you visited the mall or the supermarket with your parents to the number of times you went with them to work. As an adult, earning is far more important than spending.

As a shorthand and effective way of referring to the condition-ing our parents gave us, we use the phrase "inherited purpose." (Thanks to teacher Brad Swift for acquainting us with this phrase.) Inherited purpose is a good way to describe parental conditioning because the conditioning is much, much more than mere ideas. If you memorize Hamlet's "To Be or Not to Be" speech or the names of the first 40 presidents of the United States, you have done nothing more than fill your mind with ideas that have no effect on your behavior.

In contrast, this inherited purpose serves as an internal map—a guide for where you are, what things mean, and where you should be going. Unfortunately, the map is very much out of date because it was constructed as children. Today you have far more freedom, resources, and responsibilities than you did when you made the map. Imagine trying to find your way around a growing city, such as Atlanta or Dallas, using a map from the 1980s or earlier. You would be lost much of the time, experiencing undue frustration and de-lay. A similar result occurs from using the inherited purpose to guide your adult life.

Your inherited purpose is dynamic, because it guides your val-ues and behavior. Inherited purpose forms the basis for how your mind filters information, the generalizations, distortions, and deletions that we discussed in Chapter 4. Your inherited purpose forms your basic ideas about yourself, the world around you, and your power. The things your parents taught you about money also affect your opinions about yourself and your outlook on life. Childhood conditioning affects you whether you chose to con-form or rebel. The important question is whether the values, mo-tivation, and behavior derived from your inherited purpose move you closer to or farther from earning the income you want from work you love.

There are three possibilities about this inherited purpose:

1. You are one of those very rare people who inherited a noble purpose from your parents. This noble purpose includes earning the income you want doing work you love, and you are doing that now. Congratulations to you. Use this book to expand your contribution. (Incidentally, we haven't met any-one like this.)

2. You have discarded an inherited purpose that did not serve you. By doing this you have made the transition to earning

the income you want doing work you love, based on your true purpose. Once again, congratulations to you.

3. You are living your inherited purpose, perhaps earning less than you want doing work you don't like.

Now some examples of inherited purpose. (You may find yourself listed here.)

- Be strong and don't feel.
- Take care of others before yourself.
- Don't disturb anyone.
- Don't disappoint anyone.
- Act helpless and dependent to get love, care, and attention.
- Follow the rules.
- Rebel against rules.
- Look good.
- Don't make us ashamed of you.
- Accept the blame for everything.

It is beneficial, but not essential, to identify your inherited purpose at this point. When you declare your true purpose (later in this chapter) and start living it, your inherited purpose will object, fearing its eventual demise. It will object more and more loudly until you confront whatever it is. Whatever your inherited purpose, you can be pretty sure it produces very little in the way of satisfaction, joy, or prosperity.

The degree to which you want to blame someone for what happened (or didn't happen) in your childhood indicates the degree to which unresolved feelings hold you back from the success and satisfaction you deserve. It's no one's fault. Blaming your parents is futile, even if you have a "case." By "case" we mean even if you can prove they are to blame.

Blaming yourself is foolish, too. Typically, children are not completely aware of their own powerlessness and inability to affect events. For this reason, they often blame themselves (and continue to do so into adulthood) for events they could not have controlled, such as the divorce or even death of their parents. Even without these extreme events in your life, it's foolish to think your parents would have treated you better or at least differently if you had been smarter, prettier, more talented, or better in some other dimension. Remember, it's no one's fault. Most likely your parents had the highest intentions for you but a flawed strategy for bringing them about. Remember, your parents did the best they could with the information they had.

Besides, the actual events of your childhood are far less important than what you concluded from them. The events are over, but the conclusions remain if you haven't changed them. This fact is why some people from traumatic childhoods do well financially while others from loving and supportive backgrounds struggle on and on with money. Consider, also, that if you believe the events from your childhood matter more than your conclusions, you are giving your power away to something you cannot change. You can use the methods in this book to change your conclusions, but no one can change the content of the past.

When we mention parents, most people think of those people they grew up with, who now live in Miami, Phoenix, Poughkeepsie, or in the graveyard, Heaven, or Hell, if they have passed away. Those folks are only one of three sets of parents we all have. We have:

1. The people we grew up with.
2. The parents who live in our minds—the committee in our head that evaluates, criticizes, and comments, without invitation, on thoughts, feelings, and behavior.
3. Your true set of parents: life itself. The parents you grew up with are the manifestations of life itself you used to get here. Thus, we are all manifestations in the unbroken stream of life that began at the Big Bang or at a religious creation.

A Word of Caution

Solutions are much more important than problems. What your mind focuses on inevitably increases. Focus on the problem only enough to get through the denial and to formulate an effective solution. The problem is always more complex and more familiar than the solution (often the problem is more dramatic), so you may tend to become stuck on the problem. Some people spend a long time in therapy that results in a deep understanding of the *causes* of their problems. We believe causes are far less important than solutions. You're special; your problems are not.

It's no one's fault. If you want to blame your parents, then you have to blame their parents and their parents before them. Pretty soon you are blaming everyone back to the beginning of time. Anyone can see this makes no sense.

Relating to Your Parents as an Adult

Some otherwise confident and accomplished adults say they feel like 10-year-olds around their parents. These are people not yet free of their inherited purpose. Here several suggestions to move your relationship with your parents to an adult–adult level.

RELATE TO THEM SEPARATELY

Obviously, except for some stepparents, your parents knew each other before you got here. Possibly they support each other in denying and suppressing the topics they prefer to avoid. You may even be delightfully surprised to know them as individuals. Additionally, you now have some control over the degree of intimacy in your relationship with each of them. There are no rules about how your relationship with them should be now that you are grown up, although the expectations of all concerned on this topic may be huge. You can choose the place in the spectrum that suits you from formal civility to warmhearted affection.

ASK THEM TO RETIRE

By the time you're 18, your parents' work is pretty much complete. However, since no one comes along to tell them this, you may have to do it yourself. Point out that they will remain your parents forever, worthy of the love and respect accorded their position. The only difference is they no longer need to do the work. They have become Mom Emeritus and Dad Emeritus. Remember, they have thought of themselves as your parents for a very long time, responsible for guiding and supporting you. All of us all enjoy feeling useful. Thus, you may need to discuss their retirement with them more than one time before they agree. Should they persist in offering unsolicited advice and criticism, you can gently threaten them with Parents Anonymous—smile when you do this.

STOP TRYING TO CHANGE THEM OR GET THEIR APPROVAL

I (PL) remember telling my late mother, "Look, Mom, I am grown up now, so there isn't much you can do to change me at this point. So, please retire, so we have a more friendly relationship as adults." This works both ways. Of course your parents should be different from how they are. But you'll be happier and wealthier, too, when you cease trying to change them, especially if you are trying to get their approval. Likely their disapproval is a habitual attempt to control you. Now that you are grown up, it is up to you whether you grant them that control.

Family Dynamics

A family is a dynamic psychological and emotional system. A functional family operates for the maximum benefit of all members. A dysfunctional family functions to perpetuate the inherited or acquired neuroses of the authority figures. The system consists of interrelated bonds, boundaries, rules, and roles. Once again, some of the bonds, boundaries, rules, and roles worked for the benefit of all concerned, and others did not. Some things must have worked well in your family, no matter how dysfunctional it was, or you could not have survived.

Your View of Your Parents

It is unreasonable to believe your parents were perfect and were able to raise you without making a mistake (usually *many* mistakes and omissions, as well). Nor should you think they are the worst people on earth. You could not have survived your childhood if they were. It is probably reasonable to say they were well-intentioned people with flaws—perhaps even serious ones. Whatever they did or didn't do, each of us is responsible for recovering from our upbringing.

They were probably wrong about money. This doesn't make them bad people, just flawed.

What follows is a discussion of each element of family dynamics: bonds, boundaries, rules, and roles.

Bonds

Family bonds are lifelong, for better or worse. Even if you live for over a century, your relationship with your parents will never fade from memory. The most important bond in any family should be that between husband and wife. This bond acts as the example the children absorb about intimate relationships, and this is the bond that will remain between the spouses after the children have grown up and left. In some destructive cases, the strongest bonds are not those between wife and husband. If the husband's strongest bond is to his work and the wife's strongest bond is to the children, they will discover they have little to give each other once the children are grown, and perhaps sooner.

Once I (PL) had a client, *Oliver*, whose younger sister, Martha, had died after a long, debilitating childhood illness. The illness caused Martha to be almost completely helpless for several years before her death. She received constant parental attention, way more than he. It is hard to imagine the devastating impact of the loss of a child. Although it must stand out as the most severe tragedy, these people did not handle it well. After Martha's death, the parents' strongest bond continued to be to their deceased daughter. Family holidays were marked with parental comments such as "If only Martha could see this." Her birthday was celebrated each year as if she were still there.

These family bonds affected Oliver. He had made repeated attempts at starting businesses, but always got into difficulties that required his parents to rescue him. Ironically, he had just enough temporary successes to maintain his parents' willingness to help him out.

After some intense discussion about his personal history, we concluded that his inherited purpose was to compete with his sister for his parents' attention by being helpless as she was. When he saw that his sister had unintentionally given her life to get their attention, he realized that getting their attention was a game he couldn't and didn't want to win. He forgave himself and his parents, declared his true purpose in life, started a flower business, and broke the pattern of needing to be rescued.

BOUNDARIES

Boundaries have a lot to do with manners. They can be compared to little islands of respect surrounding each person. The specifics of boundaries vary somewhat according to culture. Generally, we don't touch people unless invited to, we don't ask them about their personal life when we first meet them, and we expect similar courtesies. Respect for boundaries is a cultural expectation.

From my (PL) consulting experience, I've learned boundaries have the biggest effect when they are violated. Childhood sexual abuse is the most grievous boundary violation I have encountered. There is a built-in genetic expectation that fully grown members of any species will care for (or at least not harm) the younger members of the species. This expectation probably became part of the genetic makeup sometime after life evolved beyond the single-celled organism. Childhood sexual abuse is a violation of this social contract. To my knowledge, there is no society in which sexual activity with children is acceptable.

One of my clients, *Angela*, suffered extreme childhood sexual abuse involving her father and other male family members. This unresolved experience caused her a wide variety of personal problems, but here I will discuss only their financial implications. Angela had an extraordinary talent for seeing color and detail. But she worked in a low-paying job for a printing company, doing color separations. People doing similar work in the film industry typically earned three to five times as much.

This woman exhibited characteristics that are common to sexual abuse victims. All the sexual abuse victims I have met have absorbed the "Don't tell" message. Additionally, Angela carried residual shame about what happened and about the fact she enjoyed some of it. Shame is highly toxic to wealth. Shame carries the erroneous idea there is something irreparably wrong with you. This notion leads to the belief you don't deserve the good things in life, such as acceptance, affection, and money. The recovery of sexual abuse victims begins when they realize that the shame is an erroneous and unwarranted reaction to an experience they could not control and did not choose. This realization provides them with previously unknown freedom to receive the good things in life the shame had kept away.

When Angela realized she was not to blame for the abuse and with the ensuing resolution of her shame, she was able to increase her income significantly by working freelance in the film industry. In addition, her personal life improved greatly.

Rules

Every family has rules. Some, such as "Look both ways before crossing the street," are of obvious lifelong benefit to everyone. Others are childhood rules, which are actually counterproductive after you are grown up. Here are 10 examples:

1. Sit down and be quiet.
2. Children should be seen and not heard.
3. Don't brag or say good things about yourself.
4. Do as you are told.
5. Don't do anything without permission.

6. Take what you are given and don't ask for more.
7. Don't take money from friends.
8. Don't take money from strangers or talk to them.
9. Don't rock the boat.
10. You can't have your cake and eat it, too.

Many of these are excellent rules for a five-year-old. If you are 25, 35, 45, or older and still obeying them, however, these rules will hinder your financial success.

Here is what may happen if you continue to follow these rules as an adult:

If you follow rules 1, 2, and 3, you feel uncomfortable about public speaking, job search, or selling anything. Job search and selling have a great deal in common. The former is far more difficult, because the product and the salesperson are identical. It is the ultimate sales job; your survival is at stake. Job candidates are unemployed salespeople, selling their skills in a very competitive environment. A job search is intensely emotional and much more difficult if you have never learned to sell. In many surveys, people have named public speaking as their most significant fear—clearly an irrational fear, caused by childhood rules. After all, the casualty rate among public speakers is quite low.

Remember that the fear you experience when learning to sell has nothing to do with the prospective customer or the current situation. Instead, it is actually about breaking family rules.

If you follow rules 4 and 5, you're likely to have a job. People who own a business soon discover there is no one to provide instructions and no one whose permission is required. Success in your own business requires the willingness and ability to operate on your own authority.

If you follow rule 6, you accept the salary you are given and feel very uncomfortable discussing a raise. Asking for what you want is always a bit uncomfortable, because you run the risk of rejection. Following this rule makes negotiation out of the question, meaning you can never receive anything better than the first offer anyone makes.

If you follow rules 7 and 8, you have a less than satisfying relationship with your boss. If it is not OK to take money from friends or from strangers, whom does that leave? Known enemies! This may seem a mere play on words until you consider the sometimes suppressed animosity between employers and workers that seems to be expressed only from time to time in labor strife. Job satisfaction is impossible if you view your employer as an adversary.

If you follow rule 9, you perform at less than your best or sabotage your success. Why? Excellence *always* rocks the boat.

If you follow rule 10, success does not seem to be worth the price. People try to prove this to be correct by creating endless obstacles and struggles. With this mind-set, you will create losses that you attribute to your progress and that make you wonder whether it is worth it.

It is not a good idea to rebel against all the rules our parents gave us, although we know a few people who try. Surely your parents taught you some wise rules.

WHAT HAPPENS WHEN YOU BREAK THESE RULES?

These rules are more than intellectual furniture. Intellectual furniture means knowledge with little or no emotional impact. $C^2 = A^2 + B^2$ would be an example. This formula, the Pythagorean theorem for calculating the measurements of a right triangle, is something most of us learned in the sixth or seventh grade. Trigonometry is very different from the childhood rules we are discussing here. The difference is the childhood rules were enforced. It doesn't matter what the methods were; they may have been extreme or not, ranging from brutal beatings to being unfavorably compared to a sibling to being sent to bed without supper. All the methods share an intense, negative emotional component. In other words, failure to follow the rules made you feel bad. This is the reason why when as adults we step outside these rules, the emotional memories of the enforcement flood awareness. For some people, just thinking about breaking the rules does this.

Stepping beyond these counterproductive rules is bound to feel uncomfortable. Knowing this makes it easier to accept the discomfort and move forward with your own business. The discomfort does not mean there is something wrong with you or that you are in any danger if you choose to violate these rules.

Financial success requires you to defy these rules and become a rebel for your own good. Rebellion has a well-deserved bad reputation, often expressed in self-destructive behavior like reckless driving or dangerous addictions. We are not referring to this sort of rebellion, but rather to stepping beyond the artificial bounds of politeness imposed before you learned to think for yourself.

Perhaps the particular rules that hold you back have been operating in your consciousness without awareness for decades. Once you are aware of the existence of these childhood rules, you can catch yourself when you hear them functioning in your consciousness. When this happens, simply laugh at their feeble attempt to stop you by remembering you are grown up now.

The rules in your family may have been different from the 10 examples listed. Ask yourself what your parents taught you (both by instruction and by example) about money and about proper behavior. A list of such items may turn up rules that no longer serve you.

LIST YOUR PERSONAL CHILDHOOD RULES

Take a moment now to start a list of the childhood rules in your household. You'll discover that some of them are still highly useful, while others may be holding you back from your dreams. Do this now. Remember, the more you put into these exercises, the more you will benefit.

One of Phil's clients, *Edgar*, was a skilled Internet programmer unhappily employed in Corporate America. He dreamed of starting his own business, but was afraid to. In addition to many of the 10 common childhood rules, his father was a vigorous advocate of getting a job with a good company and staying there. Until he started working with Phil, Edgar had been following the common childhood rules, as well as his father's admonitions about the importance of the financial security that comes from a job with a big company.

He began selling a $5 to $20 item (this is described in detail in Chapter 13) and began to deal with some of the feelings and thoughts that comprised his inherited purpose. After about six months, he broke free of his inherited purpose and started his own Internet business.

ROLES

Family roles appear to be the most important aspect in the development of inherited purpose and, therefore, have an effect on adult behavior usually more significant than boundaries, bonds, or rules.

For this reason, we'll present three examples of people breaking free of inherited purposes that came from unconsciously adopted family roles.

Some part of the reason why people bear and rear children is to perpetuate their own genetic characteristics in the world. Therefore, in varying degrees, an important childhood message our parents gave us is "Be like me." Sometimes parents punish children for behavior they themselves do, but almost no parent is so bold about this as to tell a child, "Do as I say, not as I do." As children, we either conformed to or rebelled against this message; the choice formed a part of our inherited purpose.

Additionally, we needed to find a way to fit into the social structure that existed in our family before our arrival. It is rare that children try for a role that has already been taken, because of the resulting competitive sibling rivalry. The role we adopt enables us to fit in, be accepted, and perhaps even be useful. These roles are dynamic and change with major transitions in the family. Job loss, death, divorce, and relocation may cause family members to change roles, because the challenge caused by the new situation may bring out a previously unseen portion of their personality.

To generalize a few examples of family roles, there are caretakers, providers, comedians, lost children, rebels without a cause, good students, sick children, confidantes, beauty queens, and star athletes. Whether one role is better than another is an individual judgment. The deciding issue is whether you have chosen the role consciously or whether the role represents an unconscious choice made a long time ago as a child to fit in with your family.

People Who Discarded Family Roles and Moved on to True Purpose

The examples that follow of Mary and Beverly are almost polar opposites. Theirs and George's story illustrate that what is right for one person is not right for another. Mary was a social worker, very unhappy with her career when I (PL) met her. When she declared her true purpose, the reason she was unhappy in her work became evident. Nothing in the purpose she declared was even remotely related to social work. After some discussion of her family history, we discovered the caretaking part of her social work job was a role adopted in childhood. She was the oldest sister in a large, poor family with both her parents working long hours.

The true purpose she declared showed strong interest in helping people maintain their health. She spent a couple of weeks researching business opportunities in this field. Then she bought a distributorship in a network marketing company offering health products. She began selling these part time while staying, at least temporarily, at her social work job.

She was much happier and successful, too, in her network marketing business. Her ability to support other people and to deal with their problems from her experience as a social worker served her well in her relations with customers and the distributors who signed up to conduct the business down the line from her. Her natural ability to motivate others and to provide them with a vision of their own potential aided her in creating prosperous distributors in her group.

Beverly was an attorney working as a research specialist in a large law firm. Although she had risen rapidly because of her hard work and ability to uncover the arguments her colleagues needed for their trial presentations, her dissatisfaction increased yearly. A single mother, she agonized about the long hours she spent away from her three children, her true source of joy. She worried they were growing up without her.

Her true purpose revealed that her most important values related to children in general and her children in particular. Beverly realized her inherited purpose was about law and arguments came from her father, a federal judge. A preoccupied man, he paid her little attention unless she contentiously discussed the cases he had heard. As a child, she had used these discussions to get her father's attention.

On her next vacation, she took a temporary job at a local day care center and loved it. After the vacation, she switched to part-time hours at the law office, simultaneously working part time at the day care center. She put together a plan to purchase a center.

Her research skills came into use when she gathered information about the centers in her town to identify the best ones to buy. She bought the best one available and quit the law firm. Within a few years, she had expanded to a chain of several centers.

George was a Training participant who was a highly talented pianist and composer with far greater problems than even the usual Starving Artist. George was receiving welfare checks and had been for quite some time. In fact, George was a third-generation welfare recipient. His parents and grandparents before him had lived most of their lives on welfare. George was aware that his purpose involved musical expression, but unconscious allegiance to his role as a helpless dependent of the government stood in the way of making his music pay.

George had produced a cassette of his music and was looking for music gigs. After a few months, he had learned and applied most of the methods described in this book, but he was still dependent on welfare.

I was impressed by his diligence during this time and tried to think of some way to help him free himself from his inherited purpose. One day, in a group Training course, I suggested he try something radical. I suggested he recite and accept the very negative thought that was holding him back. By observing him, I had deduced that this was "My financial problems are caused by genetically transferred character defects I can do nothing about." He agreed to do this and said the phrase once to each of the other participants, who responded simply with "I understand."

By the next week his business had taken off, and he was finished with the Welfare Department. I believe this worked for him because the phrase he repeated was the exact thought that had been holding him back. Simply acknowledging its negative truth set him free from the role he had inherited from two generations. Much of his adult life had been a struggle to deny the power of this thought. By allowing it to be expressed in the external world and discovering nothing bad happened by doing so, the negative thought lost its power over him. I don't think this would have worked if he had not been so highly motivated to break free from his family tradition. If he were not so motivated, it could have simply become another excuse.

I have included this story to show that sometimes it is necessary to uncover new methods. Your motivation and desire to succeed are what will get you where you want to go, and the methods are only tools to do so.

From these three examples, you can see how the family role becomes an identity with a specific personality and its own outlook on life, habits, traits, and ways of thinking and dealing with reality. Pretending to be someone else is hard work, if for no other reason than the constant anxiety that someone may find out you are faking it.

Your Purpose in Life

Purpose is a strategy, the strategy you have designed to express your important values. Everyone has a strategy, whether it was consciously designed or unconsciously adopted from childhood experience.

Inherited purpose is the action part of the role adopted in childhood. We accepted this inherited purpose without realizing it or choosing it. An inherited purpose can provide us with little satisfaction, because it was almost always designed to please someone else and, because we chose it unconsciously, we don't usually remember choosing it.

A purpose is similar to an outfit of clothing. One outfit is not necessarily better than another, it is a matter of individual suitability and taste. What fits you and looks good on you may not look so good on someone else. Additionally, you will enjoy much more the outfit you choose than the selection another might make for you.

For many participants in our Training sessions, dramatic and satisfying changes in their lives begin with the simple declaration of their life's purpose. This is done by asking yourself, "What am I doing here?" It's impossible to imagine a person without purpose. A person who completely lacks purpose would find it impossible to make any decision.

Here is my life's purpose: (PL)

The purpose of my life is to use my creativity, curiosity, courage, common sense, compassion, and sense of humor by setting a good example, writing, teaching, traveling, and adding to my personal fortune so that everyone enjoys the satisfaction of serving others in the way we most prefer and everyone experiences freedom and peace of mind.

And here is my purpose: (AF)

The purpose of my life is to use my entrepreneurial spirit, confidence, self-motivation, dedication, and team-building ability by developing, promoting, teaching, coaching, and mentoring others so that they are able to expand their minds, become personally and financially free, and be able to enjoy all that life has to offer.

If you experience life as a precious gift, then it follows that your life deserves a noble purpose. Not a grandiose purpose stemming from a big ego, but rather a lofty purpose that expresses your most important values in ways to benefit yourself and others.

Purpose is an internal statement with external expression. For this reason a person could follow his parents in the family business and still live a life based on his true purpose; another person could choose an occupation and lifestyle completely different from her parents and still be stuck in inherited purpose.

Better Decisions

Your life has been shaped by hundreds of decisions, some good and some not. If you do not know your purpose in life, then decision making can be a worry-filled nightmare because it's difficult to know if you have made the right decision before you see how it turns out. A person choosing between moving to Miami or staying in Minneapolis, for example, might make long lists of the good things and bad things about each location and, even after much soul searching, be no closer to the better choice. Without a framework for evaluating the information, it's impossible to see the better choice. However, a clear purpose in life makes choices easier and quicker because you have only to choose the option that most supports your purpose—the option that most empowers you to express your purpose. Once you recognize your life's purpose, you have fewer nagging second thoughts.

Respond to what your purpose tells you instead of to the distracting noise in your mind or from others who advise you of their expectations. Beyond that, clarity of purpose makes it easy to justify decisions. You simply say, "I took the choice that supported my purpose." As consultants, we refrain from advising people what business they should be in. You can make that decision far better than we by choosing a business that expresses your purpose in life. Chapter 8 explains how to free up your creativity to design a business that suits you.

Satisfying Life

The accumulation of physical goods provides only limited satisfaction. Everyone is different, but at some point the acquisition of one more physical possession becomes meaningless. Instead, satisfaction results from the expression of your consciously acknowledged important values in a way that suits you.

Both designing and expressing your consciously chosen purpose will increase your awareness of what you really want. Are your desires really OK with you? This point is important to consider, because if they are not, there are likely to be internal conflicts in designing your purpose.

How Do You Decide Which Desires to Accept?

Accepting a desire does not mean you must act on it. Accepting a desire simply means that you accept yourself while having it. Conversely, condemning your desire implies that you disapprove of yourself for having it. A little self-examination may be necessary to bring this dynamic to awareness. Do this by contemplating some desire that is not OK with you and notice how you feel about yourself.

If you have walked across the Golden Gate Bridge or been to the top of the Empire State Building or any other high vantage point, most likely the desire to jump passed through your mind. It seems to be just about impossible to look down from a high place without wondering what it would feel like to jump. Statistically, most people who visit these places, even those who accept the desire to jump and thus enjoy the experience of imagining jumping off, do not in fact jump. So accepting this desire did not cause them to act it out.

ACCEPTING DESIRES

R$ Take a minute to think about some of your desires that you do not accept—that are not OK with you. Write these down. Take your time and let it be OK to know about them. Likely these desires are accompanied by negative internal self-talk and perhaps even guilty feelings of self-condemnation. However, having a desire in no way compels you to act it out. For a moment, allow yourself to accept these desires, realizing that most humans probably have some of the same ones. By doing so, you'll immediately notice an internal shift to greater self-acceptance.

The inability to accept yourself leads to a variety of problems and conflicts, and not just about money. Shame, guilt, beating yourself up, making yourself wrong, giving yourself a hard time, and feeling depressed are some of the ways people express the inability to accept themselves.

These patterns are common to a wide variety of clients. The feelings (usually guilt) associated with condemning desires have caused some people to suppress their desire for money, as well. Make sure you take the time and do the exercise now. This book will do you no good if you skip the exercises, as you may have done in the past. Taking care of this now will set you free. What are you waiting for?

How Do You Sort Out Which Desires to Act On?

Human motivation comes from values, which are thoughts, attitudes, and opinions that each of us feel strongly enough about to put into action.

For example, if working hard is a value to you, something you believe to be valuable for its own sake, this underlying value could motivate you unwittingly to miss out on or ignore moneymaking opportunities that would empower you to work less and earn more. Most people have less money than they want, and many people feel guilty about wanting money. In other words, they condemn their desire for money. Logic leads to the conclusion that accepting your desire for money, instead of feeling guilty about it, can only increase your wealth. If you don't desire money, that is OK, too. (Although if that is the case, we doubt you would be reading this book.) Everyone we know who has been both rich and poor, and thus has had the opportunity to compare the two, has a strong preference for rich.

Relying on your sense of morality to determine which desires to act on may serve your well-being in some cases, but in other cases, especially those related to money, it may not, simply because of the often-repeated childhood message that it is not OK to want money.

It is virtually certain that you'll be wealthier and happier, too, if you rely on a consciously chosen purpose for your life to serve as the guide for choosing which desires to act on.

Parents provide the basic values education. As children, we formed the values our parents gave us into an unconscious purpose. In most cases, the childhood purpose is based on gaining the approval of the people around us on whom we are temporarily dependent or on attempting to control them to provide the nurturing we needed, or both. The important question to consider, as an adult, is whether this purpose, adopted so long ago, under very different conditions, and perhaps unconsciously, is providing you with the degree of satisfaction and self-expression you seek in your life now. Are you satisfied with the state of your health and wealth, with your relationship with a higher power, with yourself and others, and with the difference you make in the world? Achievement without purpose is compulsion and thus less than satisfying.

In a few pages we will present a method for designing your consciously chosen purpose in life. This method has been used by thousands of people in Training and in individual consultations. In some cases, people resist and procrastinate defining their purpose. The joke about the process of uncovering your true purpose is that it takes 3 weeks and 45 minutes: 3 weeks to procrastinate and 45 minutes to do it.

Money and Your Purpose in Life

Some of you may be wondering what purpose in life has to do with money. Because purpose is a strategy that we use to express our important values, it follows that our use of money is one of the important ways to express these values. Money is very, very flexible, with an infinite variety of ways to earn it and spend it. Your wealth at any point is the end result of millions of earning and spending decisions. If you live in the developed West, you probably will earn more than $1 million in your lifetime. The decisions about how you earn this fortune, and spend it, are determined by your purpose in life.

Taking this one step further, consider your purpose for money. In our consulting work, people's life's purpose and purpose for money are very useful starting points for discussion because of the pervasive effect of purpose on thought and action. Most often, people who are living paycheck to paycheck have an unconsciously chosen purpose for money that is something like "Money is to live on" or "Money is to buy the things I need." Because money responds to the commands of the human mind, the external financial experience of these people conforms to their internal thinking about it.

If you are living paycheck to paycheck, then the decisions about how to use your money are made by the bills you pay each month. This situation makes it impossible to take charge of your money. You have unintentionally turned over your prerogatives as your own financial manager to your creditors and to your letter carrier who delivers the bad news each month. Additionally, when bills exhaust all of your income, you are protected from making a mistake, perhaps unconsciously, thinking something like—"I used all my money to pay my bills. That's the best thing to do with it."

For many people the prospect of dramatically increased income is frightening. As they lack a clear purpose for their life or their money, the possibility of greater income brings up anxiety about loss or making mistakes. Having a noble and consciously chosen purpose provides you with a framework for making decisions about the effective use of your growing income.

Why Bother to Declare Your Purpose?

Life has no meaning until you give it one. Choosing a consciously declared purpose ensures that your life has the meaning you prefer. Without purpose, accomplishment is less than satisfying because it tends to be motivated by unconscious desires. Goals become things you should do, rather than things you want to do. Without purpose, decision making is unduly difficult because of lacking a framework for evaluating the pros and cons of any important choice; it may lead to a great deal of second guessing. You may have experienced the conflict of "analysis paralysis" in the past.

Declaring your own purpose is the first step in moving ahead. By choosing a purpose, you have a consciously devised filter through which to consider which desires will benefit you.

Goals naturally flow from your expression of purpose in a mental hierarchy that looks like the chart in Figure 6.1.

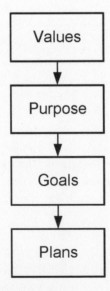

FIGURE 6.1   Hierarchy of Your Goals

The hierarchy operates, whether you are aware of it or not. If your purpose is not consciously chosen, then your unconsciously chosen inherited purpose may conflict with consciously chosen goals. Here you will learn to declare a consciously chosen purpose to express your important values.

Motivation matters, also. If you have experienced conflicts or resistance in achieving consciously chosen goals, overreliance on moving-away motivation may be the root cause. Overreliance on moving-away motivation causes a person to be primarily reactive to external events rather than responsive to internally generated goals and desires.

Consistent use of the Baseball Diamond method from Chapter 4 increases the power of moving-toward motivation. This method balances your behavior between avoiding painful situations and moving toward your internal pleasurable goals. We have uncovered a number of irrational fears that are the root of this procrastination. If you have any of these fears, realize that they are truly irrational rather than warnings of impending danger.

Fear of being different, attracting attention, or speaking up in general

People with the confidence to act on their own authority are a rarity. When you permit yourself to be motivated by a consciously chosen purpose, you run the risk of disapproval from those who are threatened by your initiative.

Unwarranted loyalty to childhood purpose or to parents in general

The movie *My Big Fat Greek Wedding* depicts the perils of violating family loyalty in an extreme manner. Clearly most families are not so xenophobic as the family in the movie that is devastated by a daughter's intention to marry a non-Greek. However, almost all families enforce certain conditions that must be fulfilled to maintain acceptance and approval.

If your parents love you at all, then they want the best for you according to their own values. Whether their values are the right ones for you is a determination only you can make. Probably some of what they taught you is useful and some is not. If you remain loyal to counterproductive values—struggle, helplessness, conformity, domination, and sacrifice—these are expressed as part of your inherited purpose. Earning the income you want from work that satisfies you is an act of defiance. It defies both societal and parental conditioning.

Fear of failure

How am I going to accomplish what I really want? A purpose is not about accomplishment at all. Goals flow from purpose. Goals relate to accomplishment. Purpose relates to expression.

Fear of loss

To the extent that a person's unconsciously chosen purpose includes using behaviors or avoiding certain behaviors in order to receive approval or to avoid disapproval from others, then the prospect of changing to behavior that is self-determined may appear to create a risk of losing approval from the outside. Consider for a moment the value of outside approval conditional on conformity. Isn't this very much like how your parents endeavored to control you? Do you prefer to make decisions on your own authority or to allow yourself to be governed by what others may think?

Preconditioned, unconscious notions of right and wrong

Perhaps you learned from your parents that it is not OK to want money. If you were punished or disapproved of when you asked for things as a child, as an adult you may tend to avoid experiencing your desire for increased income. Opportunities that could result in greater income may make you uncomfortable, usually with feelings of guilt. You may even have an unconscious strategy for avoiding such opportunities in order to feel relief from the guilt.

You can use a clearly defined purpose for your life as the yardstick to evaluate whether any desire is harmonious with the full expression of that purpose. If your purpose benefits yourself and others, then it is prudent to conclude that your desire for money is right. Recognize any uncomfortable feelings as simply residue from your unconsciously adopted purpose from childhood. Regarding money, whatever your purpose is, you'll express it more fully with money than without. Is part of your purpose to help people? To be a philanthropist? You'll accomplish much more with money than without it, and you'll be happier in the process. In fact, everything you do with money expresses your purpose, whether the purpose is consciously designed or unconsciously adopted.

THE PURPOSE OF MY LIFE METHOD

This extremely important method will help you declare a meaningful and noble purpose for your life. Now is not the time to procrastinate. You have suffered enough; otherwise you wouldn't be reading this. Do this method now. Let yourself become aware of what you are really meant to do.

Section A: List 10 to 20 characteristics you like about yourself. For example: My adventurous personality, my creativity, my caring for people and society.

1. My _____
2. My _____
3. My _____
4. My _____
5. My _____
6. My _____
7. My _____
8. My _____
9. My _____
10. My _____

11. My _____
12. My _____
13. My _____
14. My _____
15. My _____
16. My _____
17. My _____
18. My _____
19. My _____
20. My _____

Now look back over your list and check off the three, four, or five most significant characteristics to you.

Section B: List the ways you like to express yourself involving one or more of the characteristics you checked in section A. For example: Helping, caring, loving.

1. _____ing
2. _____ing
3. _____ing
4. _____ing
5. _____ing
6. _____ing
7. _____ing

11. _____ing
12. _____ing
13. _____ing
14. _____ing
15. _____ing
16. _____ing
17. _____ing

8. _____ing   18. _____ing

9. _____ing   19. _____ing

10. _____ing   20. _____ing

Section C: Think about your highest aspirations for yourself and the world, and describe these in 25 words or less.

_____

_____

_____

_____

Now go back to section B and check off the three, four, or five activities that contribute the most to making the world more the way you just described it.

Section D: *The Purpose of Your Life*. Fill in the first blank with the items you checked off in section A. Fill in the second blank with the items you checked off in section B. Fill in the third blank with the description you wrote in section C.

The purpose of my life is to use my

_____

_____

_____ by _____

_____ so that _____

_____

_____

_____.

What did you learn from discovering your purpose? Is it what you thought it was? Is it much different from what you thought it would be?

Now that you have written down your purpose, you are on your way to achieving the success you desire and deserve. Pat yourself on the back for accomplishing this. Do this now! Go on, you deserve it.

If you have not finished your purpose or if you skipped this exercise, go back and do it now. It is vitally important that you complete the methods in the order we have written them. Go ahead and design your life the way you choose, instead of what others may prefer. Do this method now!

Some participants in our Training sessions take as little as 45 minutes to define their purpose in life using the method described here. Some people take longer, and others a lot longer. It's worth doing, no matter how long it may take. Discovering and declaring your purpose is the most significant thing you can do. It's all too easy to allow yourself to be distracted by the trivia of day-to-day living and to avoid examining the most important issues. For some people, finding out how little harmony there is between their external life and their internally generated purpose comes as a big shock. Often these are the people who experience a midlife crisis when, in their 30s or 40s, they realize how hard they are working for so little satisfaction.

Clarity about purpose starts you toward significant improvements in your life. It will help you to:

- Increase your inner direction and self-reliance.
- Make decision making quicker and more effective.
- Make your financial life simpler and more focused.
- Stop worrying about the small stuff and realize you are a loving person with important business to conduct.
- Put uncomfortable feelings in their proper perspective, reducing fear of failure, fear of success, and others.
- Make everything you do a priority. If you add some skillful time management to your purpose, you can stop wasting time on activities that do not matter.

Remember that a purpose is different from a goal. A purpose is expressed; a goal is accomplished. A purpose is timeless, whereas a goal has a beginning, a middle, and an end. The goals that will be the most satisfying for you are those that are direct expressions of your purpose.

When you are satisfied with the declaration of purpose you have created, write it on a small card and carry it with you in your purse or wallet. Refer to it whenever you have a decision to make. Also, read it every chance you get to reinforce what you intend to do. The more you read your life's purpose, the more you will know exactly what to do to move yourself forward. The decisions you face will become easier and easier as your purpose becomes more a part of you.

Become Your Own Source of Permission

Adherence to the childhood rule of "don't do anything without permission" makes success in your own business an uphill struggle. There is no boss to give you permission, so you're likely to procrastinate a lot about decisions and then second guess yourself afterward.

As children, we needed permission to do almost anything. When we did not ask for it and did what we wanted, often we were punished by our parents, family, teachers, and other authority figures. Those of you who went to parochial or military schools understand this very well.

I (AF) went to a parochial grammar school and felt that I had no permission to do anything except what the nuns, priests, and teachers told us was OK. When we stepped outside the boundaries of permission, we were punished severely—sometimes to a point of borderline physical abuse. For a long time this stifled me from moving forward, and I developed a rebellious nature toward authority figures. Now that I am an adult, I discovered that this attitude served me much better to get ahead in life. I am not suggesting that you rebel against everything—just challenge the ideas and see if permission is truly required.

PERMISSION VISUALIZATION METHOD

Give yourself permission that you did not believe you had or no one else gave you before. We are our own source of permission. Most things we want to do only require our own permission. So let's give ourselves the permission that we deserve to achieve what we desire. Do this method now. It will assist you in getting through the rest of the book.

Imagine your higher power (God, Universal Intelligence, or whatever higher power means to you). Make sure this image is colorful and right in front of you at eye level in your mind. Make the colors stark and vivid like the movie *Dick Tracy* or like watching colorful fish in coral reefs.

Make sure the picture you have of your higher power is close and large. Hear any sounds, feel any feelings, smell any smells, and taste any tastes associated with this image. Make sure you are really feeling the sensation inside yourself when thinking about your higher power. Once you have this image complete and you feel the feelings inside, raise this image up in front of you to about 45 degrees above eye level, where it is still comfortable to see without having to tilt your head. Leave the image up there.

Now imagine a great big billboard with bright white lights all around it right in front of you. The lights are flashing around the billboard in a circular pattern. Now place the word "PERMISSION" in great big block letters in the center of the billboard. Make sure your image is in vivid color, bright, and large as it is in Figure 6.2.

Now raise the billboard up to the same level as the image of your higher power. Let the two images melt together to become one.

Now that you have this new image, how do you feel? Are you feeling more empowered? Do you feel that you have to have someone else's permission to move forward? Anytime you think that you have to have permission, just remember your new image. Remember, you are the source of your own permission. Having your own permission is the only thing that matters. Now you have the tool to give it to yourself. Treat yourself and use this technique any time you feel that you require someone else's permission. Most important, enjoy the freedom it gives you.

How to Stop Giving Away Your Power

Many societies practice rites of passage, ceremonies to mark the onset of adulthood. Typically these ceremonies are different for males and females. Even though the ceremonies vary greatly from one society to another, there are a couple of common elements among them. One is that the ceremonies are usually quite dramatic, sometimes even brutal, far more dramatic than graduation or obtaining a driver's license, which serve as rites of passage in western society. Perhaps the most important characteristic of these rites of passage

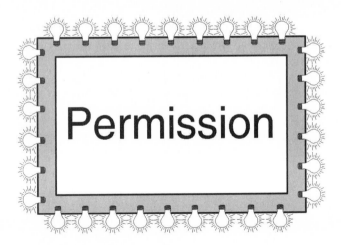

FIGURE 6.2   Giving Yourself Permission

ceremonies is that they take place in the presence of a significant number of the people. The adults simultaneously begin to treat the initiate as an adult and expect him or her to behave in that way. In a short time, the new adult catches on and fulfills the expectations that the group has for adults.

In western society, the passage to adulthood is spread over a longer period of time. Whatever your process may have been in arriving at adulthood, if you still look to others as authority figures or need to be told what to do, or if you give others the power to judge your worth, these expectations will limit both your accomplishment and satisfaction.

It is important to understand how we view the authority figures in our lives. Depending on how we see them in relation to ourselves, we may be giving away our personal power for no reason. If we view the authority figures in our lives as we did as a child, in our minds they will appear to be much larger than we are. In those cases, we may be giving them more weight than we do our own decisions. (See Figure 6.3.)

As children we are told to respect our elders, the police, firefighters, schoolteachers, and so on. We have been conditioned to elevate them to a higher level than ourselves. As adults, we may still be seeing these people the same way because our unconscious

FIGURE 6.3   Authority Figures

mind was conditioned for many years. Our parents did not mean to harm us by giving us this information. They did the best job they could with the information they had at the time.

How do we change our perception of authority figures to reflect a more realistic view? The next method will place authority figures in proper perspective.

AUTHORITY SIZE METHOD

First, understand there are no right or wrong answers here. The method will be different for everyone.

Find a nice comfortable place where you can relax. Close your eyes and take a deep breath. Relax totally. Now imagine a picture of your father—however that comes up for you in your mind. Once you have the picture of your father, imagine a picture of yourself. Once you have both pictures in your mind, place them side-by-side. Which person appears larger—is your father larger than you are, or are you larger than he is? Just remember the answer to this for now. We will come back to this shortly.

Next, clear the pictures in your mind by looking at the ceiling for about three seconds. Then look straight ahead at the wall for three seconds. Now go through the same exercise with your mother. Imagine a picture of your mother in your mind—however she looks to you. Once you have the picture of your mother, get a picture of yourself again. Once you have both pictures in your mind, place them side-by-side. Notice which person appears larger—is your mother larger than you are, or are you larger than she is?

Use this method for any authority figure in your life. For example, we used this technique when we were looking for a publisher for this book.

You now have a picture of your parents compared to you. Were they larger in size than you? Was one of your parents larger than you and the other smaller? If so, which one was larger? This is important for you to understand. If your father was larger, then you may want to look at other male authority figures in your life and see how they compare. Conversely, if your mother was larger, you may want to look at other female authority figures.

The next step is to learn how to change your perceptions about them. Pick any authority figure and imagine this person. Also imagine yourself standing next to this person. Make yourself larger and shrink your authority figure down to about the height of your knee. How does this make you feel? Do you feel more in control? Now make yourself more colorful and brighter, and imagine your authority figure dimmer, darker, fuzzier, and in black and white.

How do you feel now? Did this impact your experience? Do you feel like you're more in control now? Do you feel more empowered? Most people feel more empowered after this exercise. If you did not, repeat the method and keep making adjustments to your images until you gain that sense of empowerment. You may have to change some of the characteristics, such as brightness, focus, or location to feel more empowered. Remember, this is *your* mind, and you are free to decorate it the way you choose. If you continue to have difficulty with this method, also examine your associated sounds and feelings and change them. Have fun and stand up for what rightfully belongs to you. Take control now!

Changing the characteristics of our perceptions changes how we feel about any situation. When you changed the pictures of the authority figures in your life, you changed how you represented them in your mind. These changes will be permanent unless you choose to change them back. But why would you want to do this?

Go back and look at the rest of the authority figures in your life. Change them so they no longer control you. Use this technique with anyone that you feel may have control over you in your mind and change him or her. Do this exercise with any additional family members or other authority figures to whom you give your decision-making power.

Do this repeatedly and, especially, whenever your mind is yelling at you with sentences starting with the words "I have to," "I should," "You'd better," and the like.

If you completed this exercise, pat yourself on the back. Great job! If you skipped it, go back and do it now. True winners in life will do things that others won't. Are you a winner, or are you going to waste your time and money? The choice is yours. We know that you are a winner because otherwise you wouldn't be reading this book. Go ahead and make the most of it now. Break those old habits you used to have today.

The Power of Philanthropy

Rich people, in contrast to those living paycheck to paycheck, usually understand that money exists to express their values. This is the case even though some rich people clearly have some values you may not agree with.

Philanthropy is a method widely used by the rich to express their important values. Andrew Carnegie's philanthropy, for example, built libraries all across the United States. Don't wait until you are rich to become a philanthropist. Start now and begin to develop the consciousness that your money exists to express your values. Find a cause that expresses your values, whether that cause is social, religious, or political. Set aside a definite percentage of your gross income to donate to this cause—1 to 10 percent of your income, depending on what you can afford. Practice this consistently for three months and you will certainly notice a profound shift in your thinking about money. Clearly this method works best when done without guilt. You are not obligated to give your money away. It's your money. Use it as you like and don't let people or organizations seeking contributions use guilt to manipulate you.

Benefiting from Peer Group Influence

Most parents are concerned about peer group influences on their children. What is a peer group? A peer group consists of those people whose approval and acceptance is important enough to you that you are willing to modify your behavior, at least a little, in order to maintain your membership in the group. Now, this desire for connection and association with others is a normal impulse we all experience. The important question is whether the peer group you have chosen moves you forward or holds you back. In other words, does your natural desire for association and connection aid you or hinder you in the expression of your purpose?

Our society has mixed feelings about excellence. On one hand, our society finds excellence extremely attractive. This value transcends culture, gender, race, and all other classifications. Every four years, billions (yes, billions) of viewers around the world tune in to watch the Olympics, a display of athletic excellence.

On the other hand, our society feels that excellence rocks the boat. Show up in your peer group with a new ring way more expensive than anyone else has or with a luxury car and notice the body language. Pay close attention. This is all part of building higher sensory acuity.

In order to make improvements in any area, you must trust and believe in something inside of you that is superior to your current external circumstances. What is the general mode of communication within your peer group? Is it mostly support and encouragement for your internal aspirations? Or is it compassion for complaints about external circumstances? Now, there is clearly nothing wrong, evil, or malicious about compassion for complaints. However, as you may have already noticed, it does not move you forward. In extreme cases, people rely on their complaints for attention, significance, and connection.

If your peer group consists primarily of moaners and complainers, there are three options available to you:

1. Stay in the group and endure its continued influence.
2. Fix the people in your peer group.
3. Upgrade by finding and associating with a different group of people with higher standards and greater success.

Take this opportunity to upgrade your peer group now, by seeking others who are moving ahead and don't be surprised at how quickly everything progresses.

Clearly not everyone you associate with is a member of your peer group. There may be people in your peer group or even role models whom you don't see very often, perhaps even some you do not like very much. You may consider some people who do not know each other to be part of your peer group.

DEFINE YOUR PEER GROUP

Make a list of those people you currently consider your peer group. Ask yourself if there is anyone in the group whose continued approval or acceptance requires you to hold yourself back or who might be uncomfortable when you achieve the extraordinary gains you plan for yourself. Now that you have your list and you have determined whom you want to be with, what have you learned? Have you noticed who empowers you and who does not? Identify the people you want less contact with and more contact with. How do you feel about what you have discovered?

Knowing your purpose will improve your perceptions about money. This is because, instead of the many conflicts you used to have about money, money becomes simply an aid in the expression of your purpose. Counterproductive thinking and behavior related to competition, consumption, and comparison disappear. It quickly becomes obvious that comparing yourself to others, whose purpose is different, is absurd.

Purposelessness taken to an extreme makes your life a futile attempt to satisfy the most recent desire that springs from your unconscious mind to conscious awareness. Such a meaningless existence satisfies no one. Make sure you do this exercise. You may be surprised to find that the people you currently associate with do not serve your greater purpose.

CHAPTER 7

STOP WASTING
YOUR ENERGY

*Feelings related to facing a challenge can make you stronger and
more alert, but only if you give up fighting against the energy
that is there to help you.*

Money and Emotions

Money is a more emotional topic than commonly believed. It's expressed in numbers, creating an illusion of logic and precision. However, money is not just numbers, but numbers that record the passage of money. When you walk on the beach, the footprints you leave in the sand are not you, but a record of your passage. Numbers record the passage of money. Far more important than the numbers is how you feel about money. There is no topic more likely to cause very intense arguments for couples. In less intimate relationships, feelings about money are almost invariably suppressed.

Money takes the blame for a lot of problems that are actually caused by feelings we all are most determined to avoid and least willing to acknowledge. Money is simply the symbol that brings up the unresolved feelings. It's possible that money has caused far more pain than you wish to feel again. I (PL) have taught courses about personal finance since 1976. At the beginning of each course, people always are somewhat surprised when I start talking about how money and feelings are so closely related. After a while, a different sort of surprise takes its place—amazement that this association had not been discussed before.

One participant in a Training session commented, "These money issues are visceral. They are about survival."

Uncomfortable feelings often relate to some unpleasant event in your personal history. If you broke your leg at age six, you probably have unpleasant suppressed feelings associated with that experience. But remembering the event and the suppressed feelings associated with it cannot hurt you. The event is over. Not only can the associated feelings not hurt you, they cannot be as intense as they were when your leg was actually broken, simply because it isn't broken anymore. Obviously, any remembered pain will be less intense. Associated with the actual broken leg would be fear about how it would turn out—specifically whether you would walk again. Remembering the event from today's perspective, you know how it turned out. The uncertainty has been resolved by the passage of time, so the fear that you feel with the memory is less intense.

POWER OF PERCEPTION METHOD

We explained in Chapter 4 how a person's experience is determined by the perception he or she holds of it. Next you will learn to apply this power of perception with a natural and very rapid method for resolving the pain of past financial upsets so they no longer slow your progress. Do this now rather than skipping ahead.

R℘   First, a brief warm-up exercise so you can understand the power available in changing your perception.

Imagine you are sitting near a swimming pool. Feel the sun, see the sparkling water and the diving board high atop its ladder and platform. Watch as a person climbs the ladder to the top of the platform high above the water, walks on to the board, and jumps into the pool. Give yourself a minute to really get the picture clear and bright in your mind.

Now, notice your emotions about what you just saw. How intense are they? How would you rate their intensity on a scale from 0 to 10, where 0 is neutral and 10 is intense emotional overload?

Now imagine yourself at the same swimming pool. Give yourself a minute to get back there to feel the sun and see the water, platform, and diving board. Now imagine it is you climbing the ladder to the platform. As you do this, feel the metal railings in your hands, the alternating flexing of your leg muscles as you climb, and the rough wooden rungs of the ladder beneath your feet. When you reach the top, look down at the people sitting around the pool and notice how small they look from your new vantage point high above the water. See the diving board in front of you, walk out on it, and feel it wobble as it bends under your weight. Feel your toes curl over the end of the board. Then jump off and feel yourself plunge into the water far below. Give yourself several moments to really feel the feelings.

Now notice your emotions about what you just experienced. How intense are they? How would you rate their intensity on a scale from 0 to 10, where 0 is neutral and 10 is intense emotional overload?

Almost without exception, people report far more intense feelings with the second experience. Why is this? In both cases, some part of your mind is aware that you are reading a book. The difference between the two experiences is your point of view, or your perception.

The first time you imagined you were watching the event; the second time you imagined you were in it. The emotional intensity changed because your perception changed. The first time you experienced the event from the observer or dissociated position. The dissociated position typically reduces emotional intensity. The second time you imagined that you were the person climbing the ladder and jumping into the water. You saw the event through your own eyes or from the associated position.

EMOTIONAL RESOLUTION METHOD

Let's move on to practical ways for using our power of perception to aid wealth accumulation.

On a separate sheet of paper, make a list of past negative experiences about money. These could include instances when you spent money foolishly, when you lost money in an investment, job loss, when someone stole from you or failed to pay you as agreed. It doesn't matter whether the event occurred very recently or when you were a small child. Write them all down. Also, include negative experiences about money from your original family because, as a child, you were dependent on your parents for financial security.

Now picture yourself in each of these experiences. Make sure you see yourself in each event as you remember it, rather than seeing it through your adult eyes. Seeing yourself in the event is the way to be sure that you are dissociated.

Now make a second list of positive experiences with money, extending from the recent past back to childhood. These may include accomplishment of an important goal, the promotion of one of your parents at work, a significant increase in income, or a successful investment, for example.

Now let yourself see each of these events, one at a time, from the associated position, through your own eyes, as if they were happening now. If you see yourself in any of the memories, this means you are not associated. Change this by stepping into yourself and seeing each event through your own eyes.

People whose lives seem to be emotional roller coasters tend to see almost all of their experiences from the associated position. In contrast, people who are detached and without emotion tend to see most events from a dissociated position. Nobody's life is perfect. Use this simple method of choosing the appropriate perception (associated for pleasant events and dissociated for unpleasant ones), so that life is as enjoyable as possible and so that you are freed from the negative past events that might prevent effective action.

From Struggle to Flow

Helplessness leads to power! This statement sounds ridiculous to most people the first time they hear it because it does not conform to the traditional intellectual logic or analytical thinking that we learned in school and use every day. Nevertheless, it is highly logical in the emotional sense, as you will soon discover.

What would it be worth to you to give up struggle? How much of your creative energy might you be wasting now on struggle?

In the 1980s, I (PL) lived in San Francisco. One New Year's Eve, I was pondering my choice of a resolution. I wanted to avoid the usual ones we make and pick something that would truly make a difference for me. After discarding a list of things I could do, I began to think about this differently, considering instead "What could I give up?"

From the recesses of my mind came the answer, "struggle" loud and clear. Immediately I noticed strong ambivalent feelings associated with the possibility of such an outcome.

"My life would be much better without it."

"Will this turn out to be more struggle?"

These were just a few of the emotionally charged thoughts that raced by.

I knew I had never done this or anything like it before. My previous goals had involved accomplishing something or getting something. Never before had I intentionally given up something. This project would require a method different and more dramatic from anything I had used in the past to accomplish goals related to gaining something. I knew I required a method to alert my awareness as fully as possible whenever struggle occurred. Here is the method I decided on: Whenever I notice that I am struggling, I will lie down. I thought this had a definite possibility of success, because it would be virtually impossible for me to struggle while lying down.

With my awareness focused on noticing indications that I was struggling, it quickly became evident how pervasive my tendency to struggle was—even related to everyday events. Although I did discover that lying down temporarily ended the struggle, I found myself lying down in places where I would rather not do so. After lying down on city sidewalks several times, I made the radical decision to go home and lie in bed to have cleaner and more comfortable surroundings.

At first the urges to "get up and do something" were almost overwhelming. I saw these as counterproductive to my desire to give up struggle and stayed put. I left the bed only to attend to essential hygiene functions for a short period each day. After a day or so, waves of helplessness came to my awareness. These feelings were unusual to me; obviously they were related to my self-imposed limitations on action. I saw that my past struggle was actually a strategy I had designed unconsciously to prevent me from experiencing feelings of helplessness. These helpless feelings were now coming to my awareness because I was intentionally preventing myself from taking any action.

I realized that I used to ask myself, "How could you be helpless? Look at how busy you are!" As the days wore on, it also came to my awareness that the world seemed to operate as well as it had before I stopped participating. The utilities still provided service, people collected the garbage and cleaned the streets without any intention from me.

Then I was beset by a dilemma. The prospect of spending the rest of my life in bed did not appeal to me. "How will I know that I am done with struggle?" or "How can I be sure that I won't revert to struggle when I do get out of bed?" I wondered.

I concluded that there really could be no way to know whether I had succeeded completely until after I got out of bed. Additionally, I realized that the expectation of complete success was related to perfectionist tendencies that probably had contributed to the struggle in the first place. "I don't need to be perfect in my quest to give up struggle. Instead I can declare that a significant reduction in struggle is sufficient to constitute success."

So I began to review the past situations where I had struggled. My self-imposed limitation on action quickly put me in touch with the underlying helplessness associated with each of these situations. By allowing the feeling of helplessness to be OK, I found I could eliminate my previously impulsive reaction to avoid this feeling by struggling. If I could do this well enough, then I would be likely to experience an overall significant reduction in struggle after I got out of bed. My review of past incidents when I had struggled went on for a day or two more. I was starting to consider the project complete and a return to activities more usual for me than spending 23.5 hours a day in bed.

"Wait a minute!" I thought. "What about the future?" By this time I sensed that I had made peace with past experiences of struggle and underlying helplessness; I found the feeling delightfully empowering. I was beginning to experience the truth of the statement that helplessness leads to power. As you might imagine, I was strongly motivated to extend this new feeling of resourcefulness into my future.

To ensure this, I spent several more days in bed making written and mental lists of as many possible future situations where my tendency to struggle might arise. I discovered that simply thinking about these possible future scenarios where struggle was likely was sufficient to bring up the feelings of helplessness that previously had evaded my awareness. In the past I often was aware of feelings related to events that had not happened yet (stage fright and fear of rejection, for example), but the usefulness of this emotional phenomenon had not occurred to me before. By accepting the helplessness associated with events that had not occurred yet, I could make a definite change in how the future turned out. By seeing possible future events differently, I was training myself to respond differently. At this point, I was able to understand that helplessness had been a factor in all my troubling emotions. Anger can be well characterized as determination contaminated by helplessness, fear as helplessness to avoid unpleasant future events, and sadness as helplessness to prevent loss.

Struggle is nonproductive action that produces only the internal result of suppressing helplessness. By this I mean that if you are struggling, then you don't have to face your feelings of helplessness. You can tell yourself, "I am not helpless—at least I am struggling." Yet struggle (nonpurposeful action) serves only to continue the suppression of helplessness.

For this reason, accepting my helplessness as a feeling instead of fighting it as an unacceptable condition produced not only a significant increase in capability but also a sense of serenity about the challenges I faced. I think it will for you, too.

No, I don't think you will have to stay in bed for several weeks.

One reason this project took as much time as it did was that I did not know where it would lead, so I really didn't know what I was looking for. Since then I have shared this story with thousands of people who have been able to accept helplessness much more quickly.

Two very important things to remember:

1. Helplessness leads to power.
2. Helplessness is a feeling, not a condition, and therefore it is temporary.

Possible Origins of Struggle

From our study of the dynamics of the human mind, we find no inherent reason that life must be a struggle. No doubt you have noticed, also, that some people turn even simple tasks into confounding problems, while other people flow through life with a degree of ease unknown to the first group. Free will provides all people the prerogative to choose those actions that support the expression of whatever purpose we choose, as well as to design and select the internal sensory representations that produce the behavior we prefer. So why is life a struggle for many people?

Birth Experience

In his groundbreaking book, *Birth without Violence,* (Inner Traditions Intl Ltd. 2002), Frederick Leboyer, M.D., draws on his experience as an obstetrician to present a strong indictment about the negative effect of modern birthing methods on newborns. He argues that the birthing procedures commonly in use have been designed for the convenience of attending doctors without consideration for the newborn. His strongest and most well- founded argument is against cutting the umbilical cord before newborns have time to learn to breathe on their own. In so-called normal birth, the umbilical cord is cut as soon newborns emerge from the birth canal. This premature separation from the umbilical life support system requires newborns to begin breathing immediately or suffer brain damage due to oxygen deprivation.

Because the amniotic fluid that filled and protected the lungs in the womb must be expelled immediately, before breathing can begin, the practice of suspending newborns in an inverted position evolved. Gravity quickly removes the amniotic fluid, and the newborn has learned to breathe in a situation of fear and panic of death by suffocation.

Dr. Leboyer proposes that the umbilical cord be left intact until the newborn naturally expels the amniotic fluid and learns to breathe on its own. He argues that this gentle birth procedure eliminates trauma to the spine caused by its rapid straightening, eliminates trauma to the sinuses caused by the amniotic fluid draining out, and produces an ease about life and breathing not experienced by survivors of so-called normal birth.

Some people may point out that birth happened a long time ago (it did) and that they do not remember it (most don't). Some may even argue that newborns are incapable of experiencing pain—but they have to be people who haven't spent any time with newborns. Breathing we do all the time. Patterns of struggle imprinted on the breathing mechanism at birth are likely to be a contributing factor to the pervasive belief that life is a struggle. This is something for you to consider if you are thinking of having a baby. Similar struggle patterns may be operating for you, especially if you felt squeamish or uncomfortable while reading the preceding section or if you noticed that your breathing stopped.

How Unresolved Guilt May Be Affecting Your Financial Life in Unknown Ways

Why the topic of unresolved guilt? Parental and societal training unintentionally leads most people to accept the income that is offered from work they tolerate. A significant percentage of the people we have worked with have broken free of past conditioning by successfully dealing with unresolved guilt from various sources.

The definition of guilt that makes the most sense is that guilt is self-punishment in a universe perceived to be unsafe. If you did something wrong in an unsafe universe, it would seem a good idea to punish yourself first in an attempt to beat the much bigger and stronger universe to the punch. Thus, guilt is truly its own punishment. Additionally, guilt is less selective than you may believe. Guilt about some issue completely unrelated to money may be limiting your financial success without your awareness.

Forgiveness (which means giving up the claim of retribution, including retribution against yourself) frees you from guilt. There is also the possibility that failing to resolve guilt for unacceptable behavior in the past may unconsciously motivate you to repeat the behavior in order to justify it.

Unresolved guilt may be affecting your financial life by:

- Lowering your sense of what good you deserve.
- Stopping you from asking for what you want.
- Stopping you from knowing what you want.
- Stopping you from taking those risks that would get you what you want.
- Causing you to say yes when saying no is much more to your benefit.
- Causing you to attract people who drain your energy and money with no hope of benefit to you, resulting in justified resentment on your part. Such a dynamic may cause you to view your success as the result of good luck and others' failure as the result of bad luck.
- People stealing from you.
- Inexplicable losses of money.
- Making decisions for you in other ways.

No one would want to be completely free of guilt. If you were to behave in manner outside of your own morality, you would feel guilty. This sort of guilt is healthy. Healthy guilt provides a window to our conscience. For example, it is probably natural to feel guilty for breaking agreements, intentionally deceiving others, telling lies, and the like. Anticipation of such guilt actually aids us in avoiding destructive behavior. A person without such a sense of guilt is without a moral compass; consider recent events with famous politicians, professional athletes, and others. Complete lack of awareness of guilt renders a person psychopathic.

Actually, the origin of the unresolved guilt is far less important than our being aware of that guilt and changing it. Nevertheless, some of its possible sources are:

- Societal guilt about money
- Parental guilt
- Religious guilt
- Survivor's guilt

SOCIETAL GUILT ABOUT MONEY

Guilt about money and its backlash, which can be called class envy or resentment of rich people, is so intense in our society that reasonable discussion about public policy related to taxation is just about impossible. The income gap between the highest-earning and lowest-earning segments of the population steadily increases, and the promise of middle-class financial security is rapidly becoming a fantasy. (Here we are referring to the typical middle-class dream of homeownership, sending kids to college, and saving for a comfortable retirement.) If you feel guilty about becoming rich, then you will tend to avoid or fail at those steps that will make you rich, in order to avoid the discomfort of the associated guilt. Conversely, if you resent rich people, you will tend to avoid riches, so as to avoid the possibility of receiving the same resentment that you now project onto rich people. There may be many reasons why you cannot afford a Rolls-Royce; the fact that someone else has one is not one of these reasons.

PARENTAL GUILT

Personal and societal expectations regarding parenthood are unreasonably high. Parenthood is one of the toughest jobs in the world, and there is little useful training for it. Unfortunately, the only training most people receive at this is from their own parents. Although you have the ability to influence others, you do not control them, including your children. You probably made lots of mistakes of commission and omission in raising your children. If you did the best job you could and your children turned out below your expectations, this is OK. Further self-punishment serves no one.

RELIGIOUS GUILT

Thankfully all of us in the United States have freedom of religion. You can have whatever religious beliefs you like. The issue here is how religious beliefs affect your finances. No matter what religion you belong to, there are rich people who are members. It is OK for you to be one of them. One religious model of life says that we separate from God at birth and remain so until death. From this assumption comes the conclusion that the purpose of life is to earn a reunion with God at some unknown time in the future. Such a reunion is often believed to be conditional on adherence to an elaborate system of morality. This morality often includes the idea that money is evil.

If you believe that money will corrupt you, you are corrupt already. There are lots of popular sayings about this: "Money is the root of all evil." "Power corrupts. Absolute power corrupts absolutely." Money projects power. No question about that. However, it's a big leap of logic to state that money is the cause of the corruption. In fact, money *cannot* corrupt you.

There are corrupt and degenerate poor people and corrupt and degenerate rich people. The difference is that money enables rich degenerates to express themselves more fully.

Having your own business is a wonderful thing. It's your creation whereby you serve others by expressing those values that are most important to you. The more money you earn, the more able you become to serve even more people by the expression of your important values. The idea that money will corrupt you assumes that money has the power to change your values. If money has that much power over you, then your values cannot have been very strong in the first place.

Religion that keeps you poor borders on medieval superstition. It is time you were free of this. This model produces struggle and lack. Unity with the Source of Sources can only aid in your prosperity. Another way to say this is that the creator of the universe did not create Mercedes automobiles so that you could not have one.

SURVIVOR'S GUILT

Survivor's guilt is the result of a natural but erroneous conclusion made by the survivors of catastrophic events: that there is some relationship between the fact that the victims died and the survivors did not. Survivors of air crashes, wartime combat, the Nazi Holocaust, as well as other manmade and natural disasters experience survivor's guilt to some degree.

I (PL) grew up in a small town in New Jersey (pop. 7,000). Ten people from my town went to Vietnam, and I was the only one to come back. Many of the casualties were people I knew. As I recovered from the war experience, I sought therapy about survivor's guilt. In time I recognized that the fact that those people were dead and I was alive had nothing to do with each other.

I believe that survivor's guilt is the primary component in posttraumatic stress disorder (PTSD). One characteristic all PTSD sufferers have in common is that they survived while others did not. Survivor's guilt tends to keep the PTSD in place far longer and far more severely than need be, because the guilt makes the events more painful to talk about and leads sufferers to think they should feel bad.

It may aid millions of fellow Vietnam veterans and other sufferers from PTSD to understand that PTSD is not a disorder at all. There is nothing wrong. PTSD results from the natural functioning of your unconscious mind. In a life-threatening situation, your mind puts feelings aside and 100 percent of your awareness focuses on dealing with the danger. Later, after the event, your unconscious mind brings forth the suppressed feelings to your awareness so you can resolve them after the danger has past. Sometimes this may be years later.

In my case, when I returned home, I experienced inappropriate reactions to sudden loud noises, such as diving facedown into snowbanks in response to buses backfiring, and intense nightmares causing me to awaken bathed in sweat. The awareness that all of this was part of a natural process rather than an indication that something was wrong, coupled with simply talking about it, aided in problem resolution. If you experience PTSD from any traumatic event, ask yourself whether you would really want to be the kind of person who would go through a traumatic experience like that and *not* be affected by it.

People who suffer from survivor's guilt often tend to seek validation as, at least, a temporary relief from the guilt. Thus, the mature Private Ryan in *Saving Private Ryan* asks his wife to tell him that he has led a good life.

The effort of suppressing guilt only increases its power. Surely carrying around guilt of any sort limits self-expression as well as income production.

Your feelings are the subjective experience of your passion. How much of your passion do you put into what you don't want? How much passion do you put into what you do want?

Feelings have two components: the energy itself and your opinion about the feelings. You have no control over the energy itself, but you do have complete control over your opinion. And your opinion determines what any feeling means about you or to you.

Your opinion (remember, you control this) is the more important part, because it determines how the energy affects you. Your opinion may take many forms, but the essential aspect is whether the feeling is acceptable to you. If it is acceptable, then the energy is available for the activity of your choice. If it is not acceptable, the energy becomes much less useful and, in some cases, even destructive.

How we respond to feelings of threat, anxiety, regret, guilt, and joyousness define our personality at the deepest level. For example, some people give up in the face of failure; others become more determined. Some people graciously accept compliments; others deflect them with embarrassment. Some people love taking risks; others are very conservative.

Lacking conscious direction, feelings are energy in raw form. Work is the expenditure of energy in a purposeful way. We have all read about "how to" work more effectively: Set priorities, plan your work, and work your plan, be persistent, and the like. But to be truly useful, any discussion about working more effectively must deal with managing your energy itself in a better way. You experience your energy as feelings or sensations. No matter where you start—with your bank balance, education, abilities, or experience— learning to use your energy better will improve your financial situation and your satisfaction with your work, as well. You'll have a better experience of life, regardless of your current circumstances.

Feelings: Genetically Programmed Responses to Challenges

The challenge that causes feelings may be external or internal, real or imaginary. Standing before an audience of two thousand, about to present an important speech, anyone would experience an increase in energy from the very real and present challenge. It's also possible to sit at home by yourself and think about presenting a speech to two thousand people. A few minutes of this and you will experience the same increase in energy, even though the challenge is completely imaginary. In intensely emotional situations, the mind does not differentiate between something that is real and something that is imagined.

Later, when we talk about planning, you will discover that a plan is the natural *intellectual* response to a challenge and learn how to use that response to aid your accomplishment of any goal.

Admit Powerlessness over Your Feelings

Most people fear public speaking, although it's not dangerous. You are safer giving a speech than driving on the freeway, but almost no one allows fear to prevent highway travel. Trying to explain why you are afraid will not make you a better public speaker. Analyzing the cause of your feelings is unproductive.

You could spend years in psychotherapy to learn why you are terrified of public speaking. Even an accurate answer to why you have this fear would do very little to increase your public speaking confidence or effectiveness. Another problem with wanting to know the why of what you are feeling is the tendency to look for a scapegoat. Whether you find the correct scapegoat or not, your search for one still makes you a victim. A bit of humor is useful. Blame your uncomfortable feelings on the hairy elephants, which are explained in the following fable. This probably isn't an accurate conclusion about the source of your stage fright, but it's definitely more useful than whatever the so-called accurate answer may be. This answer helps you to realize that, since you obviously can't do anything today about the hairy elephants, you may as well admit that you can't do anything about the terror of speaking in public, either. Such an admission of powerlessness, if you have the courage to make it, enables you to give up your struggle and experience the terror as it is. The struggle is only your perception. Stopping this struggle leads to acceptance of the terror and the ability to function with it and even use it to your benefit.

For these reasons, it's mostly useless to try to determine the cause of your feelings.

This fable is useful in understanding the origin of feelings. Like all fables, the moral of the story matters more than the objective truth.

Once upon a time, long ago and far away, there were two kinds of people—the Fuzzies and the Smoothies. The Fuzzies were people who got an increase in energy when presented with a challenge, and the Smoothies were people who did not. This seemed quite normal to everyone and the two groups lived in harmony, even married one another, much as right-handers and left-handers do today.

One day, after hunting, they were seated around the campfire. One of the Fuzzies, who got an increase in energy when faced with a challenge, had been chosen as their sentry. The Fuzzy sentry saw a huge herd of woolly mammoths stampeding toward the camp. Responding to the increase in energy in his body, he raced to the campfire, hair standing on end, shouting, "Run for your lives! Run for your lives! The hairy elephants are coming."

The other Fuzzies heeded the warning and ran; many survived the stampede. The Smoothies, who did not experience an increase in energy in response to the challenge, were unwilling to leave the comfort of the fire. "You get so excited about everything," they commented, and stayed where they were. All of the Smoothies eventually were trampled by the mammoths. None survived. Thus, none of the Smoothies became our great-, great-, great-, great- great- (etc.) great-grandparents. That explains why we are the way we are today.

So, when you wonder why you feel any particular sensation—"Why am I angry today?" or "Why am I afraid to speak up?"—the answer is "It's because of the hairy elephants." While it isn't the most accurate answer, it's the most *useful* one.

The moral is: Your feelings are your natural response to any challenge. And your feelings have the potential to help you. Whether you are able to take advantage of the potential benefit depends on you. Begin today to develop your sensory acuity and use your feelings as feedback to help you succeed.

It's very difficult to determine the exact cause of any feeling, because the increase in energy is so deeply programmed into our genes. You could conclude that your anger when someone insulted you was caused by their insult. Perhaps. Another possibility is that the anger was there all along and the insult merely brought it out. After all, there are people who simply laugh at insults, rather than react angrily. An honest assessment of your emotional life may lead you to conclude that your effort to identify the cause of your feelings is, in fact, an attempt to justify them in a society where feelings are not OK. Ask yourself which side of the cause-and-effect equation (discussed in Chapter 4) you are living on right now.

The Primitive and Ancient Design of Our Emotional System

Anthropological evidence suggests that our brain and the rest of the human emotional system are of ancient design, unchanged in thousands of years. Thus, our emotional system was designed to aid survival in an environment far more violent and primitive than most of us face today. In a primitive environment, added energy is essential to meet most challenges. This is less so in our modern society. A traffic jam is the classic example of a situation where the added energy isn't useful in meeting the challenge. In order to function stress-free, we must be able to experience added energy and at the same time do nothing about it.

Feelings Do Not *Mean* Anything

Feelings are not in the realm of meaning. Weather, for example, doesn't mean anything, either. Feelings can be thought of as internal weather—sometimes stormy, sometimes rainy, sometimes windy, and other times calm, tranquil, and pleasant. Like the weather, your feelings show up without invitation, leave without saying good-bye, and defy prediction. In other words, you have no choice about your feelings. Despite efforts to control them, they occur whether you like them or not. If there were an earthquake where you are now, everyone present would feel afraid whether they wanted to or not. We have no choice about this increase in energy. The choice we do have is how our feelings affect us. Remember, feelings are nothing more than feedback. It's how you choose to use the feedback that makes the difference.

You are the one who gives meaning to your feelings. On their own, they don't mean anything. The first step to understanding this idea is to recognize that, since feelings are simply energy, there are no good feelings and no bad feelings. There are simply feelings; we *judge* them to be good or bad. Once you judge any particular feeling to be bad, you begin a struggle to change it to something better, by ignoring it, hoping it will go away, ingesting a substance from an external source, or stuffing it down someplace where no one can notice.

We waste a great deal of effort suppressing our feelings: The energy that our bodies give us to deal with the challenge is wasted, and the energy used to suppress the original energy is wasted. No wonder people feel stressed. This push/pull of energy is similar to driving on the freeway with one foot flooring the accelerator and the other flooring the brake pedal. By doing so, you will wear out your car very quickly, and your gas mileage will be terrible.

Feelings Are Not OK in Our Society

There is an essential conflict about feelings. One side of the conflict is that we all have feelings, they are OK, natural, and normal. The opposing side is that we live in a society where feelings are not OK. Most people are afraid of their feelings. Discomfort and shame about feelings is learned in childhood from parental admonitions such as "Big boys (girls) don't cry," "Don't be a scaredy cat," "It's not OK to be angry," "If you can't say something nice, don't say anything."

This conflict about feelings produces suffering for some, bizarre behavior in many, and strange standards for almost everyone. If you were to sit in a park and cry (letting your feelings out) for a long enough time, duly appointed representatives of officialdom eventually would remove you to an institution for examination and perhaps treatment, despite the fact that you are hurting no one. Compare this to the drunken driver (who uses alcohol to keep feelings in) who must cause considerable damage or even death before being institutionalized. In our society, feelings are accorded little importance, discussion, or consideration. Fears and hurts lead the parade of feelings that are never discussed, especially by men.

It feels wonderful to experience passion. Consider the intense feelings that sports fans allow themselves in connection with their favorite teams. Supporting your favorite team provides the opportunity for passion without consequence. It's an impossible stretch of logic to think that *your* cheering and enthusiasm affects the outcome of the game. If you are a rabid sports fan, consider investing that same energy into increasing your income, where the payoff is higher and more rewarding. In your financial life, the expression of your passion has positive consequence in your bank account.

You Can Choose Your Response to Feelings

Although we try to control our feelings, we really have very little choice about them. Your response to your feelings is more important than the feeling itself. The hero isn't without fear. Rather, heroism and cowardice are simply different *responses* to fear. Different people respond differently to feelings and to stress. The various responses are usually learned during childhood. Some get a stomachache, some become aggressive, and others withdraw and pout. Consider stress as a sign that your body is providing you with additional energy to meet some challenge, rather than a sign that something is wrong. Your body cannot tell the difference between danger and anxiety. For this reason, it's sometimes necessary to look more closely than usual at emotional responses to reassure yourself that there is no danger.

Our feelings defy logic. That feelings are not logical does not invalidate them, however. Balance is essential. Logic without emotion causes results just as devastating as emotion without logic. Sometimes we feel sad when we receive what we want, sad when we lose what we don't want, and afraid in situations where there is obviously no danger. Different people respond to the same feelings in different ways, which accounts for the unpredictability of human behavior. Witnesses to intensely emotional situations, such as wartime combat, serious earthquakes, or other disasters, have observed this phenomenon. In an intensely fearful situation, some people freeze, others panic and do precisely the wrong thing, while others rise to the occasion and seem to know exactly what to do.

You can probably think of many examples of people who experienced frustration and anger from a setback. Some lose their temper, yell, scream, and hit things; others withdraw, sulk, and suffer in silence; still others use the energy that the setback provides to become even more determined—the more positive response. People also respond to loss in different ways. Loss produces sadness for everyone, but some people deny the loss and are unwilling to cry about it; other people spend the rest of their lives in mourning; while others seem to emerge from a loss in even better condition than before.

Your opinion about your feelings—whether you judge them to be good or bad—determines how they effect you. When we judge feelings—and the energy they produce—to be bad, that energy isn't available to us, because we struggle to suppress it. Often we decide which feelings are acceptable and which ones are not arbitrary, without careful consideration and based solely on habit. Remember, feelings are neither good nor bad. Good and bad are merely judgments that we make about them. We can compare feelings to electricity: simply energy, neither good nor bad. We can use electricity to cook your dinner or to murder a cat. Neither use determines anything about the electricity. The decision as to whether a feeling is acceptable to you is of paramount importance because it determines whether you can use the energy for your benefit.

Acceptance of energy brings you into the present moment. Being in the present moment enables you to deal with the situation that is producing the energy, usually fear. For example, I (PL) have fought fires at sea. In such cases, you have two choices: put the fire out or take your chances abandoning ship. It's essential to accept the fear, so that your mind can focus on the operational aspects of the problem: Where is the next fire extinguisher? How can I get more water? How do I cool it down? It's just about impossible to focus on the solution to the problem if your mind is distracted by possible future consequences: the ocean temperature, the distance to land, and the time until your possible rescue from a lifeboat.

In our society, there seems to be a very wide variation in what feelings are acceptable. This fact indicates that we decide which feelings are acceptable quite arbitrarily. Because the decision about the acceptability of different feelings is arbitrary, it's as possible to change your judgment about particular feelings as readily as you can cultivate an appreciation for food that is new to you.

Some people love roller coasters; others hate them. Aficionados feel excited and thrilled by the rides; others feel nauseous and terrified. The aficionados accept the feelings that roller coasters bring up, but the others judge them as bad. Thus, acceptance determines the difference between excitement and fear.

Some people enjoy sad movies. Video rental stores offer a section for tear-jerkers. The tragedies that befall the characters offer fans a more acceptable and positive perspective about their own troubles. People with zero tolerance for such movies may find them uncomfortable because of their own unresolved feelings of loss. Thus, acceptance determines the difference between gratitude and sadness.

No one would claim that developing an appreciation for roller coasters or sad movies is going to make much of a difference in your financial success. Yet many activities related to your career and finances bring up intense feelings like these. How you deal with these intense feelings significantly determines your financial success.

Accept Anger to Increase Resourcefulness and Determination

To most people, anger is the most socially unacceptable emotion. A person whose life is consumed by fear or sadness or even by jealousy or gluttony can expect at least some compassion. Rage-aholics get no such compassion.

Nevertheless, we all feel angry sometimes. Because anger is so socially unacceptable, we tend to justify our anger, if it is not OK with us. This justification process creates a downward emotional spiral. Say you feel angry, and you do not accept this response. You seek to justify your anger by focusing on your valid reasons for feeling angry. Focusing on these reasons naturally causes the anger to intensify, which creates the need for additional justification. Do this long enough and consistently enough, and you will become depressed.

A variation of this pattern can be seen in intense arguments between couples. He is angry with her and says, "You said you would make dinner and now I am left to do it." Now she is angry because of his criticism, so to justify her anger, she says, "I am sick and tired of you nagging me after I have to deal with those kids all day long." Now he is angrier than before, because she doesn't seem to be listening, so he focuses on additional complaints he has about her. And back and forth they go. What is really happening here? The anger is not OK with either of them, so each strives to justify his or her own anger by expressing, but not really saying, "My anger is justified and yours is not" or "My reasons for feeling angry are really important and yours are trivial." Not accepting your anger can ruin an otherwise excellent relationship very quickly. Instead, take a breath and let your anger be OK. It doesn't mean anything about you. Letting it be OK empowers you to use the passion that is present to get what you want instead of wasting it seeking justification for the feelings you condemn yourself for. Just as anger that you have not accepted is determination contaminated by helplessness, anger is also intense determination in disguise. Letting it be OK for you to feel anger strips it of its disguise.

Things to Remember about Feelings

Uncomfortable feelings don't mean anything about you. Instead it's you who gives meaning to your feelings. Uncomfortable feelings no longer need to be a reason to avoid something that would otherwise benefit you. You are not alone. Everyone has weird feelings. If you don't notice the weird feelings of others, they probably don't notice yours.

Feelings are an extremely poor basis for decision making, because they are temporary and irrational. Your best decisions will be those based on the choice that most supports your true purpose.

Feelings are energy. Suppressing them wears you out and causes stress. Expressing them constantly will drive people away. Accepting them as they are is far and away the superior response, not only for your productivity and effectiveness, but for your well-being, too.

The End of Procrastination

Does time seem to slip away with your accomplishing less than you'd like? Do you find yourself procrastinating on tasks that turn out to be far easier than you had made them in your mind?

Notice how procrastinators think: "I'll do it tomorrow, next week, when it stops raining, when I feel like it and so on." As mentioned earlier, the way you interpret your feelings determines how they affect you. Procrastinators interpret fear to mean "STOP." Now, in some cases this is not a bad interpretation of fear. If you have $10,000 of credit card debt, then your fear of economic destitution can be useful when it tells you to stop this. However, procrastination implies the postponement of action toward something you want to accomplish. Do not wait for fear to go away before acting. Because feelings are genetically programmed responses to any challenges, we do not control them. Change your interpretation of fear to "GET READY." Fear means you should get ready to meet the challenge at hand.

No More Procrastination Method

 Here is a method we learned from our friend, author and teacher Jeffery Combs. Do this right away.

Gather together:

- A supply of index cards or sticky notes
- Paper clips
- A supply of dollar bills

Write down the tasks you are currently avoiding, one for each index card or sticky note. Then write down the date and time when you want to complete each one. An example might be:

Graphics designed and organized for my new book. Noon Friday April 4, 2005

Make sure to state the goal, date, and time precisely, as in the example, so that your mind has no doubt about what you mean.

Then use a paper clip to attach two single dollar bills to each of the cards or sticky notes on which you have written. Add the tasks to your calendar book or whatever scheduling system you now use and place the cards, with the money attached, on your refrigerator or near your phone or computer, so that you are reminded of them frequently.

When the date and time indicated on each of the cards arrives, either you have completed the task or you have not. If you have, take the money and buy yourself a treat. If you haven't, cut both bills into shreds. If you haven't done the task but you still want to do so, set a new date and time, attach two new dollar bills to the card or note, and work through the process again.

Clearly, how quickly this method works for you depends on how deeply entrenched your habit of procrastination is. Very few people find it necessary to shred their two dollar bills more than twice. If you have some goals you have been procrastinating about, do this exercise now. Do not wait another minute. You have been putting it off already. By taking this action, you will begin to break an old pattern that does not serve you. What have you got to lose except a bad habit?

DEAL WITH YOUR FEARS IN ADVANCE

R$ Do this exercise now! Get rid of the fear that is holding you back from achieving your success. This exercise will eliminate any fears that may arise when you do something new or something you have not been able to master because fear has stopped you. This method will work with any situation that currently creates fear and anxiety. Let's get started.

Imagine a situation in which you are uncomfortable: cold calling, public speaking, or something similar.

Now imagine you are in a theater seeing yourself on a stage or a movie screen going through the experience you picked. See yourself accomplish it flawlessly. Make sure to add as much detail as possible. Can you associate any sounds or feelings? Any smells or tastes? The more details you can add, the better this method will work.

If you see something you do not like about this experience, start again from the beginning and make any necessary changes. Keep making changes until the scene is absolutely perfect, just the way you like it.

When it is perfect in your mind, run through it faster a few more times. Make sure you see yourself going through the experience flawlessly, just the way you want it to happen.

This "new you" whom you have been watching has the ability to achieve the desired outcome. The capabilities are now there. You see this new you as totally confident in achieving the results you desire. There is one more step: integrating the new you with the current you.

Imagine in your mind's eye that you see this new you with all the ability to perform perfectly in front of you. Now open your arms as if you were going to give this person a big hug. Have the new you come right in front of you, then draw the new you inside yourself. Become one with this new you. Feel that person and all the abilities and capabilities being integrated into your self. Just enjoy the feeling as you now become one with the new you.

How do you feel? Do you feel confident that you can perform in the situation you picked? Do you feel that you can easily and effortlessly attain your outcome? Do you feel that you have the ability and capabilities necessary to do it? If you do not, go back to the beginning. Make sure you see the situation happening flawlessly and exactly the way you want it.

The more details you add, the better. Also make sure you go through the episode several times and experience it happening exactly the way you want it to.

Now go through the situation you picked earlier for real. Go out and perform as you saw yourself do in your mind. Take action now! Your performance will be great! When you accept the passion that is your feelings, you are unstoppable.

CHAPTER

YOUR MIND IS
NOT A DEMOCRACY

*If you keep thinking what you have always thought, then you
will keep getting what you always got. Instead of putting up with
what you always got, you learn how to intervene intentionally on
the unconscious thinking process that has produced results in the
past. Gain reliable access to your creativity, instead of awaiting
inspiration, and learn to apply the natural, empowering psychological reaction that occurs whenever you commit to a goal. You
will also acquire certainty about accomplishing any goal and discover why it is essential to run your mind as a dictatorship.*

If you are confused about what you should want, the mere topic
of goals causes you frustration and upset. If you haven't completed the method for declaring the purpose of your life in Chapter 6, go back now and complete it. Without clarity about your
purpose, frustrating conflicts about goals are inevitable. Clarity of
purpose vastly simplifies and focuses goal setting. By determining
the purpose of your life, much of the conflict surrounding goal
setting is removed, and you are empowered to choose goals that
are expressions of your purpose, not ones based on what you were
supposed to do or want.

Everyone has goals; some are chosen consciously and others unconsciously. Some people consciously choose goals to maximize satisfaction, self-expression, and wealth or some other combination of
important values. Once you take responsibility for your results, you
will recognize that even the upsetting aspects of your current situation actually were created in the past by unconsciously selected
goals. Other people settle for these preprogrammed, unconsciously

131

chosen goals they have adopted from their personal history, producing results that are different from what is consciously intended.

If you are in this latter category, go back to the Purpose of Your Life method in Chapter 6. Goals naturally flow as an expression of your purpose in a mental hierarchy that looks like Figure 8.1.

This hierarchy operates based on conscious choice and unconscious programming. If you have not consciously chosen your purpose, then your unconsciously chosen inherited purpose likely will conflict with consciously chosen goals.

Motivation matters, also. If you have experienced conflicts or resistance in achieving consciously chosen goals in the past, overreliance on moving-away motivation may be the root cause. Such overreliance causes a person to be primarily reactive to external events rather than responsive to internally generated goals and desires.

Consistent use of the Baseball Diamond method in Chapter 4 increases the power of moving-toward motivation. Use the method to balance your behavior between avoiding painful situations and moving toward your internal pleasurable goals.

Two very important and almost immediate events inevitably occur when you establish a meaningful goal for yourself. For some people these events occur so subtly that they fail to notice them in

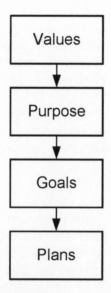

FIGURE 8.1   Hierarchy of Your Goals

the daily activity of their busy lives. We want to point them out so that you notice them when they occur and use them to your benefit. These two events may occur in any order.

Very quickly, sometimes instantly, upon establishing a goal, your mind begins to attract the resources you require to accomplish that goal. Also, your mind will dutifully cooperate to accomplish the new goal by letting you know which of your past thoughts are opposed to your accomplishing the goal.

Let's say that your new goal is to double your income from $60,000 per year to $120,000 per year within the next 12 months. One event is that almost immediately your mind is filled with possible ways to do this. Before you set the goal, you had not been thinking of ways to increase your income, so why would your mind bother to produce any useful ideas for you? Pay particular attention to the people you meet after establishing a new goal; your mind will naturally attract into your presence not only the ideas but also the people and other external resources you require.

The other event is that your mind cooperates with accomplishing your new goal in another way, by bringing to your attention the thought patterns that stand in the way of timely and convenient accomplishment. Before you had set the goal of doubling your income, your mind may have been thinking, "This is all the money I need to get by" or "It is not worth the effort or risk to earn more." These types of thoughts definitely will hinder your accomplishment of your new goal. So, almost immediately after establishing your new goal, pay close attention to what may seem to be objections in your mind. These comprise very useful information; your mind is dutifully saying to you, "In the past you told me to think these thoughts: '$60,000 is all I need to get by' or 'I can't do this' or 'I shouldn't want more money.'" You must change these old thoughts to achieve your new and different goal. Use the Power Affirmations method in the next chapter to change specific, limiting thoughts like these.

Creativity

Creativity and analysis are two of the major functions of your conscious mind. The creative function thinks up new ideas. The analytical function evaluates things in light of information and experiences already stored and attempts to assign cause and effect; it figures things out. One function isn't better than the other; both must be developed for a person to lead a happy and productive life. Since our educational system develops the analytical function almost exclusively, here the focus is on achieving reliable access to the creative function.

If you don't use your creativity, you are living with half your mind tied behind your back. Most people grossly underestimate the power of their own creativity, because it was squashed so strongly in school. Creativity isn't just for artists, writers, and musicians. All of us can use our creativity better. So vast is our creativity that even the most creative people use only a small portion. If you remember any of your dreams, you can get an inkling of how creative you already are. The issue then isn't how much creativity you may possess, but whether you can access it and express it usefully. Dreams may be thought of as images and ideas popping out of the unconscious mind while you sleep. You will be learning to access that same creative function while awake.

How Creativity Is Squashed

Creativity is handicapped with the idea that there is *one right* way to do some things and with the idea that questions have *one right* answer. Your creativity was stifled at any early age. For example, most of us allowed our parents to convince us that there is one right way to eat. If you have traveled, you know that, when eating, British people carefully pile food on the curved side of their fork. Continental Europeans use their knife right-handed to push food onto their fork, held in the left. Americans, although obsessed with efficiency in other areas, have somehow decided that the right way is to hold the knife in the right hand and the fork in the left while cutting food, and then to put down the knife and transfer the fork to the right before eating. Our clashing of metal eating implements probably amuses Asian people who use efficient chopsticks.

This one right way theory is strongly reinforced in our educational system, where rigid adherence to multiple-choice tests determines course grades, who graduates, and who goes to college. A multiple-choice test cannot measure someone's ability to think creatively. Life doesn't come with answers laid out for easy selection. Instead, you will enjoy far greater satisfaction by using the creative part of your mind to create opportunities for yourself.

It is even possible to obtain a Ph.D. degree, the pinnacle of educational achievement, without doing anything creative. Although there are exceptions, most Ph.D. dissertations deal with cause and effect. "The Cause and Effect of the Second World War" and "The Cause and Effect of Global Warming on Our Environment" are typical titles.

Clearly, some questions have one right answer. It's not practical to use creativity to balance your checkbook, for example. However, adult life, after your school days are over, presents very few questions with one right answer. Most practical problems require a degree of intuitive judgment that goes beyond that.

Figure 8.2 shows the very different functions and capabilities of the two major parts of your conscious mind: the analytical function and the creative function.

The Analytical Part of Your Mind

The analytical part of your mind figures things out, solves mathematical problems, balances a checkbook, and evaluates probable outcomes of a wide variety of actions. It's concerned with cause and effect.

Functions of Your Mind	
Analytical	**Creative**
Cause & Effect	New Ideas
Why?	How?
The Past	The Present and the Future
Logic	Intuition & Feelings
Reasons	Commitment beyond Reason
Good/Bad or Right/Wrong	Better/Worse

FIGURE 8.2   Functions of Your Mind

The analytical part is concerned with the question "Why?" Since this is the only question it knows how to answer, "Why?" is the only question that it will ask. If your car will not start, "Why?" is a useful question. The cause of the problem, in this instance, is an essential piece of information. The proper remedy is different if the car has no gas than if the battery is dead. Once the "why" has been discovered, the problem changes to one requiring the creative part of your mind to answer other questions, such as "How can I charge the battery?" or "How can I obtain gasoline?"

Everything related to cause and effect is in the past. Historians and economists study the past to understand the present and to forecast the future. Scientists experiment with the physical universe to determine rules that will apply in future instances. Sociologists study large numbers of people to predict future trends. This sort of analysis of the past works reasonably well for the physical universe and for large numbers of people, but works very poorly when dealing with yourself or just a few other people.

Logical people like to think that they make decisions for reasons and often insist that others do the same. Even the most logical person uses the creative part of his mind, however, if only to gather alternatives for consideration. In some cases, you may have made decisions intuitively—using your creative mind—and then invented reasons later.

The analytical part of the mind tends to evaluate possibilities according to criteria that are dualistic, almost like a moral code. Clearly, we are presented with temptations regularly that challenge our ethics—some decisions are actually moral or ethical issues. Difficulties occur if the only standards of evaluating possibilities are good/bad or right/wrong. People using only these standards tend to seek the right job or the right person—their standards of perfection are so high that excellent, but less than perfect, opportunities are too quickly discarded and satisfaction is almost impossible.

Do not allow such perfectionism to prevent you from using the methods in this book. They are probably new to you. Anything worth doing is worth doing poorly at first until you learn it. Watch a toddler learning to walk and falling repeatedly. If you had applied standards of perfection while learning to walk, you would still be crawling.

The analytical part is very poor at making changes, because it's concerned with the past and justifying it. If you rely on it completely, the only changes that you will make will be after conditions become so intolerable that you are willing to accept almost any change. Thus, you must use your creative function effectively to make the changes that you now want.

The Creative Part of Your Mind

For most of us, the creative part of our mind has received very little training and no validation. Nevertheless, all of us have far more creativity than we are currently expressing. This is equally true for the most creative person and the least creative person that you know. Learning how to access the creative part of your mind and to use the information that it contains can bring you a far richer, more rewarding, and exciting future than you may have imagined.

The creative part of your mind generates new ideas. Your curiosity about new things and experiences lives here. When you were young, you were very curious. To the chagrin of parents worldwide, toddlers want to put everything into their mouths. After a while, the socialization process made you follow rules that were made and enforced for the benefit of those designing them. This process sharply reduced your fascination with new things. The sense of fascination makes learning and education exciting. Unfortunately, by the time we started school, this sense has been suppressed in most of us.

The creative part of your mind is interested in "How?" In most issues involving your own behavior and that of others, "How?" is a far more useful question than "Why?" For example, you may know people who spend hours thinking about and talking about why they do not have the income that they want. But "Why don't I have the income that I want?" isn't a useful question. Even if you were to come up with the right reasons why you do not have your desired income, it's unlikely that this answer would bring you much closer to achieving your desire. In this case "How?" is a far more useful question. A good answer to the question "How can I obtain the income that I want?" may in fact lead you to your goal.

LEARNING TO ASK BETTER QUESTIONS

R℞   Pay close attention to your internal self-talk. Write down your thoughts for five minutes without censoring any. You don't have to share these thoughts with anyone. When you are done, look at the questions you are asking yourself. Are there lots of "why" questions? "Why" questions usually seek reasons or justification. They do little to move you ahead. Each of the methods in this book offers a way for you to consciously intervene to change the unconscious thinking you had been using up to now. Doing this ensures that your future brings you the results you consciously intend. Our shorthand way of expressing this is:

$$\text{The Future} \neq \text{The Past}$$

The future does not equal the past.

Instead of "why" questions, train yourself to ask "how" and "what" questions and others like them:

- How can I move ahead more quickly?
- What do I need to change to progress more easily?
- How can I get others to help me?
- What other capabilities do I have to possess in order to succeed?

The creative part of your mind lives in the present and thus deals with your intuition and feelings. It has the ability to invent new ideas for future use. You use your creativity in the VCR method in the appendix to give your mind a new and more resourceful view of a past event. To apply the skills of goal setting and planning that you will be learning, you must use your creativity.

Commitment beyond Reason

There may be times in your progress toward a significant goal when, by any sense of logic or reasoning, the right decision is to give up. At this point, you may have little to show for all the effort that you have invested. Success appears to be so far away that it's worth much less than the additional effort required. Struggling harder in this situation isn't the answer. Instead, renewing and strengthening your commitment is far more effective. Commitment is a function of the creative part of your mind and defies logic.

Commitment is a matter of focus. It relies on your ability to focus on the things that you choose as important and to pay no heed to those you decide do not matter. An example of this from my (PL) life is that in the mid-1960s, I served as commanding officer of a ninety-five-foot Coast Guard patrol boat engaged in search and rescue operations in the offshore waters of New England. The North Atlantic winter isn't pleasant on a boat that small. Although weather conditions were a constant consideration, they did not determine whether we went on a rescue. We dealt with the weather to survive, but we totally ignored it when deciding whether to proceed or, once underway, to continue. This commitment was so strong that there really was no decision at all. We just went. "You have to go out, but you don't have to come back" is the mind-set required for search and rescue.

Better/Worse

Very few things are perfect. Almost every situation or possibility has disadvantages. Clearly different solutions have different disadvantages. It's a good idea to give up your search for the ideal and, instead, begin to make small improvements. Instead of looking for the ideal, look for something better than what you have. As you begin to make small improvements in all areas of your life, you will discover that some are quite minor; then sometimes you will accomplish some improvement that has a far greater effect than you had anticipated. The expectation of perfection causes some people to overlook the small improvements that they could make. For example, you will always have financial problems of some kind. Winning $10 million from your state lottery would solve your current financial problems. But it would create problems in areas where you don't even have areas now.

Access Your Creativity for Problem Solving

For most people, creativity is similar to an unused set of muscles. Next we will take your creativity to the gymnasium and get it into better shape so that you can use it in any situation, whenever you want.

Scientists have the reputation of being coldly logical. If you think of science as a collection of unchangeable rules governing the behavior of the universe, then science is, in fact, logical only. The most successful scientists, however, consider science to be a method—a method of testing and verifying assumptions about how things work. The testing and verification aspect of science can be dry and logical, but good scientists use their creativity to devise the assumptions to be tested and clever ways to test them. For this reason, almost every scientific breakthrough involves some leap in logic, some intuitive assumption that no one had tested before.

The zigzag in Figure 8.3 describes the method you already use for solving problems. First your creativity comes up with a solution. Then you shift gears to the analytical part of your mind where you analyze the possible results of the solution. The solution probably has pluses and minuses, which the analytical mind evaluates. If the solution has greater disadvantages than advantages, then you will discard it and perhaps feel upset and de-

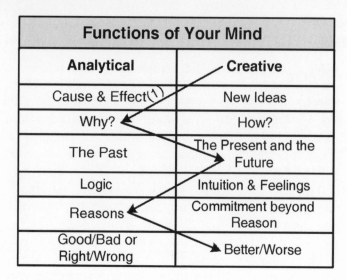

FIGURE 8.3   How Your Mind Solves Problems

pressed that the problem isn't solved yet and try to forget about it for a while. Then, at a later time, when your creativity invents a different solution, the same analytical process occurs once again in evaluating it.

This method is time-consuming. Coming up with possible solutions uses the most time. We'll be showing you how to speed things up greatly by creating 20 solutions to any problem in less time than it usually takes to invent just one. Considering a large number of possibilities increases your chances of getting a suitable one. It's much faster than creating one solution, analyzing it, discarding it, creating another solution, analyzing that one, and so on. It uses the combination of speed and writing to tap into your creativity.

DISCOVERY WRITING METHOD

In the Discovery Writing method, speed is very important. Usually when you learn something new, you start slowly. Discovery Writing is different, because speed is required to make it work. With all of our education focused on training the analytical part of our mind, it's likely that this part thinks it can figure out the answer to everything. So part of the challenge to accessing your creativity reliably is to make the analytical part of your mind be quiet temporarily. Writing as fast as you can does this.

When you use the Discovery Writing method the first time on a "real" problem, there is a very strong tendency to "think" about it. "Thinking" here means trying to devise a solution using the analytical part of your mind. So start with a couple of obviously absurd problems for practice. Try "20 uses for a tomato" or "20 things that float."

R℞ This method will give you a peek at how creative you already are. Think of this as building your creative muscle; it's like weight lifting for the mind. You have to work it out and push it to the limits. Otherwise, it will not grow. Imagine what it would be like to apply this limitless creativity to the opportunities and challenges facing you today.

Write at the top of a sheet of paper "20 Uses for a Tomato" or "20 Things that Float," and number from 1 to 20 down the left. Do this now! Give yourself two minutes to complete a list. Write as fast as you can. *Speed* is the only thing that matters. Neatness, accurate spelling, or "correct" answers are not important. Don't censor any ideas, just write as fast as you can. It's even OK to write "I can't think of anything to write" or "This is so frustrating that I can't think straight." Write in whatever language your mind gives you even if it is a language you never heard before. It may seem like you are accomplishing nothing by this exercise, but you are strengthening your creativity by simply acknowledging its output without criticism.

After the two minutes are up, look the list over and evaluate what you have written by drawing a circle around those items that actually are uses for a tomato or things that float. When we teach this technique in Training sessions, sometimes people ask, "What if some of my answers are wrong?" Do not consider the items on your list as "answers." There is no right or wrong here. They are possibilities, some better than others. The list increases your choices, thus increasing the possibility of having a good choice not considered before.

Once you can make a list of 20 possibilities in two minutes or less for an absurd problem, you are ready to move on to "real" problems. For most people, "real" problems tempt them to "think." Don't think, just write. Think *after* the list is made. Some practical lists that you could make are:

- 20 businesses that express my purpose
- 20 things I *could* do to increase my income
- 20 ways I *could* reduce my expenses
- 20 skills I *could* use to enjoy life more
- 20 people who *could* help me with this problem
- 20 things I *could* learn from applying this material
- 20 things I *could* do to express my purpose

We have italicized the word "could" in the preceding examples to emphasize that in making your list, you are looking for *possibilities*, and not answers. Only after the list is finished do you analyze it to identify a good solution.

We include the following two problems to appeal to the rebellious part of your mind, which can be very useful, if you don't take it too seriously.

- 20 important phone calls I know I should make but must continue to postpone
- 20 reasons that I must continue procrastinating about starting that diet (going to the gym) (quitting smoking)

Your first list may not provide a useful solution. That is fine. Making another list only takes two minutes. Even if your list does not provide a useful solution, at least you now know that some solutions exist, just not one that you can use yet. This knowledge tends to reduce anxiety, making the problem easier to solve. A mind filled with fear is a mind without options. The converse of this is also true: A mind with options is a mind without fear.

What Do You Want?

Limiting your desires to what you do *not* want produces comfort without satisfaction. Free up your thinking by using the Discovery Writing method to uncover your desires, even if you are unaccustomed to expressing them. Consider making lists with these titles:

- 20 things I want to be
- 20 things I want to do
- 20 things I want to have
- 20 improvements I want in my relationships
- 20 improvements I want in my financial life
- 20 improvements I want in my health
- 20 things I want to learn
- 20 improvements I want in my spiritual life

After you complete each list, circle the desires that are most important and most real to you. Remember, at this point you are not concerned with how you will accomplish these desires. Goals answer the question "What?" Chapter 14 presents a plan to accomplish your goal. Jot down in your calendar the most important items from your lists so you remember to do them. Later in this chapter, you will be formulating them into SMART goals.

Take a moment to consider what you learned here. Were there times in the past where a new solution to a lingering problem would have been far more useful than what you did? How else might you use this speedy method?

Remember that your creativity is similar to an underused muscle. When you visit the gym for a workout, you are in better condition for a while after leaving. The same is true with your creativity. Most people discover that as little as two minutes per day of Discovery Writing is enough to recondition their creativity so that creative solutions come to them much more quickly in their everyday life.

The solution you are looking for may not come to you while you are making one of these lists. Near the beginning of writing this book, we made daily lists of possible titles. After several weeks we still had nothing we liked well enough to use. One day while driving my car (PL), "Wealth Without a Job" came to me. This felt right. Andy agreed. We spent another week continuing to make lists of possible titles to ensure we found nothing better. Even though the lists we made did not produce the title, they did, in fact, free up creativity sufficiently for the final title to pop out into awareness. This is a fairly common phenomenon.

THE RIGHT BUSINESS FOR YOU

Surely you have been exposed to impassioned pleas offering you business opportunities too good to pass up. Perhaps they are good, but if they do not express your own values and interests, you are unlikely to get very far with them. Aptitude tests also are of limited value because you'll be successful only to the extent that you use your aptitudes to express the values and interests that matter to you. Besides, the passion called forth by expressing your most important values and interests will motivate you to gain any of the aptitudes you lack.

METHOD FOR CLARIFYING THE BUSINESS FOR YOU

 Here you will be using your creativity to define a business for yourself by asking three important questions:

1. Whom will I serve?
2. Why would they do business with me?
3. How will I serve them?

Here is the author's completed business definition:

We serve independent businesspeople and emerging entrepreneurs in their desire for financial freedom by teaching internal self-management and business skills not taught in schools.

Next, you will be designing your own business definition. You do not have to start at ground zero, because you have already declared the purpose of your life in Chapter 6. This statement of purpose provides a broad overview of the values that matter to you, how you intend to express them, and why. To save time and to eliminate unsuitable business possibilities, refer back to your statement of purpose.

Here is the framework for your business definition:

I or we serve (1. Identify customers) in their desire for or to (2. The benefits you wish to offer) by (3. Identify the work you will do).

Some of you no doubt have a clear enough picture of the business you want or already have so that you could write out your business definition without using the next steps.

If you are not at that point, use the previous method to define the business you want. You will be making three lists to assemble your own business definition. You'll make rapid progress by starting at the end with list 3 and working toward the beginning of your business definition. Start by creating a list of possibilities to fill the final blank in the sentence. Remember to set your timer for two minutes and write as fast as possible. No thinking.

1. 20 *possible* characteristics of the customers I want
2. 20 benefits I *could* offer to customers
3. 20 things I *could* do to serve others

From the items on these lists, pick the most suitable entries you created to produce a business definition that suits you by filling in the blanks yourself.

I (or we) serve *List 1* in their desire for *List 2* by *List 3*.

Your Mind Is Not a Democracy

Your mind isn't a blank slate. It's already filled with ideas, thinking patterns and ways of perceiving yourself and the world. These developed from past experiences and many have been in your mind since childhood. Some of your thinking patterns don't serve you; some do. What they all have in common is that you think they are right. In other words, you have accumulated evidence over the years proving these conclusions to be true and accurate. When you add some new idea, such as a goal you wish to accomplish, there is no accumulated evidence to prove it. Planning and creativity are natural partners. Planning is about the future. Since the future hasn't happened yet, it cannot be analyzed, but has been created. Access to your creativity is essential for making useful plans.

You must have goals to have any satisfaction in life. Since birth, and perhaps before, your consciousness has been busily creating your reality based on the thoughts that you think. Your best past thinking has brought you to your current circumstances. There is no reason to expect your mind to stop doing this any time soon. Your mind already has an agenda or goals defining what it will create for you, assuming you continue thinking what you have been thinking. Unfortunately, these goals are most likely unconsciously chosen, and they may not be things you would most prefer or even like. Everyone has goals. For some people they are unconsciously chosen from personal history; for others they are based on their true purpose and a sense of those values they wish to express.

A goal is a new idea. Unless it is trivial, you can't prove you can do it yet. Figure 8.4 represents the impact of a new goal. The dashed rectangle represents your mind; it is dashed because ideas come in and go out all the time. The X's represent your limiting beliefs, thinking patterns, and experiences from your past as related to this goal or to goals in general. The X with the circle represents any new goal you have just added to your mind.

Notice that your past thinking greatly outnumbers the thought representing your new goal. At this point, if you hold a mental election about whether you could accomplish your goal, the results would be an overwhelming no. The democratically obtained result will always favor an outcome where your goal seems impossible because you haven't accomplished it yet. Democracy may be a fine way to run a government, but it's poorly suited to mind management. So, if you truly expect to make the changes you want, you must make your mind a dictatorship, with yourself as dictator.

The same dynamic affects any new goal. Let's say your new goal is to climb Mount Everest—a lofty goal, accomplished by very few. In this example, the uncircled X's represent your past thinking on

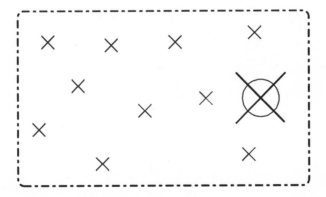

FIGURE 8.4   Your Mind Is Not a Democracy

this subject. Everyone is different, but you may have limiting thoughts such as:

- I don't know how to do this.
- I am afraid that I may fail.
- People will think that I am crazy for trying.
- I may succeed and not be satisfied.
- My mother will worry about me.
- I may be injured.
- It will take too long.
- I have had big dreams before and failed.
- I sure don't understand math.
- I'm afraid I'll become one of those arrogant overachievers.

The nos would easily win an election given the number of them compared to your lonely goal on the diagram. Not so obvious from the diagram, there is another reason the nos would triumph: Your mind will try to convince you its past experience proves your limiting thoughts are "true." There is no evidence showing you have climbed Mount Everest yet.

From this example, we'll take the limiting thought, "People will think that I am crazy." You "know" this is "true," because several of your friends mockingly questioned the sanity of such a dangerous goal. At the most difficult parts of the climb, you may be the one thinking that you are crazy for trying this. This limiting thought will continue to nag at you until you find a way to accept it.

It's possible that the worry about your friends' opinion of your sanity could distract your attention at precisely the moment requiring the most concentration, causing your foot to slip, resulting in an injury that scrubs your climb. This is one example of how we can unintentionally sabotage our best intentions without realizing it. If we focus on our old limiting beliefs, they will bring about more of what we have been getting instead of what we want.

You probably haven't attempted a climb of Mount Everest. You probably have, however, unconsciously sabotaged your progress toward some important goal because you were unaware of some limiting thought about it. Setbacks you blamed on "bad luck" or "circumstances" are often the acting out of limiting thoughts about the goal that you did not recognize. Such thinking is living on the effect side of the equation discussed previously.

How have we been conditioned to think about goals? Think back to the goals you had in childhood. They probably had two very important characteristics that no longer apply as an adult: Someone else probably chose them, and there was an undue focus on measurement.

The first measurable goal experienced was toilet training—a crappy topic that we will not dwell on. Success or failure was clearly measurable, there probably were consequences for failure, and this goal may have been imposed by an authority figure.

Then came school. The frequency and the precision with which the school system attempts to measure our children are ludicrous. Does anyone believe that the high school valedictorian with a 3.98 grade point average is better prepared for adult challenges than the runner-up with a 3.96 average? As students we did not decide to attend school for all those years or that we needed two years of a foreign language to get into college. If you received a job offer from an employer who planned to measure your performance with the frequency and precision used in the school system, you probably would decline the offer.

Goals Are Not about Measurement Anymore

I (PL) worked with a client, Roberta, who was a talented graphic designer. Before hiring me, she had been financially dependent on her boyfriend, who had recently left her. I always ask new clients to figure out the starting point for their income. She calculated an average of what she had earned over the past couple of months and told me she was starting from a very low average of $14 per week. Then we discussed her goal for income. She wanted $4,000 as a weekly average. After a couple of weeks she told me, "You know when you gave me that talk telling me that goals are not about measurement anymore, I didn't completely understand what you meant. But now I've got it, my starting income was $14 per week. Last week I earned a little over $1,000, and my goal is $4,000 per week. So that means I am succeeding because I am moving toward my goal." As adults, goal getting is far more satisfying if you make the process primarily about direction, not about measurement.

SETTING SMART GOALS

When we set a goal to achieve a particular outcome, the goal must be SMART. What is a SMART goal? A SMART goal is:

Specific
Measurable and Meaningful
As if now (present tense)

Reach out and Reasonable
Time

Let's look at each of these components of a well-designed SMART goal and determine why each is so important.

Specific

If it is not stated specifically, your unconscious mind will not know exactly what you want. Sometimes unconscious minds have a sense of humor. They may produce an outcome you do not want but that satisfies what you asked for. Remember that the unconscious mind takes the path of least resistance to produce what you ask for. This is why it is essential to state your goal specifically.

Specific also means it must be stated in the positive. Ask for what you do want. Do not ask for what you don't want. Remember that the unconscious mind does not understand negatives or negation. If you use negatives, the unconscious mind will produce exactly what you don't want.

Specific also means specific to expressing your purpose. Check back and read over your purpose of life statement. Working on (even thinking about) a goal that is out of harmony with your purpose creates internal conflict, making the goal far more difficult to accomplish. If your goal is not in harmony with your purpose, then change one or the other.

Measurable and Meaningful

If the goal is not measurable, how will you know you achieved it? If your goal is to be happy, how do you measure that? Happiness is a state you can have any time you choose. You must state your goal in such a way that it can be easily measured. When writing your goal, ask yourself: "What evidence do I require when the goal is achieved so I will know 100 percent for sure that I achieved it?" Another way to determine measurability is to ask: "Can it be carried in a wheelbarrow?" If yes, it is measurable. If your goal is huge, you will need a huge wheelbarrow to hold it.

For example, your goal may be to feel ecstatic. The feeling of being ecstatic is not measurable. There are varying degrees of this feeling, and it will be different for everyone. Obviously, the feeling of being ecstatic can't be placed in a wheelbarrow.

The goal must also be meaningful to you. If it is not, you will lack the necessary motivation to achieve it. It is best if your goal aligns with your purpose. Ask yourself "Does this goal express my purpose?" If it does, then it is meaningful. If not, pick a different goal.

As If Now

You must be state the goal in the present tense. This is critical. You cannot change the past or the future. The only change you can make is in the present. The changes you make in the present will affect the future, but you cannot directly change the future. If you state your goal in the future tense, it will remain in the future forever. However, if you state it in the present, as if you already have it now, you will produce the results you want.

Reach Out and Reasonable

The reach-out part of the goal should stretch you beyond your current situation. You do not want to make the goal too easy; otherwise you will not feel satisfied when you achieve it because you were not stretched. Every human being wants to grow and stretch, whether they realize it consciously or not. Do not limit the size of your goal based on your current capability or results. The tools in this book will add vastly to your capability. If accomplishing your goal does not require that you gain new skills and learn more about what interests you, then it is not enough of a stretch. Remember, if you reach your goals easily now, then you're not stretching yourself enough. Make the goals bigger!

The goal also must be reasonable—it must be attainable. Perhaps you'd like $1 million by tomorrow morning. This is not reasonable unless you already have millions of dollars that you can use to achieve the goal. If your goal were to achieve $1 million in five years, this would be reasonable. Remember, scale back dreams as necessary to make them achievable.

Time

You must include a specific date by which you will achieve your goal. If you do not state a specific time in your goal, it will always remain in the future. Your unconscious mind will take the path of least resistance and produce only what you ask it to produce now. When you put a date on your goal, your unconscious mind knows that it must figure out a way to achieve what was asked of it. It will find a way to produce the outcome in the specific time frame you asked.

There is some art involved in selecting these dates. Use your feelings as a gauge to know whether your dates are reasonable. If you wonder "Why bother to get started?" then the desired completion date is too far away. If the date throws you into a panic, it's too close. Experiment until you come up with a date that challenges and energizes you. Here is an example of a SMART goal:

I now have $1 million in my prosperity bank account on December 31, 2009.

This goal assumes that you have little or a moderate amount of income. It also assumes the goal was set in the year 2004. This goal would not be appropriate for someone who already has close to $1 million in a bank account currently or with a $500,000 income. For those individuals, the goal would have to be increased to include the reach-out requirement.

Now check to ensure your goal is SMART. Is the goal specific? It is stated positively and asks directly for what you want. Is the goal measurable? The evidence necessary to know if it is achieved is a bank statement that shows $1 million. It can also be placed in a wheelbarrow. Is the goal stated as if now? It is stated in the present tense by "I now have." Is the goal a reach-out and reasonable goal? This goal is a reach-out goal and will make you stretch. It is also reasonable because a five-year time frame will allow you enough time to generate the income you must have to satisfy the goal. Does it have a specific time frame? The outcome is achieved on December 31, 2009. Thus our goal meets all the criteria of a SMART goal.

EXERCISE: DEVELOP YOUR SMART GOALS

 Take a few minutes right now and write down your top five goals. Make sure they are SMART. Take action now to achieve what you desire and deserve. No more procrastinating! The way to achieve your goal is to take massive action now. Do you want to cheat yourself or treat yourself?

Once you have your SMART goals written, copy them onto a 3-x-5 index card. Carry the index card with you. Any chance you get, take out your goals and read them. The more you do this, the more your unconscious mind will grasp on to them and make them a reality for you. Read your goals at least twice a day—once when you wake up and right before you go to sleep. Make sure you have a good mental image of what your goals are. The more clear, vivid, colorful, detailed, and rich the images are, the more sold on and committed to the goals your mind becomes. Make sure you add your favorite sounds and the feeling you will have when you achieve your goals. You will keep building your images of your goals as you continue to pursue them.

Next you will learn how to install your new goals into your future. How you think about time is very, very important. Whenever you consider doing anything in the future, you must at least unconsciously place it into your internal representation of your future in order to evaluate whether you want to do it. Also, everything you remember is perceived through your personal internal representation of the past.

For these reasons, we will first be asking you to become aware of how your mind now represents time to you.

Your Traditional Perception of Time

Time is a concept that we first represent externally. Yes, we all have a diurnal rhythm that tells us it is time to wake up and time to sleep, but this rhythm is short term. If you don't know that today is Tuesday, for example, there is nothing inside of you to give you that information. You can, however, tell what day of the week it is by consulting a calendar or a daily newspaper. This means that we built the structure we now use to perceive time from external events.

If a child asks, "How long until Christmas?" and you respond, "Twenty-three days," the child is likely to ask "How long is that?" This child has not yet built a structure to represent time. We develop this structure sometime in early childhood, certainly by the time we get to school, where events occur at specific, announced times. Thus you most likely formed your own perception of time, including the past, present, and future, at an early age, and you may not have considered it since. The perception of time is a person's timeline.

HOW DO YOU PERCEIVE TIME NOW?

Recall brushing your teeth this morning. Remember as many details about this as possible. Good. Now recall brushing your teeth five years ago, also with as many details as possible. What differences are in these two images of the same event at different times? Most people report they perceive the more recent event as closer to them. Our minds naturally perceive time in a linear structure.

Figure 8.5 presents eight examples of how your mind may represent time to you; or it may do so in a completely different way. In the eight diagrams, you see the individual from above (note both ears and nose), looking at various kinds of timelines. In the upper left-hand example, the individual sees himself as off to the side of the timeline with the past stretching out to the left and the future to the right. In the lower left-hand diagram, the individual sees herself in the flow of time with the past and the future stretching in the same directions as the previous example and the present moment inside her body.

There are other possibilities. Some people report they see the past and the future as the same line stretching away from them. Others report they see the future as a spiral fading away into the distance. Some people represent the future not as a line but shaped like a quarter of a pie with their point of view at the sharp point of the slice.

There is no right answer here. What you want to determine is how your mind represents time to you now. How your current perception of time affects you matters more than what it is.

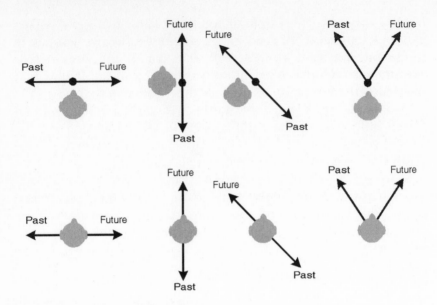

FIGURE 8.5   Timeline Examples

MODIFY YOUR TIMELINE FOR MAXIMUM RESOURCEFULNESS

When as a child, you first constructed your perception of time, your mind may have accepted the first representation that came to it; perhaps it has not made any modifications since. It is also likely that you didn't design your internal representation of time to make you as effective as possible.

One client saw her past and the future as the same line, which explained why the changes she wanted had been impossible. Another person saw a gap between himself and the beginning of his future. Changing this internal perception eliminated habitual procrastination. Now experiment with possible alternative ways for your mind to represent time.

EMPOWER YOUR PERCEPTION OF TIME

By now you are probably enjoying the benefits of doing the exercises as you read. Relax for a moment and imagine your past, stretching back away from you. What direction does it go in? Perhaps it is front of you or behind you; perhaps it goes off at an angle to one side; perhaps it is slanted slightly up or down. However, you see it is fine. Now imagine that your perception of the past connects to you with a 360-degree ball joint. This enables you to change the orientation of the past so it extends away from you in any direction. Slowly swing your representation of the past through different directions, like swinging your straight arm from your shoulder joint. Watch it point, up, down, left, right, straight ahead, and behind you, and all other combinations. As you do this, notice how you feel. Most people find that one direction causes them to feel most empowered. This most empowered direction may be the same one you had originally or it may be different. Once you have found this most empowered direction for the past, leave it there. If your most empowered direction is different from the original one, from time to time you may have to consciously reset the direction of your past to the new orientation by taking your mind through the process you just did.

Now do the same thing with your perception of the future. Clearly the future matters way more than the past, so we will pay it particular attention. See your future stretching away from you. Once again imagine that your future connects to you with a 360-degree ball joint, enabling you to swing it in all directions, front, back, left, right, up, down, and all combinations. As you do this, notice if a particular direction causes you to feel most empowered. Leave your perception of your future in that position. Most likely this will be in front of you.

Now we will examine your most empowered perception of the future more closely. Does your representation of the future start where you are, or is there a gap between where you are and where your representation of the future begins? If so, notice how it feels when you fill in this blank spot, so your future begins now.

How wide is the line that represents your future? Experiment with different widths. You are free to decorate your mind in any way you like. Some people prefer to see their future as a narrow line; others as a footpath; still others prefer it to be as wide as a ten-lane freeway. Try different widths to discover which is the most empowering to you.

What about color? What color is your representation of your future? Would you like a different color better? Experiment with different color combinations so your future looks most appealing to you.

What supports your perception of the future? Some people prefer to see their future suspended in space; others add graceful stone arches beneath it like a Roman viaduct; still others add cables similar to a suspension bridge.

What symbols appear in your future? If you like, add symbols of success like roadside billboards to your future. What do you want in your future? Add symbols that represent the success, health, wealth, recognition, or whatever you seek onto the timeline that represents your future.

You may find it necessary to repeat this exercise from time to time until this new vision of yours becomes the way you naturally perceive your future.

INSERTING YOUR GOAL INTO YOUR TIMELINE

 In this section you will be installing your SMART goals one by one into your new vision of the future. Most people discover that this method works best if they read over the entire method first. Consider having someone guide you through this process instead of trying to do it by yourself. If no one is available or you do not feel comfortable sharing this experience with anyone, make sure you understand the process completely before you go through it. Perhaps make a tape recording to help guide you through the process. (If you do use a tape recording, make sure to allow pauses that are long enough for you to complete each step of this process. Remember, you are new to this method. With practice, you will become faster.)

By now you should have established your goals. If you have not determined what your goals are, go back now and establish your goals now! If you do not have goals, your results will be determined by others. So take the time and do this now. For those of you who did the exercise, pat yourself on the back and congratulate yourself. In Chapter 14 you will create plans to accomplish these goals.

Now it's time to review your goals and make sure they are SMART goals. Check to make sure your goals are specific, measurable and meaningful, written in the present tense (as if now), reach out and reasonable, and have a date (time). Do this now. Do not deprive yourself of the success you desire and deserve by using goals that are not SMART.

Now that your goals are SMART, let's place them in your timeline one at a time. Your unconscious mind will help you to do so by reevaluating the events that lead up to achieving your goals. Doing this will tap you into and attract into your presence the necessary resources to achieve the outcome you desire. It will realign all the events from then to now in order to support you achieving your goals.

Now pick the first goal you want to insert into your timeline. Determine the last step necessary for you to know that you have achieved your goal. For example, if you were taking a trip to Europe, what is the last thing that has to happen to know that you achieved the goal? Some people know they have achieved the trip when they make the travel reservations. Others know they have achieved the goal when they step onto the plane or land at their final destination. Make sure you determine what is the very last thing that must happen for you to know that the goal is achieved. Do this now.

Make an appealing internal sensory representation of yourself arriving at this very last step. Do this using all of your senses—sight, sound, feeling, smell, and taste. Now make a picture of you completing the last step and achieving your goal. See this picture through your own eyes as if it were happening now and feel the feelings of having achieved the goal. Now improve the experience of achieving your goal by making the accompanying pictures brighter, bigger, and closer in stark, vivid color and panoramic. Add as many details as you can; the more, the better. If your experience is vague and not detailed, use your imagination and keep adding more details until you really get excited.

Add sounds to your experience. Let yourself hear people telling you what you'd like to hear about accomplishing the goal. Add your favorite music in the background. Make it loud and stereophonic. Now add the feelings that you will have when you achieve your outcome. Make sure they are as intense and pleasurable as possible. Keep making adjustments until the experience feels best to you. Make sure your feelings are as intense as you can make them.

Also add smells and tastes to achieving your goal if possible. Add any internal dialogue necessary to enhance the experience. For example, you might say, "This is great!" Keep adjusting your experience until you get the most positive and intense feeling possible. Do this now.

Now step out of the experience and see yourself in the picture with the goal accomplished. Make sure that you can see your own body in the experience. You should now be dissociated. Dissociated means you see yourself in your mental picture. Refer back to the Emotional Resolution method from Chapter 7 for a reminder of the power of choosing an associated or a dissociated perception. So, see yourself (dissociated) with the goal accomplished.

Next, take this same internal representation of achieving your goal where you can see yourself in the picture. Take it with you on your journey above your timeline. Float high above the present moment. Make sure you are well above your timeline, looking down on it as if from an orbiting satellite. Give yourself a vantage point that allows you to see far back into the past and way out into the future, but still lets you see events happening down on your timeline.

Take the internal representation you are carrying and energize it with four deep breaths. Take a deep breath in through your nose and out through the mouth. As you breathe out, blow all your life energy into your internal representation. Do this three more times to really energize it. That's right.

Now look toward the future end of your timeline. Float out into the future to the exact date that your goal will be achieved, taking your internal representation with you.

Let go of your internal representation, and let it float right down into your timeline. Let it float down as if it were a sheet of paper floating down on air. Watch as it plugs itself into your timeline.

From your accomplishment date on your timeline, look back toward the present. See the events from the date the goal is accomplished all the way back to now. Watch these events reorganize themselves to produce your desired outcome. You may want to see this reorganization happen a couple of times to aid you in envisioning a clear path to your goal.

Once you are finished watching the events reorganize themselves, come back to now. Float back down to now and come back into the room. Look up at the ceiling for two to three seconds. Doing this ensures that you are ready to continue with the next part.

Congratulations! You have installed the first goal into your timeline. Use this method to install your other goals. If you have set smaller goals in order to achieve larger ones, make sure that they are SMART and that you place them into your timeline as well.

Gain Certainty about Any Goal in Seconds with the Filing Cabinet Method

The more certain you are that you will accomplish any goal, the more effectively you will get there. Remember a time when you were about to achieve a goal that you were very certain you could achieve. How easy was it for you to achieve that goal? Did the obstacles seem to be simple to overcome or maybe even nonexistent?

Now remember a past goal that you weren't sure you could achieve. Do you remember a lot of obstacles? Did they seem difficult to overcome? How difficult was the goal to achieve? Did it take a long time to complete? Now that it is complete, was it really that difficult, or did it just seem difficult at the time because you were uncertain?

Now think of an important goal. If you don't have one in mind, refer back to the section on SMART goals. Ask yourself, in percentage terms, how sure are you that you will accomplish this. Take a moment to jot down this percentage. Do this now! In order to achieve the goals you want, you must take action. Do not delay.

Now think of a fact of which you are 100 percent certain. It might be your gender, or the color of your eyes, or your nationality. Or you may choose the fact that the earth is round, the sun will shine again, or the location where you currently live—something you could prove in court if necessary.

Now notice exactly where this fact is stored in your mind. (Perhaps in the front or the back or on one side. Look carefully enough inside to find its precise filing location.)

Now find a location in your mind that you can easily find, and imagine a file cabinet. Take your chosen fact and move the certainty of that fact into the file cabinet. Now pick a second fact that you are absolutely certain about. Move the certainty of that fact into your file cabinet where you stored the first fact.

Now think of the goal you referred to at the beginning of this exercise and find its precise location in your mind. Grab onto this goal in your mind, carefully remove it from its present location, and move it into your file cabinet with the other facts of which you are 100 percent certain. Actually experience moving the goal into the file cabinet in your mind.

Now pick a third fact that you are 100 percent certain of. Move the certainty of the fact into your file cabinet. Add as many additional facts as you wish. The more facts you place in your file cabinet with your goal, the better this exercise will work for you.

Check for completeness by asking yourself, in percentage terms, how certain are you that you will accomplish the goal. Take a moment to jot down this new percentage.

Repeat adding facts into your file cabinet until you are 100 percent certain.

MENTAL FLEXIBILITY FOR PEAK PERFORMANCE

Mental rigidity makes improvement difficult, perhaps impossible. The rigid mind is absorbed in justifying the past rather than in improving the future. Using what you learn in this chapter, you will be able to prevent your negative thinking from getting the better of you. Learn why positive thinking alone produces results that are most often minor and temporary. The Power Affirmations method allows access to the unconscious thinking that is limiting success. It is a method that changes your thinking to facilitate accomplishment and to eliminate annoying internal chatter.

TRUE OR FALSE QUIZ TO PROMOTE MENTAL FLEXIBILITY

 Take out a sheet of paper and number it from 1 to 6. Answer true or false to these questions. Please, no changing answers after writing them.

1. The sun rises in the east and sets in the west.
2. The sun neither rises nor sets in any direction. Rising and setting is an illusion caused by the rotation of the earth on its axis.
3. $1,000 is a lot of money.
4. $1,000 is a small amount of money.
5. Everything is the same.
6. Everything is different.

Let's see what your answers are. Six true answers earn 100 percent, as do six false answers. Each of these statements is true or false, depending on your perception. If you were lost in the woods with a watch and no compass, knowing that the sun rises in the east and sets in the west would help you find your way out. However, a rocket scientist calculating the correct trajectory for launching a rocket from earth to Mars would simplify the calculations by assuming the sun to be stationary.

Whether $1,000 is a lot or a little money depends on the situation. At the supermarket one answer is correct; at the Mercedes dealer the other one is.

Similarly, perspective determines whether two things are the same or different. At the subatomic level, matter is empty space and energy, so all of it is the same, but microscopic analysis reveals differences even in simultaneously minted coins.

How Our Mind Proves Ideas to Be True

Over the years, you have allowed yourself (consciously or unconsciously) to be convinced that the contents of your mind are true. If your friends refused to play with you when you were a toddler, you may have thought, "No one likes me." The defensiveness that such a thought would create would surely make you less likable. Additionally, it might make you oversensitive about how people treat you, and you might interpret even normal behavior as rejection. It's possible that you cause people to reject you because of the belligerent attitude that the thought "No one likes me" would cause. After doing this for a while, you have built your case—you have unconsciously gathered sufficient evidence to prove that no one likes you. As you are the one who convinced yourself that such limiting thoughts are true, you are the one who can convince yourself of something different and better.

As you begin to shift your thinking, it's a good idea to consider your mind an unruly puppy that you wish to house train. You might scold the puppy sometimes being firm but gentle. You would not blame the puppy for not knowing to do its business on the paper.

Power Affirmations: Design the Life You Prefer

Most people are familiar with using affirmations, to mixed results. Here you will learn the most effective way to use affirmations to apply the creative power of your mind so results are certain.

The most significant drawback of most methods of using affirmations is reliance on repetition. Relying on repetition alone assumes that your mind is similar to a piece of sheet metal. If you just pound on it long enough, you can change it into a shape that works better.

Such repetition often involves saying to yourself positive phrases or sentences over and over. This method does nothing to deal with underlying limited thinking. It is about as permanent as a nice new paint job applied on top of the rusty surface of a car.

Your mind is like a computer. Your brain can be compared to computer hardware, and the thoughts that occupy it can be compared to computer software or programs. Computers include instruction manuals. The human mind does not, however. Consider this book a brief instruction manual for running your mind to your benefit.

Your computer arrived from the supplier with certain programs and settings preinstalled. For example, the borders on the screen were probably blue. If you hate blue and prefer green, you can manually alter the default conditions, causing your machine to generate green borders. Similarly, your mind is preprogrammed with unconscious beliefs that have created results (desired or not) up to now. You will discover that many of the limiting beliefs were adopted unwillingly or unconsciously during childhood and have remained unquestioned ever since. This chapter shows you the most effective way to change the unwanted default conditions of your mind so that you are free to produce more favorable results.

How you think is everything. Life is a reflection and creation of thinking. Thoughts cause actions, and actions cause results. Our decisions, our reactions to events, our motivation, and our external circumstances all result from our thoughts, attitudes, beliefs, and emotional dynamics.

So long as you attribute your well-being to something you do not control, you will experience pain. Thus, acknowledging that you create your own results by virtue of your own internal thinking process opens a door to a whole new world of satisfaction, wealth, and accomplishment.

When you turn on your computer, you do not get access to all of the software it contains. Most computers will not allow you to access all the software simultaneously, and in most part of the software remains inaccessible to users. Your mind has many similarities to this. You are not aware of the specific thoughts that you use to digest your dinner or that cause your leg to jerk when your knee is tapped. More specifically, the thoughts that inhabit your mind affect your success and satisfaction in all areas of your life, whether you are aware of the specific thoughts that cause specific results or not. When you want to upgrade your computer's performance, you can buy better hardware or better software. The analogy falls apart here, because brain transplants exist only in science fiction. Yet while upgrading your mental hardware is not an option, you can upgrade your mental software—your thoughts—whenever you want. (See the solutions presented in Table 9.1.)

Lying to Yourself

Your mind differs from a computer in that it possesses the ability to distinguish between truth and falsehood. Any new information that comes into your mind is automatically compared to what is already there in a test of validity. Some of the information already in your mind is clearly not beneficial, but nevertheless it is perceived as true, given the evidence of your experience. In other words, your computer already contains some software, programming in use for many years. These may be thoughts that no longer serve you, but any method that deals with your mind cannot work very well unless it helps you deal with what is already there. If you don't believe your affirmations enough to see them as reasonable possibilities, then you are lying to yourself.

For example, no one's mind would argue with the statement, "The sun will rise tomorrow." Conversely, almost no one's mind would completely accept the statement, "I am certain to win the lottery tomorrow." Such statements are too near the extremes of credibility (almost completely believable or almost completely unbelievable) to be useful as affirmations. The challenge then is to formulate affirmations in

TABLE 9.1 Common Problems with Solutions

Affirmations	
Lying to yourself.	Use affirmation preambles.
Relying on repetition alone.	Use the interactive method, example at end of this chapter.
Desire to control.	Forget about *how* you will get what you want; instead focus on receiving your desire.

such a way that your mind can accept the truth of them and yet have them offer the change that you want. Let's say that you are working with the affirmation "Everyone supports me in increasing my income." If your reservations about this statement are so strong that they cause you to wonder about its truth, take a step back by using one of the affirmation preambles to make the statement less definite and less absolute, or to add to the affirmation a reason to believe it. You can add these preambles to the beginning of any affirmation to make it more believable or acceptable. (You may have to modify the syntax of the sentence so that the grammar is correct.) For example, most people find the statement "It is OK for me to think that everyone supports me in increasing my income" easier to accept than the same statement without the preamble.

Affirmation Preambles
- It is OK for me to . . .
- It is OK for me to think that . . .
- Now that I am grown up, . . .
- Since I am a child of God, . . .
- It is within the realm of all possible events that . . .
- I have permission to . . .
- I am good enough to . . .

If you write the affirmation "I am a wealthy man with a large and growing income," it is possible that your mind will be unwilling to accept this. However, if you include in your statement some verifiable facts about yourself, acceptance becomes easier. For example, "I am a tall, brown-eyed, American, wealthy man with a large and growing income."

Relying on Repetition Alone

Some books about affirmations recommend constant repetition as the primary method for persuading your mind to accept a new idea. Our method is far more effective. It allows, even encourages, the parts of your mind that object to the new idea to speak up, so that you can deal with the objections with affirmations composed for this purpose.

Desire to Control

Each of us has control of our behavior and thoughts and nothing else. Affirmations will not necessarily change your reality, but they can change your willingness to take action to change your reality, and they can change your perception of reality. In those instances where perception actually is reality, it may seem that your reality changes. For this reason, usually it is not useful to limit the manner in which your desire may come to you. Make the statements in your affirmations as broad and general as possible. For example, we don't recommend using as an affirmation "My spouse now does what pleases me"; "It is now easy for me to see the good intention in the behavior of others" would be a better choice.

Which Affirmation to Use?

Because the method you will be learning is interactive, it is not essential to start with exactly the "right" affirmation. The process encourages your mind to lead you to the most effective affirmation. On page 175 we provide a list of affirmations to start with. You can apply the method you will be learning to every area of your life. Thus, we present a menu of affirmations for your choice. Pick the one that produces a strong emotional reaction in you—either it makes you feel wonderful, or it produces an uncomfortable churning in your stomach or tightening in your jaw.

I (AF) want to tell you my experience with our affirmations method. I know some of you may be thinking affirmations really don't work. Perhaps you've used them with no change in results.

I used to agree. I used affirmations diligently in the past, repeating them hundreds of times a day, with little or no results. I was ready to give up on them until one day I heard Phil, as a guest speaker on a teletraining call.

The call started out with an introduction of Phil and his topic "Affirmations." I thought, this is going to be a waste of time and I was about to hang up. Affirmations don't work.

Phil started his presentation and said: "Just speaking affirmations out loud won't produce permanent, significant results." This got my attention.

Phil discussed the method we are sharing with you now, and it made sense to me. I ordered a copy of *Money Is My Friend* and a copy of "Power Affirmations," which was then an article.

I used the methods and made progress very quickly. For the first time I really got in touch with what was in my mind. I was able to quickly and permanently change the thoughts that were holding me back from achieving success. By using this information daily and working with different affirmations, I was able to clear out all that chatter that had been running through my mind—the disempowering garbage we have all experienced.

Since then I published my first book, *Profiting in Turbulent Times*, have written this book with Phil, and have three other books in the works. I have increased my consulting business and have the privilege of working with Phil, combining our talents and abilities to deliver Training that help people overcome obstacles very quickly and permanently.

In sales situations, I can really hear what my prospects are telling me instead of letting my mind get in the way. I used to think about what to say before the prospect ever finished. I assure you this was not effective and sales were almost nonexistent. Now I can really listen and have quiet in my mind while others speak. By really listening, I learn a lot about what my customers want and need. My sales have increased very quickly. Eliminating the chatter that distracted me made accomplishment both easier and quicker. You will discover this too as you use these methods.

BASIC METHOD: SET OF 10

R℥ Choose an affirmation from the list on pages 175–177. We are going to demonstrate with "It is OK for me to have strong emotions."

First write the affirmation in the first person: It is OK for me to have strong emotions. Most people discover that writing by hand is more effective than typing because of the higher engagement of visual, hearing, and feeling senses when we actually use pen and paper.

Then write the objection or negative reaction your mind comes up with. Put this reaction in parentheses to show that it is of less importance than the affirmation. This statement is your response: (I feel guilty when I lose my temper.)

Recording your negative response to your affirmation is a key part of this process. By writing down your response, you are allowing the scared little person we all have inside, but prefer to ignore, to have his or her say. By composing a new affirmation to deal with the response, you reassure the child that you are capable of taking care of it. The scared little child merely wants to be heard; by recording your response, the internal chatter subsides.

Then compose a new affirmation to change the thought in your response. To paraphrase Regis Philbin, "Is that your final answer?" Of course, you do not want the negative responses to be your final answer. *Now it is easy for me to remember to take a breath and think before I speak. (For identification purposes, we add an asterisk at the beginning of the new affirmation.) Then you write, "It is OK for me to have strong emotions" twice more in the first person, each time with a response and a new affirmation to change the response. Allow your mind to produce responses spontaneously without censorship. Doing so you will result in different responses each time.

Now write your affirmation in the second person, using your name: "George, it is OK for you to have strong emotions." Do this three times, each time recording your response and composing a new affirmation as you did before.

Then write your affirmation in the third person, using your name: "It is OK for George to have strong emotions." Also do this three times, each time recording your response and composing your new affirmation as you did before.

The final step is to write your affirmation, "It is OK for me to have strong emotions," once in the first person with no response.

Three times in each of three persons plus the final one in the first person equals a set of 10. With a little practice, you'll complete a set of 10 in about 15 minutes.

Using all three persons (I/me; you; he/him/she/her) enables you to deal with all the objections your mind has on a subject, whether these ideas are ones that: you thought up yourself (first person); other people told you (second person); or other people said about you (third person).

You may have thought up the objections in your mind on your own. When I (PL) was a child, my mother had a lot of faith in doctors. If I complained about not feeling well, she immediately took me to the doctor. After a few such trips, I noticed that the doctor always did something unpleasant to me, so I concluded on my own that "Doctors hurt me" and learned to avoid complaining about illness. As an adult, I realized that my compulsive avoidance of doctors did not serve optimum health and used affirmations to dissolve this thinking. This was a conclusion that I made on my own, and so it was in my mind in the first person, "Doctors hurt me."

It is possible that ideas got into your mind in the second person. If your parents told you regularly, "You are an excellent student. I am glad that you are so smart" or "What's wrong with you? How can you be so stupid?" this information entered your mind in the second person.

Third-person sources require a bit more explanation. Observe the behavior of two or more adults in the presence of an infant. In almost every case, the infant is the topic of conversation. The adults discuss the infant as if he or she were not present, offering opinions about the baby's personality, bowel movements, progress toward toilet training, resemblance to relatives, and lots of other personal characteristics. Today if two people had this same conversation about you in your presence, you would be justifiably offended.

People seem to assume that since infants cannot speak, they can't understand. However, if you observe an infant in this situation, you'll see that he or she is taking in every word (unless the baby is asleep). Infants pay attention because they want to learn to speak, and they will do so by imitating those around them. Negative conclusions can enter your mind if you overhear others discussing you.

WHAT LANGUAGE TO USE IN AFFIRMATIONS
IF ENGLISH IS YOUR SECOND LANGUAGE

You'll make far more rapid progress writing affirmations in your first language. Childhood rules and conditioning were imparted to you in your mother tongue. Write your affirmations down in your first language, even if you must consult a bilingual dictionary to do so.

Dealing with Responses to Your Affirmations

Specific thoughts can limit your accomplishment and peace of mind. You can't change what you don't know about. Positive thinking produces results that are usually minor and temporary because you are not aware of these limiting thoughts. By writing your response to each affirmation, your objections come to the fore. Let's say you write the affirmation "My income exceeds my expenses," and let's say that your response is "(I am always broke)."

Now, it is important to realize that the limiting thought that arose as your response has been creating results in your life for a very long time. Furthermore, these results confirm the validity of "(I am always broke)." The question then becomes: Is this thought true? It is true in the limited sense that it conforms to your personal experience. For this reason, you must question "(I am always broke)" a little further and ask, "Is this thought absolutely true?" "Absolutely" means throughout all space and time, in all cases for all people. Surely you can see that "(I am always broke)" is not absolutely true; there have been times in your life when you have had money, and other people have money, so you can, too. The

Power Affirmations Method requires your willingness to see things differently. Insisting on the absolute truth of "(I am always broke)" will cause your creative thinking to continue manifesting that experience. What you focus on in life is what you receive. By questioning the validity of your thinking at an absolute level, you can see things differently.

"I can't" is the verbal expression of the sensation of helplessness. Humans have limits. There are things we cannot do. However, many of the things about which you think "I can't" are not only humanly possible, but things that other people do every day. You may have to pay closer attention to your thoughts and language to detect the "I can't." "I can't" is almost never true. If you catch yourself thinking "I can't," and change it to "I won't," then ask yourself whether the statement is true. This may seem like a small distinction, but "I won't" returns the power of choice about your behavior to you. Just because you *feel* helpless does not mean that you *are* helpless. Remember:

> Helplessness is a feeling, not a condition.
> Therefore, it is temporary.

> An astounding truth about helplessness is this:
> Helplessness leads to power.

When a Response to Your Affirmation Doesn't Appear

Writing affirmations facilitates positive change in your reality. Your external reality is a reflection of your thinking. If you want something different from what you have, then the thoughts that created what you have now must be resident somewhere in your consciousness, even though you may be unaware of them. To change what you have, you must identify and change the specific thoughts that created the status quo.

Your mind may not willingly (at least at first) tell you what it has been thinking to create the status quo. Perhaps your mind desires to maintain the status quo because there is fear of change. Or perhaps your mind believes it is protecting you from an uncomfortable memory, some past upset or negative feelings, by not letting you know what is there. Obviously, some thought in your consciousness is in opposition to the affirmation; if it were not, the change you desire would have already occurred. So if you can't come up with a response to an affirmation, write something like this as your response: (*I know there is something there in my mind, but it is not coming out yet.)

Then write something like this as an affirmation to deal with this response: *It is safe for me to know about everything in my mind.*

Composing New Affirmations to Deal with Your Responses

With experience, you'll get better at composing affirmations to deal with your responses primarily because you will gain a better understanding of the negative parts of your mind—the parts you may feel ashamed about or have been struggling to deny. (Also, over time you will take your negative thoughts less seriously.) As uncomfortable as it may be, this understanding will benefit you greatly. Some people have reported that their responses are the exact words of one of their parents. This tends to occur most frequently in responses to affirmations written in the second person. Hence the affirmation preamble: "Now that I am grown up . . ."

Inversion is probably the simplest method of composing new affirmations to deal with negative responses. Take the negative response and invert it directly into a positive statement, adding one of the affirmation preambles, if required, for believability. Consider the next examples:

Response	*Affirmation to Deal with It*
That will never happen.	It is within the realm of all possible events that . . .
I don't know how.	I have the ability to learn anything I set my mind to.
What will people think?	I am the source of my own approval.

Acceptance of Shortcomings

Unless you can accept your shortcomings, success becomes a compulsion—a requirement. Not only does this lack of acceptance cause you to feel guilty, it also robs you of the satisfaction that comes with success. A healthy acceptance of your shortcomings removes the denial that makes problems impossible to solve. Thus "It is OK for me to _____" or "It is OK for me to think that _____" are appropriate affirmations for dealing with any response.

Dealing with Perfectionism

A healthy acceptance of your shortcomings removes the denial that makes problems impossible to solve.

Too many people tell themselves (and others) that they have low self-esteem. So-called low self-esteem is a trap. The term "low self-esteem" offers no solution; it merely describes a seemingly permanent condition. The existence of this condition sometimes trumps all attempts to improve. It goes like this: "You see, my problem is I have low self-esteem. I know I should get out and meet people, but I have low self-esteem. I know I would benefit from exercise, but I have low self-esteem." And so forth.

No one benefits from calling it low self-esteem. We prefer to call the condition "unwarranted perfectionism." In other words, the problem is not so much your bad opinion of yourself, but rather your unreasonably high expectation of how good you think you must be to be acceptable. Lower your standards of acceptability a little. Probably there are people less acceptable than you who are OK.

Religion

Examine your religious beliefs to determine whether any hold you back. In particular, examine whether any beliefs place unwarranted limits on your wealth, happiness, and self-expression. No matter your religion, there are probably wealthy members of your church.

Most books about personal success, business, and psychology do not discuss religious beliefs, perhaps because of the volatility and passion surrounding this subject. Volatility and passion are precisely the reasons why we address religion.

In our consulting work, we have discovered that the detrimental impact of self-defeating religious beliefs is, for some people, more profound than childhood conditioning from parents. Violation of childhood rules may have resulted in your being sent to bed without supper or a spanking or worse, but surely no punishment was so severe as eternal damnation. Most childhood conditioning teaches that the approval of the people you associate with is something that must be earned by loyalty to the group and by compliance with externally imposed rules that may or may not serve your best interest. Such conditioning often paves the way for belief in a religion based on the dualistic judgment of a Supreme Power creating rules that are interpreted by self-appointed authority figures.

Here in the United States and in much of the world, we are blessed with freedom of religion. Such freedom is essential to personal self-fulfillment, and we respect and are grateful for it. We are not interested in converting you to a different religion, but we do want to suggest that you may greatly benefit from a review of your religious beliefs.

Miriam is a Jew. As a child in the post–World War II United States, her parents provided temporary housing for a large number of European Jews, survivors of the Holocaust. During one of her consultations, I (PL) asked her what it meant to be Jewish. "It means I am a victim" was her response. Anyone can applaud her parents' humanitarian efforts on behalf of the stream of refugees they housed during Miriam's childhood. But Miriam felt neglected by the care and concern the refugees received. Her conclusions led her to believe that she was a victim, that suffering was required to be accepted and cared for, and that she had not suffered sufficiently to be accepted. As you can imagine, these conclusions had a devastating effect on both her career and her close relationships, until she applied the methods in this book to change these detrimental childhood conclusions.

George is a born-again Christian. He reported that his personal relationship with his savior provided him great solace during the financial crisis of credit card overspending that he was facing. I (PL) suggested that possibly he could benefit even more from this important relationship by calling on his savior for more than just solace. He felt he would be disapproved of for the mistakes he had made in accumulating the credit card debt. I asked him to request forgiveness for these errors and make the relationship more active by asking for guidance and energy to aid him in paying off his credit card balances.

Both of these people benefited greatly by reexamining their religious beliefs and kept the original religion they had at the outset. What about you? Are you putting your faith in a Supreme Power that offers you more restricted freedom of belief than the temporal power of the government that guarantees freedom of religion?

Emotional Reactions

Your emotional reaction to the material that comes to mind as a response may be far more important than your intellectual response. Whenever you have strong feelings about your response, compose an affirmation to deal with those emotions. Some examples are:

> It is OK for me to feel afraid.
> It is safe for me to feel angry.
> I am using my feelings of hostility in productive ways.

In the resolution of your personal psychological obstacles, a feeling is worth 1,000 thoughts. Feelings are richer, three-dimensional, more pervasive, and more honest than thoughts. Temporary, extremely intense body reactions are not uncommon. People report brief periods of light-headedness, dizziness, blurred vision, shakiness, spastic writing, and sleepiness in response to their affirmations. Having such intense reactions verifies that you are on the right track.

Take Appropriate Action

Affirmations cannot be a cure-all. If you want financial freedom but devote all your energy to a dead-end job and are not willing to take the risk associated with a business of your own, just changing your mind won't help you much. Start with changing your perceptions of the risk you face. Affirmations can help you accomplish any goal, but direct action is required, as well.

When to Switch to a New Affirmation

Switch to a new affirmations in two cases. First, use affirmations to aid in the achievement of a particular result. Once you have achieved that result, switch to a new affirmation. Second, as you compose affirmations to deal with your responses, you may compose one that has a stronger emotional reaction than the original affirmation. If so, switch to the new one.

The results from any affirmation may not be instantaneous, because you are dealing with psychological material that likely was learned during 20,000 meals with people who gave you conflicting messages about yourself, money, sex, and other issues. However, it is rare for two weeks of daily use of Power Affirmations not to produce significant progress on any desired result.

Using Power Affirmations is similar to psychological horticulture. Weeds will grow anywhere without attention. By using this affirmations technique, you tend your mental garden, eliminating the weeds and bringing forth the fruit that you most prefer.

It is impossible to solve your financial problems with money. If you have a money mind-set that produces financial problems and you should happen to get more money without changing the mind-set, then pretty soon you will have the same financial problems, only bigger.

As many people have discovered, struggling and juggling produces limited results. This is because, like to emergency room care, it deals with symptoms rather than causes. Change to a prosperity mind-set is almost certain to take you outside your comfort zone. Dealing with the psychological and emotional issues that inhibit your progress is not always easy, but it is far easier than carrying them around in your unconscious where they confound your best efforts to get ahead.

Whatever your views about money, you are right. Your mind automatically creates financial results that are a precise reflection of your internal thinking. So whatever you think about money, the issue as to whether you are right is meaningless. Would you rather be rich or would you rather be right?

The following Sample Set of 10 demonstrates the procedures to use in creating Power Affirmations. Of course, your responses and composed affirmations will be different.

Sample Set of 10
Power Affirmations

Write the affirmation in the first person (me) followed by any objection or negative that your mind may have about it. Place this objection in parentheses ( ) to emphasize that it has less importance than the affirmation. Then compose an affirmation that would cancel the validity of the objection. Precede this affirmation by an asterisk * to make it easy to find. (Note: We show the composed affirmation in *italics* for clarity.) Refer to main text about how to make the composed affirmations.

Complete three repetitions of the affirmation in the first person, response, and composing new affirmation.

First Person: It is OK for me to think that everyone supports me in increasing my income. (What about those people who don't want to buy?) *I can always learn something useful from people who decline my offers.* It is OK for me to think that everyone supports me in increasing my income. (I am afraid that if I believe this, I will be easily deceived by dishonest people.) *It is always OK for me to say no.* It is OK for me to think that everyone supports me in increasing my income. (What about those people who are not interested in what I am offering them?) *I know how to find out quickly whether people are interested.*

Repeat the process in the second person (you). Use your childhood name (Skipper in the sample) to make this affirmation more effective.

Complete three repetitions of the affirmation in the second person, response, and composing new affirmation.

Second Person: Skipper, it is OK for you to think that everyone supports you in increasing your income. (I remember my parents telling me that there are people that I should watch out for.) *I forgive my parents for the mistakes they made.* Skipper, it is OK for you to think that everyone supports you in increasing your income. (If I make more money, I will just have to pay more taxes.) *I am grateful that the government does not take all my income.* Skipper, it is OK for you to think that everyone supports you in increasing your income. (What about the people that don't have the money to pay for what I am offering?) *I have the freedom to change my prices whenever it is to my benefit.*

Repeat the process in the third person (he or she). Again, use your childhood name to make this affirmation more effective.

Third Person: It is OK for Skipper to think that everyone supports him in increasing his income. (All kinds of people, will approach me with requests for gifts or with silly investment schemes.) *I can say no without feeling guilty. *I know when it is right for me to be generous.* It is OK for Skipper to think that everyone supports him in increasing his income. (I am afraid that some people will think they have been cheated.) *I trust myself to be responsive to people's reasonable complaints.* It is OK for Skipper to think that everyone supports him in increasing his income. (Why not?) *I am grateful for my ability to change my mind.*

Now write the affirmation in the first person, without a response and without a composed affirmation, to complete the set of 10.

It is OK for me to think that everyone supports me in increasing my income.

PICK YOUR OWN POWER AFFIRMATION

 Pick the affirmation that produces the strongest emotional reaction for you from the following lists. Then write a Set of 10.

Affirmations Menu

GENERAL

- I am the one who tells my mind what to think.
- All parts of my mind are cooperating with each other.
- I forgive those teachers who forced me to write sentences as punishment.
- My thoughts have infinite creative power. I am focusing on what is desirable in my life and consciousness.

SPIRITUALITY

- I am always in the right place at the right time, successfully engaged in the right activity.
- I am living in a safe and friendly environment filled with people who love me and support my purpose.
- I am experiencing ever increasing amounts of God's love and grace.

SELF-ESTEEM

- Disapproval is OK with me.
- The more I like myself the way I am, the more I am the way I want to be.
- I forgive myself for thinking that my feelings meant something bad about me.
- I am proud of myself. I am proud of what I do. I am proud of who I am.
- Even though I have character defects, I love and accept myself completely.
- It is OK for me to have strong emotions.

RELATIONSHIPS

- I am now receiving assistance and cooperation from those people everywhere necessary to accomplish my desired results.
- I am ready to meet the (wo)man I want, who loves me and who wants a relationship.
- When I mean yes, I say yes; when I mean no, I say no.

TIME

- My mind is more than flexible enough for me to use time most effectively.
- Time is on my side.
- I am using my time in effective ways that express my purpose.

FINANCE AND CAREER

- Success makes me more determined. Setbacks make me more determined. Everything makes me more determined.
- Everyone is supporting me in increasing my income.
- Now that I am grown up, it is OK for me to receive income and support from various places at once.
- My competitive spirit empowers and motivates me to earn, receive, and accumulate income far in excess of my requirements.
- I am calm and attentive while selling.
- All parts of my mind are cooperating to produce the action that creates wealth for me.
- I made it through birth, infancy, toilet training, childhood, adolescence, and the rest. Now I am expressing myself the way I choose and freely receiving all my positive desires.

RESOLUTION OF GUILT

- God is my Father.
- I am free of those religious views that in the past kept me poor. I step forward to claim all the good that God has for me.
- I am not my past. I am a child of God.
- I now possess the foresight to think through my behavior to its ultimate results.
- I forgive myself for allowing guilt to make decisions and hold me back. Now I am using self-acceptance and massive action to lead straight to my goal.
- I am alive and they are dead and these two things have nothing to do with each other. (for survivor's guilt)

HEALTH

- My body knows how to heal itself.
- I am developing the right habits for better health.
- I am receiving excellent advice from health professionals.
- I am healing myself by accepting the energy I refer to as symptoms.

You probably have noticed that many of the affirmations contain participles, such as "developing" and "receiving." These forms make affirmations more active for you.

10

OVERALL BUSINESS MODEL

Learn the essential aspects of any successful business, the importance of managing your time, and working effectively with your employees.

This chapter is aimed at readers new to owning their own business. It's goal is to eliminate confusion so that you can create a business structure. Even if you have had your own business for a while, it's worth reviewing the fundamentals to ensure your long-term success. Remember, excellent athletic coaches focus on fundamentals to improve performance. The broad perspective offers the opportunity to step back and evaluate essential issues you may not consider every day.

Top-Down View

Perfectionist tendencies can keep you bogged down in urgent but unimportant details that leave you no longer in control of your business.

Would you rather be right, or would you rather be rich? Throughout this book, we have taught you to revolutionize your thinking in general, not only about income-producing activities. Earning the income you want from work you love is an act of defiance—it defies both parental conditioning and societal conditioning.

In your own business there is no one to tell you what to do. A very, very important decision you make every day is how to use your time. In a job, you may spend much of your time on urgent details. It's different in your own business.

In this chapter, we will stand above the details for an overall look at the essential functions of any business. Up to this point, you have been learning the skills required to construct a winning mind-set about money and business. This chapter provides you with the broad perspective about a business. The next three show you how to apply what you have learned to excel at negotiation and selling.

What Does a Business Do?

The simplest explanation of a business is this: You need only three things to be in business: a customer, a price, and a product or service you can deliver. If you lack any of these three items, you are out of business until you can make up the lack.

Any business can be thought of as dealing with four essential functions. As a business owner, your task is to constantly maximize the productivity of each of these functions.

1. Finding prospective customers
2. Presenting your product or service, so prospects buy
3. Producing your product or service, delivering it and collecting payment
4. Follow-up

These four elements are present in every business model. By breaking down your business into these four components, you can make improvements and pinpoint problems.

FINDING PROSPECTIVE CUSTOMERS

To find customers, focus is crucial. Don't waste money advertising to the general public if only a small segment is interested in what you are offering. An informative Web site is very useful. Purchase a small amount of print advertising to refer people to the site. A Web site offers lots of space to tell about your products and services; you could never afford this amount of space in the print media. Spread the word about your business in ways different from those of your competitors. Write a magazine article about your business. Ask your local paper to do a story about you. Become a public speaker and create an interesting speech about some aspect of your business.

PRESENTING YOUR PRODUCT OR SERVICE SO PROSPECTS BUY

What makes your business different? What is so good about what you offer that people would feel foolish doing business with anyone else, regardless of price? In most cases, despite the existence of e-mail and the Internet, the telephone probably will be your most important sales tool. Expect to spend 10 to 20 hours per week making phone presentations to prospective customers. The amount of time you spend at this is self-regulating because the less business you have, the more time you devote to finding new customers, and vice versa.

PRODUCING YOUR PRODUCT OR SERVICE, DELIVERING IT, AND COLLECTING PAYMENT

The smaller your business, the greater the importance of personal service. Although you may never compete with a major corporation based on price or efficiency, customer service is where a small business can shine. Remember, it is almost always easier to keep a current customer than it is to find a new one. The customer from hell is the exception. Let your competition deal with customers who consistently demand price concessions and pay slowly or not at all. Perhaps you can't afford to turn away business at the outset, but after a while you will discover that 20 percent of the customers create 80 percent of the problems. Unless your business is a regulated utility, you can choose your customers. Your business will profit and your peace of mind will increase after you politely decline business from the problem creators.

FOLLOW-UP

Turn your customers into salespeople. Always ask for referrals and references. There is nothing wrong with asking your satisfied customers to put in a good word for you. Not all will agree to do so, but some will. It is almost always appropriate to ask your customers if they know other people or businesses that can use what you are selling.

Hiring Your First Employee

Success will make you busy. Unless you learn to delegate tasks, your income will become very limited by the number of working hours in a week. When you're working 60 hours a week, even earning the income you want from work you love gets to be a drag.

When I (PL) started to sell a significant number of copies of *Money Is My Friend*, it became evident that I needed help or the time I spent packing and shipping would reduce the time I had available for selling. I had to find a part-time helper.

When you need your first employee, you won't be able to afford or use a full-time person. Your first hire should be a part-time helper who can run errands to the post office, copy center, and bank as well as take care of some of the simpler and more tedious computer work, such as printing and data entry. It's a perfect job for a trustworthy college or high school student who wants to learn about business. A part-time worker who frees you up even just a few afternoons a week can make a big difference.

When you have to do everything yourself, your creativity may be limited by the knowledge that implementing any new income-producing idea means additional work for you. When you hire an employee, he or she can implement some (perhaps all) of a new idea. Your management challenge is to use the time the part-timer frees up to produce income more rapidly than the salary you pay. Some small business people even have several part-time employees with very different skills, before they hire a full-time employee. Remember, though, even the most conscientious employee may not be as motivated as you and will require supervision.

Network Marketing

As you investigate various business opportunities, you are sure to come across network marketing. Hundreds of businesses in fields as varied as tax advice, nutrition, discount travel, health and beauty products, and health insurance offer entrepreneurial opportunities. Associating with a good network marketing company provides several significant advantages compared to starting a business on your own. The advantages are:

- You work for yourself but not by yourself.
- There is the possibility of earning from the efforts of others.
- There is the possibility of earning residual income.
- The company solves the business problems of finding and maintaining sources of products to sell.

The major disadvantage to network marketing in our experience is the low percentage of people who make a full-time living at it compared to the number who get started. With the information you have already gained and what is to come, your results will surely be far above the average.

One of our clients, Henry, had been with his network marketing company for several years. During this time, he built a sales organization with more than 50,000 people. He enjoyed a middle-six fig-ure-annual income. He had no doubts about the promise of network marketing, but was dissatisfied with the very small percent-age of people in his organization who participated enough to be earning even one-tenth of what he earned. He knew he had to do something different to help those people. Conventional training and methods didn't seem to work to produce the results he knew were possible.

Henry examined several choices and decided to hire us to im-prove both the retention and the productivity of the people in his downline organization. The information in this book represents a part of the Training sessions we gave to them. Henry was quite pleased with the results of our unconventional methods for his or-ganization. His retention rate improved dramatically, and more people were working their business full time.

11

NEGOTIATION

Negotiation is an intense emotional experience for many people. Learn why the negotiating tactics you practiced as a child fail to work as an adult.

If you are hesitant about negotiation, it is almost impossible to get more than what anyone offers you. Negotiation skills are not just for diplomats, business executives, and labor leaders. They are for you, too. Most likely you negotiate more often than you realize. Some of your desires can be fulfilled without other people. Losing weight and learning a musical instrument are examples. Relations with your colleagues, subordinates, boss, friends and family, customers, and vendors all involve negotiation.

Apprehension about negotiating is a cultural peculiarity. It is probably based on fear of conflict or fear of rejection. No matter, the apprehension is not a genetic trait of all humans, and thus it can be overcome. In some cultures people love to negotiate and are insulted if you are unwilling to participate in the game. Some American automobile dealers are using advertising themes like this: *"Negotiating car prices is a hassle. Buy your next car from us. We don't negotiate. We already have low prices, so we have done the negotiating for you."* With the information in this chapter, you won't be duped by such claims. Car dealerships need customers, or they wouldn't be advertising. It is doubtful they will refuse a reasonable offer. Paradoxically, as you improve your negotiating skills, a car dealership that advertises nonnegotiable prices could be the place for the best deal because staff members there are out of practice at negotiating.

TABLE 11.1   Negotiation Matrix

Negotiating Factor	Child–Parent Mode	Adult–Adult Mode
Your View of the Counterpart	Authority figure	Equal
Number of Sources	One	Many
Negotiation Method	Justification of desire	Make offers to other person and consider theirs. Continue until agreement is reached or until you realize that one cannot be made.

Negotiation Matrix Explained

The negotiation matrix (Table 11.1) provides a convenient way to evaluate your behavior. Our first negotiating experiences came as children. Negotiating from the Child–Parent mode gives all the power to the adult and will leave you at a disadvantage. Because children have little power, you are more successful as a negotiator moving your behavior to the far right (Adult–Adult) column.

YOUR VIEW OF THE COUNTERPART

To a child, almost everyone is an authority figure. If you view your counterpart as an authority figure, then it is natural to conclude that the other person's desires, statements, and opinions are more important than yours. In this position, it is too easy to rationalize acceptance of whatever is offered, rather than asking for what you want. People often have this attitude when approaching a lending institution for a loan. Yet lending institutions derive their income by making loans. It is neither useful nor pleasant to approach a lending institution on bended knee in the posture of a beggar seeking a handout, any more than you would beg your local grocery store to sell food to you. They need your business as much as you need them. Regardless of whom you are dealing with your negotiation will be more successful if you view the other as an equal, whose desires are no more and no less important than yours. This is a good time to remember what you did in the Authority Figure exercise in Chapter 6.

NUMBER OF SOURCES

An early and common conclusion we made as children is that goodies all come from one place: Mommy or Daddy. As adults, this is no longer an accurate view. You can have multiple sources of income and anything else that you want. Realizing that there are many places to obtain what you are negotiating for helps take the pressure off, because it is not a catastrophe if you cannot make the deal.

NEGOTIATION METHOD

Infants have little in the way of goods and services to offer but simply receive nourishment, shelter, love, and affection as a result of parental generosity and responsibility. What anyone can offer in a negotiation increases with age. Infants, with limited communication skills and lacking much to offer, pitch fits to get what they want. Nine-year-olds seeking permission to go to a movie and believing they have nothing to offer the authority figures whose permission is required strenuously justify the desire with long lists of reasons. Savvy teenagers who want to use the family car on prom night can offer a wide variety of services to obtain the required permission.

As adults, things are very different. First, you have a lot more to offer the other person. Second, in many cases, your reasons for wanting what you are asking for are of little concern to the other person. An understanding employer may empathize with the financial pressure you feel from mounting bills but will not feel these justify giving you a raise. The issues that matter are what you can offer your employer in increased productivity and responsibility.

EVALUATING YOUR NEGOTIATING EXPERIENCE

R$ On a separate sheet of paper, list the transactions you have made with a value in excess of $5,000. (See Table 11.2 for an example.) No skipping ahead. Do this now! If you find yourself procrastinating, go back to the exercises on eliminating procrastination, then come back.

TABLE 11.2 Past Negotiation Experience

Approximate Date	Description	Approximate Amount
1992	Bought House	$ 80,000
1993	Bought Car	$ 8,000
1995	Accepted Job Offer	$ 45,000
1996	Salary Negotiation	$ 50,000
1998	Sold House	$ 95,000
1998	Signed Year Lease on Condo	$ 12,000
2001	Bought House	$170,000

MAKE YOUR OWN LIST OF TRANSACTIONS

 Depending on your age and experience, your list may be longer or shorter than the sample, and your numbers may be larger or smaller.

Go back over your list and add up the amounts of the transactions that are less than satisfactory. These are the transactions where you believe you could have or should have done better. It is likely that you could have done 10 percent to 20 percent better in each of the unsatisfactory transactions if you had used better negotiating skills. Ten to 20 percent of the amount may come to a big number, which will serve as a powerful incentive for improving your negotiating ability.

By referring back to the negotiation matrix, you will no doubt discover that you were far more successful in instances where your behavior was as described in the Adult–Adult column.

Accepting Conflict

Negotiation is the process that resolves a conflict to the satisfaction of all concerned. Several consumer rights groups have published reports showing that women pay more for the same major purchases than men. It is probably fair to say that women are less comfortable, in general, with conflict than men. Once I (PL) was a guest on a radio talk show, discussing the issue of negotiation and conflict with the host. A female caller asked, "Why does negotiation have to be that way?" Her question is a bit like asking why water is wet. Conflict is the inherent nature of negotiation. The conflict exists before the negotiation starts. The buyer wants to pay the lowest price and the seller wants the highest price. A completed negotiation results in a satisfactory resolution of this conflict.

> Negotiating is supposed to feel a little uncomfortable.
> Plunge ahead anyway. It's OK.

Six Negotiating Rules to Remember

Rule 1. *If you are negotiating with a company or organization, find a person with the authority to agree to what you are asking for.*

Almost without exception, your first contact with any company or organization is with an employee who can only follow prescribed instructions. If you want anything different, you must work with higher-level people to make the deal you want. Focus your energy on finding a person empowered to give you what you want. Until you find that person, your requests are futile.

Rule 2. *There is never a deal you have to make.*

Before you begin any negotiation, plan your limits on the range of what you are going to offer and what you will accept. Avoid these dangerous self-fulfilling prophecies:

"It is too good to be true."
"I'll never find another deal like this."

If it sounds too good to be true, it probably is exactly that. Generally, if you negotiate from the position of scarcity, you will have problems. Unless you are purchasing one-of-a-kind items, there are always other possibilities. If you feel you must make a particular deal, you run a high risk of regretting it later. Before entering any negotiation, write down for yourself your opening offer and also (depending on whether you are the buyer or the seller) the most you are willing to spend or the least you are willing to receive. Complicated transactions involve the exchange of

- goods
- services
- money
- rights
- risks
- time

In these transactions, it is essential that you have written out beforehand the ranges that you are willing to accept.

Rule 3. *Beforehand, have a plan for the possibility of no deal.*

If you are unwilling to contemplate the possibility of a particular deal falling through, then it is likely that you have violated rule 2. Knowing in advance what you will do if an agreement cannot be reached relieves the pressure to make the deal work.

Rule 4. *It is always OK to go back to the beginning and start over.*

A common apprehension about negotiation is that your counterpart will lead you along and get you to agree to something you really didn't want or cannot afford. If at any time you feel confused or unsure, it is OK to ask that your counterpart go back to the beginning and start over.

Rule 5. *Sign nothing until you have read and understood every word.*

It has been said that verbal agreements are not worth the paper they are printed on. Once a written agreement is signed, the transaction will be interpreted according to the documentation, making any prior or subsequent verbal statements irrelevant. It is your responsibility to satisfy yourself that the document accurately reflects the discussion and that you understand everything it says. When the other person presents a document for your signature, give yourself time to read it carefully before signing. It is acceptable and advisable to excuse yourself for long enough to do so. Remember that any preprinted agreement presented to you for signature has definitely been written to benefit the writer and not you. Sign nothing until all of your what-if questions are answered.

Rule 6. *Consult an attorney if needed.*

At times you will require an attorney. You may negotiate with your attorney, just as with anyone else. There is a distinction between hiring an attorney and seeking legal advice. Hiring an attorney means you explain to him or her what you want and the attorney draws up the papers. Seeking legal advice means that *you* draw up the papers and consult an attorney, before signing, to receive advice about suggestions or potential problems related to the document you have prepared. In the first instance, you will be paying a lawyer's hourly rate for what amounts to legal secretarial services. If you can easily afford to pay this, you save a little time. If you cannot afford it or don't want to, commonly available legal guides show you how to draft any kind of agreement, from purchase and sale of real estate to divorce. Once you have the agreement drafted, you only pay the attorney's hourly rate for reading it and providing counsel.

WHAT DID YOU LEARN?

Now look back over your list of transactions over $5,000. Identify the transactions where you are less than satisfied with the result. In light of the negotiating suggestions you have just read, what mistakes can you identify? What can you do better in your next negotiation?

Negotiating with Your Children

Some of the wisest parents negotiate service agreements with their children. These agreements, documented and often posted on the refrigerator, consist of the name of each child, a list of the agreed-on tasks, and places to check off when the job is completed each week. The compensation (allowance) is also shown on the refrigerator. Documents such as these seems to build children's sense of self-esteem and ability to assert themselves in the world. They give children an idea of what the world outside the home is like.

CHAPTER

SECRETS OF COMPELLING COMMUNICATION

Make your communication more influential by actually putting yourself in the other person's shoes. Learn to understand the internal psychology of others.

Forget about persuading and convincing. The sales method we teach involves neither. Judging yourself by your ability to persuade others is the primary source of the emotional overload that many people associate with selling. If you allow your well-being to depend on something that you do not control, then you will experience pain. This is the essential concept and prime advantage of taking responsibility for your results, and it is the significant feature of the sales map you will be learning.

In sales situations, the customer makes the buying decision. Yes, you as the seller have influence, but you do not have control. Our sales model puts you in control and dramatically reduces the emotional overload or emotional pain people often associate with selling.

Chapter 13 takes you step-by-step through the process of making a sale using a Sales Map. This Sales Map has three simple objectives—present your customer with compelling value, collect decisions, and be willing to receive—all of which are within your control.

Here we present essential information about communication to make your selling far more effective and far less frustrating than before. The value you present is only compelling if your customer sees it as so. We explain how to identify and characterize other people's internal thinking so that what you present appears most compelling to each individual. People are different. They purchase different things for different reasons. When you finish this chapter, you will know what to listen for so you can present your product or service in the most effective way to each customer you contact.

The process consists of two parts: (1) categorize your customer's motivation and thinking method by knowing what to listen for and (2) be flexible enough to tailor your communication to suit each individual.

Have you ever seen some Americans in foreign countries? Unable to speak the local language, they try English, then *loud* English, and sometimes even English with a foreign accent to make themselves understood. Have you ever felt similar frustration, even with people who understand English? You make your communication most compelling and most influential by tailoring your message to the recipient.

We influence each other continuously. Whether you consider yourself a salesperson or not, you are sure to benefit from increased ability to influence others. For example, if you are a parent, it is imperative that you be a better salesperson than the local drug dealer.

"Walk a mile in another man's shoes" is a poignant adage pointing out the impossibility of understanding others from your own point of view. You gain far greater understanding of people by seeing the world as they see it. In Chapter 7 you used your power of perception to reduce the emotional intensity of past negative experiences and to increase your enjoyment of past positive experiences. Dissociating (seeing yourself in the picture) reduces the emotional intensity of any event; associating (seeing the event through your own eyes) increases emotional intensity.

In this chapter you learn to understand others more quickly to build an emotional connection. These methods are most effective when you consider the other person's perspective as well as your own. These different points of view are perceptual positions. So far we have discussed two perceptual positions: associated and dissociated. These were sufficient for dealing with ourselves. Here we add a third because we are dealing with other people. The third position is the view of the other person.

Three Perceptual Positions
Position #1—You (associated, seeing reality through your own eyes)

Position #2—Observer (dissociated, seeing reality, including you and the other person, from the outside)

Position #3—Other person (dissociated from yourself, but associated into the other person's perspective)

Perceptual Position #1: Associated

In position #1, you experience an event through your own eyes. (This is also referred to as being associated.) In this position you see the pictures, hear the sounds, and feel the feeling of the event.

PERCEPTUAL POSITION #1 EXERCISE

 This exercise demonstrates to you what you already experience consciously. Do this exercise now. Do not wait. This is very important in building your sensory acuity.

Recall a pleasurable event. As you remember that event, see it through your own eyes. Make sure you hear any sounds associated with that experience. Now check your feelings. Are they there? If you are looking through your own eyes, you should be able to feel the feelings you experienced. If you see your body, you are not associated. Make sure that you can experience the event associated.

Let's try another one. Remember a time when you were totally motivated. Float down into that time, and be fully associated seeing the experience through your own eyes. Make sure to add any sounds to your experience. Do you feel totally motivated?

Perceptual Position #2: Dissociated

In position #2, you experience the event from an observer's point of view. (This is the dissociated position.) When you are dissociated, you see your own body in the event as an observer would. This position is useful because it removes emotions that are attached to the event. This way you can evaluate the situation for effective behavior.

PERCEPTUAL POSITION #2 EXERCISE

 Now think of a time when you had a mildly unpleasant experience, such as an argument with someone. See the experience through your own eyes, hear the sounds, and feel the feelings associated with that experience. How do you feel? Probably not so good reliving that experience.

Now step out of your body; see yourself and the other person in the event. Make sure you are not seeing the event through your own eyes. What did you notice? Where are the feelings now? Did you notice the bad feelings disappear? At this point you should not have any feelings about the situation. It should feel neutral.

Do you understand how this method can be useful in your success? Do you see how you can use it to improve your behaviors?

Position #2 is a useful way to check whether your behavior in a particular situation was effective. If you find that your behavior was not what you wanted, you now have the opportunity to correct it. When you get good at using this method, you will be able to change your behavior instantly and make the necessary adjustments to achieve success. How could you use this in your daily life?

Perceptual Position #3: Other Person

In perceptual position #3, you are experiencing the event through the other person's eyes. When doing so, you gain the other person's perspective looking back at you. It's the same as walking in the other person's shoes. This method is also particularly useful because you can feel what the other person felt looking at you and listening to what you said and how you said it. It is also useful in changing your own behavior toward others after experiencing your own behavior from their perspective.

PERCEPTUAL POSITION #3 EXERCISE

R$ Now let's look at the same event in the previous exercise. Take the same event where you argued with someone else. Make sure that you are associated and seeing it through your own eyes. Play through the argument for one minute. Now rewind the argument to where it started and take position #3. Float out of your body and into the other person's body. Look at yourself through his or her eyes looking back at you. Now start the argument again and see what you notice. Was your behavior effective? Would you change your behavior if you could do it all over again? Did you get any insights into how the other person felt?

This unique perspective is useful when we deal with others. I (AF) use it to good effect to check my own behavior and to become aware of what the other person may be feeling when I don't get the response I expected. This has been extremely useful in sales and negotiations. Next time you have an argument with someone and you are not getting the results you desire, take position #3. See your own behavior and how you present your case to the other person. Use this feedback to change your behavior. It is a way to build your sensory acuity. Remember, sensory acuity is one of the five principles for achieving success.

Putting It All Together

When you fully understand and regularly use all three perceptual positions, you gain great sensory acuity. You are able to make the changes necessary to correct the situation if it is not going well immediately, which gives you behavioral flexibility. This is another key to achieving success.

You probably have experienced an event similar to this in your workplace. Imagine you are Mary telling Bill he did a poor job. You did this without considering how Bill would feel or react. Bill thinks he has been doing a good job and does not understand why he is being accused otherwise. Now, the conflict begins and an argument starts. Does this scenario sound familiar to you? Has this ever happened to you? Most people have gone through this. We know we have.

A better way to handle the situation is to take all three positions both before the event and as it unfolds. Let's say you are Mary. In your position as yourself, you notice that Bill shows displeasure through his facial expressions. This is a clue for you to take the other perceptual positions.

Now take position #3 (Bill's perspective) and observe yourself as Bill would see you. Imagine how you would feel, as Bill, if this were the first time you had been told that you are doing a bad job. Wouldn't you be upset? Most people would be. Now take position #2, the observer position, and see the event again. What did you notice as an observer? From this perspective, how could the scenario have played out differently? What things could both people have changed to prevent the unpleasantness?

Think for a moment how powerful it would be to have the mental flexibility to take all three positions as an event happens. When taking position #3 (other person), you notice it felt bad to hear this news and you became angry because no one had mentioned the problem before. Using this information, you can change your approach. You also can take the observer's perspective, in which emotions are far less intense, often nonexistent. What did you notice when no emotions were involved? Did you realize that you had more choices? By taking these two perspectives into consideration, you can turn a potentially ugly event into a positive productive experience.

Mohandas Gandhi, the great Indian nationalist leader, used this method all the time. Before meetings or negotiations with the British, he placed himself in all three perceptual positions. First, he looked at the situation through his own eyes to make sure he knew what he wanted to accomplish and say. Next, he took position #3 and saw the situation through the other person's eyes. He would think like the person he was going to meet. He asked himself: If I were this person, what would I want? How would I feel if this were presented to me? How would I react? Once he understood those two perspectives, he looked at the bigger picture and took position #2, the observer position. Taking the observer's view gave Gandhi the ability to create a win-win solution.

Gandhi was so good at this process that he was able to do it even during conflicts. He could see perspectives and change his behaviors and strategy to gain a winning outcome. He moved an entire nation to defeat the British empire without violence. Now, that's personal power!

Remember these four key points when using perceptual positions:

1. To enhance positive experiences even more, take position #1 and be associated. You want to keep the positive emotions.
2. To neutralize or remove negative emotions from an experience, use position #2 as a dissociated observer. You want to be dissociated from your negative experiences and remove the emotions. Doing this allows you to learn from all your experiences. Because people tend to suppress recall of the emotions associated with intensely negative emotional experiences, it is difficult to learn from them. Position #2 facilitates learning you may have missed due to the emotional intensity of the event.
3. To enhance any relationship in ways you probably have not imagined, use perceptual position #3 and put yourself in the other person's shoes.
4. In some situations you do not want to dissociate from a negative emotion. Fear serves you in dangerous situations, so you react to protect yourself.

Take charge now and use your personal power. Learn these strategies and use them daily.

Establishing Contact with Your Prospective Customer

MOTIVATION STRATEGIES: MOVING AWAY AND MOVING TOWARD

In Chapter 4, we discussed the Baseball Diamond Method for changing your personal motivation. You learned that people are motivated emotionally to move away from pain or to move toward pleasure. The first and simplest way to categorize and understand others is based on how they are motivated at the most basic level. At the most basic level, people are motivated either to move away from pain or to move toward pleasure. Clearly, everyone uses some of each of these strategies. It is very easy to identify which is the predominant motivating factor by knowing what to listen for and listening carefully.

You probably have experienced something like this in a work situation. A group is working on a project and falls way behind schedule. The manager offers additional rewards and bonuses to the group if the schedule is met. Instead, work slips farther behind. Then, in frustration, the manager threatens people with dismissal if the project is not completed. All of a sudden, the project gets back on schedule. In this situation, threats produced the desired results. Conversely, you may have observed times when the threatening approach produced poor results, but a new management improves performance by offering bonuses and incentives. How do you account for this?

In the first instance, the workers unconsciously relied on a motivation strategy based on moving away from pain. The incentives did nothing to motivate them. But when faced with the pain of dismissal, they magically began to perform. For people who motivate themselves by moving toward pleasure, the incentive method produces far better results.

Identifying the distinction between moving-toward and moving-away motivation in others is essential to make you communication compelling.

MOVING AWAY OR MOVING TOWARD?

 Characterize the predominant motivating factor of the people making these eight statements.

1. We have a real problem here.
2. I want to move into a different business with more growth potential.
3. This new boss is nasty and hard to deal with.
4. It would be very useful for me to learn better selling methods.
5. I am sick and tired of just earning enough to get by.
6. I am looking forward to doubling my income next year.
7. Commuting to work is an expensive waste of time for me.
8. I want to do work that gives me a satisfied feeling of accomplishment.

You probably hear statements like these every day. In the odd numbered statements, the people are expressing moving-away motivation; in the even-numbered statements, they are expressing moving-toward motivation. Now that you know what to listen for, it is pretty easy to characterize other people's motivation.

Why does motivation matter? Let's say your potential clients rely on a moving-away motivation strategy. If you describe the glowing benefits of what you are offering and go into great detail about its future results, they will be rolling their eyes around, thinking, "Yeah, sure, this guy has no idea how big my problems are." Problems and negative circumstances shape the reality of moving-away people, providing them with motivation. Instead of describing positive results for the person with moving-away motivation, get lots of details about their problem: how bad is it really, how long has it existed and what other solutions have been tried. Then say something like: "This sounds like a significant problem. Is it bad enough to cause you to take action?" Some people are terrified of making a mistake—so terrified that they postpone making decisions until their back is to the wall. Ask: "How bad do you think this situation will be in six months or a year?"

Other people are motivated by moving toward pleasure. Their vision of the future is their primary concern and source of motivation. They tend to ignore or minimize the current problems. Although the service or product you are offering may actually relieve customers of current problems, people with moving-toward motivation will quickly become bored and even irritated if you dwell on problems. Instead, focus your presentation on how much better the future will look after the problems have been solved. Describe the benefits of already having the problem solved.

Characterizing Internal Ways of Representing Information

Have you ever given a sales presentation and realized that you weren't getting your message across very well, but you didn't know what to do to change it? Remember, people think differently, and not everyone accesses information the same way.

YOUR OWN REPRESENTATIONAL SYSTEM

If you are asked, "What transportation did you use for your last shopping expedition?" you may answer, "I drove in my car." Probing more deeply: "How do you know this is accurate?" Of course, you remember, but *how* do you remember? What are the first details that come to mind as you recall this event? Do you remember the view of the scenery and traffic as you were driving? Perhaps you recall the sensations of sitting in the car with your hands on the steering wheel, or the sounds of the engine and car radio. You probably can recall your trip in all these ways. However, which way came to awareness first for you? Now as you think about your trip some more, which of these ways provides you with the clearest memory and the most details? All of us use all of these representational systems: visual, auditory, kinesthetic, smell (olfactory), and taste (gustatory). However, almost everyone has one representational system that predominates. Because the visual, auditory and kinesthetic systems are the primary ones used in communication, we will focus on them.

For all of us, our predominant representational system determines how we use language. We tend to use words and phrases that fit with our favorite system. These words are sensory indicators and sensory indicator phrases.

Throughout the western world, the primary representational system used is visual. Approximately 55 percent of westerners favor the visual representational system, perhaps due to the prevelance of television and the Internet. Approximately 35 percent favor the kinesthetic system, and 10 percent favor the auditory system. These percentages vary in different countries.

We describe our internal representations using sensory indicators and sensory indicator phrases. A predominately visual person uses words like "see," "look," and "view." A primarily auditory person uses words like "hear," "sound," and "listen." A primarily kinesthetic person uses words like "feel," "touch," and "sense." Because each of us relies on our primary sense for taking in information, the information is conveniently stored in that representational system. It is only natural for us to express the information in the same representational system as it is stored.

Those of you with a second language will relate to the following analogy. Spanish is my (PL) second language and Italian is my third. When someone begins speaking to me in Spanish unexpectedly, there are some mental gyrations required to shift gears from the English that my mind had been expecting. I can understand the Spanish, but English would be more convenient for me. When I speak with someone who speaks both Spanish and English, if his or her English is better than my Spanish, then we naturally slip into speaking English, and vice versa. To the extent that languages consist of agreed-on code, representational systems are like different languages. The big difference is that speaking one language or another is a conscious and agreed-on choice, whereas the representational systems that predominate for any one person are largely unconscious and not specifically agreed on.

Just as using a language that the other person understands makes communication easier, communicating in the predominant representational system of the other person makes your dialogue much more effective. If you have given a presentation where the audience didn't seem to get it, quite possibly you were speaking outside their predominant representational system. Here's good news: Developing the behavioral flexibility to determine and use the predominant representational systems of others is much, much easier than learning a second language.

Imagine that you are able to communicate with your significant other, parents, and friends more effectively. How would that impact your personal life? Would it be better? Would your relationships be more positive? What would happen if you communicated more effectively with your customers, prospects, or the people you work with? Would your situation improve? Could more effective communication bring you more business? Improve your bottom line? Get you promoted or a significant raise? You bet it can.

Remember, people like people who are like themselves. Because each of us favors a different representational system, it is almost as if we speak different languages. When you understand how to communicate in all the different representational systems, you will affect more people positively, make your communication more compelling, and avoid misunderstandings.

Look at the list of words and phrases for the three different representational systems. As an exercise, add other phrases to the list.

Visual	*Auditory*	*Kinesthetic*
See	Hear	Touch
Look	Listen	Feel
View	Sound(s)	Grasp
Appear	Silence	Concrete
Imagine	Question	Scrape
Clear	Resonate	Solid
Focused	Harmonize	Catch on
Hazy	Tune in/Out	Tap into
Picture	Echo	Stuck
Light at the end of the tunnel	The silent treatment	Back up your claim
Look into it	Sing their praises	Toss this around
Polished	Rings a bell	Too hot to handle
Illustrate my point	Lend an ear	Resist
Dark side	Let's talk about it	Tackle

REPRESENTATIONAL SYSTEM EXERCISE

 This exercise will help you understand and identify what representational system is being used. Read the eight statements and identify the representational system. Do this exercise now. No skipping ahead.

1. He's constantly giving me static about that.
2. That really brightens my day.
3. I'm absolutely immersed in this project.
4. This thing is weighing on me.
5. The guy is really offbeat.
6. This problem keeps staring me in the face.
7. This project really stinks.
8. This guy has a checkered past.

Did you have difficulty understanding any of the sentences? Did any seem not quite right to you? This is quite normal. The statements that felt natural and easy to understand are most likely in your own favored representational system. The others are not.

Sometimes I (AF) didn't understand what my wife, Tamar, was saying. She had the same issues with me. My predominant representational system is visual and my least favored was kinesthetic. Her predominant representational system is kinesthetic. No wonder we had a tough time understanding each other, before we realized and respected these differences.

Now I use language patterns that accommodate her main representational system. For a predominantly visual person like me, talking kinesthetically was challenging, but our communication has improved tremendously since.

Here are the answers to the exercise you just did. Congratulate yourself for completing the exercise. If you did not do the exercise, go back and do it now. You want to improve your overall communications, don't you? Do the exercise now.

The key words shown in italics help identify the correct representational system.

1. He's constantly giving me *static* about that. (auditory)
2. That really *brightens* my day. (visual)
3. I'm absolutely *immersed* in this project. (kinesthetic)
4. This thing is *weighing on me.* (kinesthetic)
5. The guy is really *offbeat.* (auditory)
6. This problem keeps *staring me in the face.* (visual)
7. This project really *stinks.* (olfactory)
8. This guy has a *checkered* past. (visual)

How did you do? Did you get them all right? If you did not, it's OK. With practice, it will become natural to you. Taking action and applying what you learned here will produce the results you want. Think of the world as your laboratory. You have subjects everywhere to practice on. By knowing what to listen for, you'll listen more effectively.

R℞ Let's do another quick exercise. Think about all the people in your life. Which ones do you get along with the best? Who seems to understand you the best even when you don't finish the sentence? Whom do you relate to the easiest? Most likely the people whom you get along with best have the same predominant representational system as you. Next time you get together, listen to the phrases they use and see if you can identify with them. Notice which representational system they favor.

Business Application of Language

People buy from people they like. When people are like each other, they tend to like each other. This concept is very powerful. When we talk to other people using only our own favored representational system, communication may not be as effective as it could be. When we use the same representation system as our clients and prospects, we become more like them. Using the words our clients and prospects prefer builds a connection and understanding.

Once you have identified a person's favored representational system, you must have the behavioral flexibility to get out of your own system and into that person's. Think about how much you can gain by doing this. How many more clients can you serve? How much happier will your clients be when they know you understand their needs and fulfill them? No more presentations where they don't get it.

REPRESENTATIONAL SYSTEM CONVERSION EXERCISE

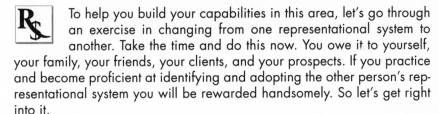 To help you build your capabilities in this area, let's go through an exercise in changing from one representational system to another. Take the time and do this now. You owe it to yourself, your family, your friends, your clients, and your prospects. If you practice and become proficient at identifying and adopting the other person's representational system you will be rewarded handsomely. So let's get right into it.

Change the following eight sentences into the other two representational systems. For example, if the sentence is written with visual language, translate it using auditory words and then again using kinesthetic. This way you will understand how to communicate with all three systems.

1. He's constantly giving me static about that.
2. That really brightens my day.
3. I'm absolutely immersed in this project.
4. This thing is weighing on me.
5. The guy is really offbeat.
6. This problem keeps staring me in the face.
7. This project really stinks.
8. This guy has a checkered past.

This exercise may seem difficult, but do not skip ahead until you have completed it. Your future depends on it. With practice, this skill will become natural to you. Come on, you can do it. Do it now! For those of you who have completed the exercise, congratulate yourself.

Here are possible solutions. Let's go through them together.

1. Auditory: He's constantly giving me *static* about that. Kinesthetic: He constantly gives me *grief* about that. Visual: He's constantly *showing* me displeasure about that.
2. Visual: That really *brightens* my day. Auditory: That really makes my day *sing*. Kinesthetic: That makes me *feel* great today.
3. Kinesthetic: I'm absolutely *immersed* in this project. Visual: This project *looms* large on my radar. Auditory: This project really *strikes a chord* with me.
4. Kinesthetic: This thing is *weighing on me*. Visual: This thing *looks* bleak for me. Auditory: This thing *sounds* terrible to me.
5. Auditory: The guy is really *offbeat*. Visual: This guy is really off *color*. Kinesthetic: This guy has really different *strokes*.
6. Visual: This problem keeps *staring me in the face*. Auditory: This problem is coming in *loud* and clear. Kinesthetic: This problem is *abrasive*.
7. Olfactory: This project really *stinks*. Visual: This project *looks* terrible! Auditory: This *sounds* awful. Kinesthetic: This project does not *feel* right.
8. Visual: This guy has a *checkered* past. Auditory: This guy's past is *out of tune*. Kinesthetic: This guy has a *sticky* past.

Did you find this exercise challenging? Was it exciting to change your language to accommodate others' representational systems? Can you see, hear, and feel the power behind this? Imagine what this can do for your business. How will things in your business improve? Will you be better able to present compelling value? Will you enjoy increased customer satisfaction and repeat business? Imagine all the possible benefits this will give you. Really feel what it would be like to achieve those desires.

Now take a look at your personal life. How will these tools help you there? Imagine how your communication has improved with your family, friends, and loved ones. Is your life more enjoyable? How do the people close to you react to you with your new skills? Really feel the difference this will make in your life.

The key to achieving success is to use the tools. You must take massive action now! No waiting around. That will serve no purpose. Use the tools every day in your life. By doing so you will make your selling and all of your communication much more effective. Practice a little at a time and notice the difference in people's responses.

Speaking Speed

Here is another indicator you will find very useful in determining the primary internal representational system of others. Generally, predominantly visual people speak quickly. They refer to the pictures in their mind when talking. A picture is worth a thousand words, so these people must speak quickly to keep pace with the pictures that come to them. Typically, these people pause as they wait for their mind to access the next set of pictures.

Primarily auditory people tend to speak at medium speed with a steady cadence, sometimes in a monotone. They access information as internal sounds. The sounds come to them at normal speaking speed.

The primarily kinesthetic person speaks s-l-o-w-l-y, using information from their feelings to guide their speech. Feeling information comes to the mind more slowly than pictures or sounds, accounting for the slower speed.

To figure out what to say, determine whether the other person has predominant moving-away or moving-toward motivation. To figure out how to say it, determine the other person's primary internal representational system.

CHAPTER

LEARNING
TO SELL
THE EASY WAY

To avoid emotional overload, the new salesperson should learn to sell in a step-by-step manner. It's essential to learn to establish connections quickly with anyone. Presenting from a script produces limited results.

Successful salespeople offer prospective customers compelling value and collect buying decisions. This is the essence of selling. It is not about persuading or convincing. You may not have thought about the sales process in this way before. New salespeople often are in emotional overload. For this reason, you will be learning to sell in an easy step-by-step way. This chapter shows you how to start with the least amount of emotional tension and also how to deal with this tension.

So-Called Conventional Wisdom about Selling

What does it take to succeed at sales? In the help wanted section of your Sunday newspaper, you'll find many listings looking for salespeople. Quite often the word "aggressive" is emphasized. Certainly you would avoid any salesperson who was aggressive with you; so would most people. It is not necessary or even desirable for you to be aggressive when you sell. However, if you are in the habit of taking what you are given and not asking for more, then the simple act of asking the customer to buy what you have may seem to be aggressive to you.

209

BECOME THE SALESPERSON YOU WANT TO BE

Even if you've never sold anything, you have a great deal of experience with people selling to you.

 Stop for a moment and make a list of 10 likes and dislikes about salespeople. Here are just a few examples to get your list started.

Likes about Salespeople
1. I like it when they introduce themselves and ask my name.
2. I like it if they are aware and knowledgeable about their competition.
3. I like it when they ask questions.

Dislikes about Salespeople
1. I dislike when they use my name in every sentence.
2. I dislike when they assume that they know what I like.
3. I dislike when they offer a discount, when I didn't ask for one.

What many people dislike most about salespeople is their interest in money. You must look on your selling as serving others. You are offering an important opportunity that has high potential to provide your customer with great benefit. If you don't think that now, then work on changing your mind. You are your own first customer. If you don't believe in what you are offering, then the only people who buy will be the ones you fool.

Money Described Most Simply

Money works the same for all, rich or poor. You have some money and everyone else has all the rest. To create a flow of money toward you, you must devise a method to persuade other people (who have all the rest) to pass it over.

There are lots of ways to do this. Almost all ethical methods of creating an income consist of providing services or products in exchange for the money of others. Yet one step immediately precedes this exchange: You must show the potential buyer that your products or services are worth more than the money you are asking. If you succeed at this, then you have a deal; otherwise, you don't. This process of showing the other person the value of what you are offering is called selling. So, in one way or another, all income is derived from selling, even if you haven't thought of it that way before. This is the case whether you're at a job interview, selling your house, or selling in your own business.

You Are Your Own First Customer

It is impossible to present compelling value if you are not sold yourself. Do you believe in what you are selling? The people you talk with are not fools. They can detect a phony as easily as you can. Are you truly interested in providing something of value, or are you just in it for the money? If you are motivated only by the money, you may be shocked to learn that you are far more transparent than you thought.

Selling is a form of self-expression. For most people, their inherited purpose creates guilt, anxiety, or fear about self-expression. If your desire for money is the sole motivation strong enough to subdue your reservations about expressing yourself, then you are in trouble. The customer hears your need for money, becomes justifiably suspicious, and won't buy.

Do you come from service or greed? The answer to this matters more than how polished your presentation is. Although it hurts to be rejected by people you are trying to help, you have to accept that rejection will occur. No one is rejecting *you*, unless you perceive it so. Instead, they are rejecting your offer.

To serve your customers best, you want to find out how they think and hear not only what is said, but also what is meant. Prospective customers must perceive your product or service as offering compelling value. Because each prospective customer is different, presenting from a fixed script can produce only very limited results. If your customers do not buy how you sell, they are less likely to buy what you sell.

Emotional Dynamics of Selling

Selling makes people nervous. Emotions are the most troubling part, especially for beginners. In our Training sessions, we used to discuss fear about selling, but we have since discovered that terror is a more accurate description of many people's feelings. Yet selling is easier than you think, especially when you understand moving-away and moving-toward motivation and predominant representational systems. Our purpose here is to make your transition to a winning salesperson as quick as possible.

Why Selling Is Uncomfortable

In almost all cases, these uncomfortable feelings have nothing to do with any danger or risk in the sales situation. Selling violates almost all of the childhood rules we discussed in Chapter 6, which are re-produced here for your convenience.

1. Sit down and be quiet.
2. Children should be seen and not heard.
3. Don't brag or say good things about yourself.
4. Do as you are told.
5. Don't do anything without permission.
6. Take what you are given and don't ask for more.
7. Don't take money from friends.
8. Don't take money from strangers or talk to them.
9. Don't rock the boat.
10. You can't have your cake and eat it, too.

Remember, your feelings are caused by the hairy elephants. The feelings are your energy and have arisen to help you deal with a challenge (in this case, the challenge of making the sale), even if they are uncomfortable at first. Feelings of terror will help you succeed if you can just let them be, rather than fighting to control them. If you stop fighting against it, then the increase in energy makes your senses more acute, you become more aware of what prospective customers are saying and really meaning. Almost everyone feels uncomfortable while learning to sell. But you only have to go through this learning process once. Practice makes it easier. Once you learn to sell, you will never need to worry about money again.

Some uncomfortable feelings are inevitable. Remember, you determine what these feelings mean to you. If you insist that fear means "STOP," you are doomed to the status quo. Why not interpret fear as excitement, meaning "GET READY"?

How to Reduce Emotional Overload

On Figure 13.1, the vertical axis is selling price. The higher the price, the more emotionally intense and difficult the sales process becomes. If you are selling a $10 item, customers are easy to find. Almost everyone has $10 to spend. You have to look much harder to find a customer who will buy your $400,000 item. Nevertheless, there are people right now driving around in your city with $400,000 available to buy a house.

Typically, you encounter customers one at a time. With the $10 item, the stakes are low. The outcome of a single sales opportunity

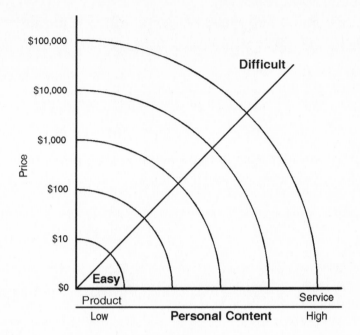

FIGURE 13.1   Evaluate Your Sales Ability

won't determine whether you pay your bills this month. But if you are selling $400,000 items, then whether you pay bills this month could very well turn on the decision of one customer. Experience is very useful to deal with the increased emotional intensity of higher stakes. It is impossible to do your best selling job if you are distracted by your fears.

The horizontal axis has two scales. First is product versus service. A product is easier to sell. With a product, customers can get much more information about what they are buying before making a decision. For example, if we offer to sell you a book, you can leaf through it to find out whether you like it before you make your decision. But if we are selling you a haircut, you know less about what you're getting. Even if we show you a roomful of people whose haircuts you like and who tell you we give the best haircuts they ever had, you still don't know what *your* hair will look like until after you have made your decision. Thus, you must trust the seller more to buy a service than a product.

The other scale of the horizontal axis refers to the degree of personal content. If we sell you a pen, there's low personal content.

If the person who designed the pen were selling it, the degree of personal content is much higher; thus it's tougher for the designer to deal with the possibility of rejection. To you, the book you are reading is ink, paper, and a cover; as such, it would be easier for you to sell than for us, assuming equal sales ability. When I (PL) began selling *Money Is My Friend*, the high degree of personal content made it very uncomfortable for me to hear no from a prospective customer.

Selling becomes more emotionally intense and therefore more difficult for beginners as you move up and to the right on the diagram. The farther you move from the lower left corner, the tougher it gets. Emotional intensity makes selling difficult because it draws your awareness inside, distracting you from what customers are telling you.

How to Apply These Emotional Dynamics to Learning to Sell

There are generally two ways to learn anything. You can jump into the deep end to sink or swim, or you can learn a little at a time, perhaps starting with a flotation device in the kiddy pool, improving gradually until your stroke becomes strong and graceful enough to challenge ocean waves. Even if you learned to swim through the sink-or-swim method, you probably could have a better stroke if you had learned in a more gradual way, simply because crisis and panic can't produce an environment for optimal learning.

Consider all the things you have learned to do. Very few of them were taught by the sink-or-swim method. For this reason, we will be starting in the kiddy pool of selling. Figure 13.2 shows the sales ability diagram from Figure 13.1, but this time it includes three numbered, shaded areas.

Mistakes of the New Salesperson

Most people starting their own business can't afford a store or factory. This prevents them from selling products, so they sell services. Nor can they afford to hire employees at the outset, so they sell the service and perform it themselves. The degree of difficulty of selling a service that you perform yourself puts you somewhere in the darkened area 1 on Figure 13.2. The fact that you are offering a service and that it possesses high personal content makes your initial endeavors in this area more difficult than they need to be.

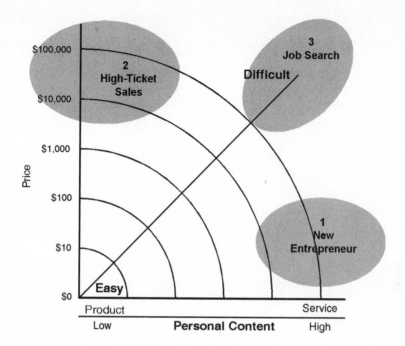

FIGURE 13.2 Sales Ability by Type

Other people start a business of their own with a different approach. Their reasoning may go something like this: "I have friends with their own business. They have told me how difficult selling is. So I will sell high-ticket items. This way, even if I have trouble selling, I can make a living with just one or two transactions per month. I will become a real estate agent!" This decision puts you in shaded area 2, where the price of the item makes the selling emotionally intense and, once again, the learning is more difficult.

Another group of people may decide to avoid their own business completely and look for a job instead. Job search places them in shaded area 3 on the diagram. Here the salesperson and the product are identical. Personal content is maximized. No wonder job search is so overwhelming.

None of this is to say that operating in shaded areas 1, 2, or 3 is bad. However, the emotional intensity of selling in these areas makes the process unduly difficult to learn. If you are currently engaged in selling activities in categories 1, 2, or 3, it is not necessary to cease these in order to improve your selling skills.

Your 30-Day Sales Course

The following suggested course of action is adopted from what I (PL) presented in *Money Is My Friend*, when I first wrote it in 1979. Since then hundreds of people I know of (and perhaps thousands I haven't met) have used it as a springboard to earning the income they want from work they love.

Simply sell a low-priced product, selling for $5 to $20. Offer it at a price greater than what it cost you, so you earn a profit on each transaction. It must be a product that you didn't make yourself. It must be something that you like, something you believe in, and something you can't help talking about. Look around your house, your car, and your office to find some small possession you delight in owning and using.

This 30-day course is a start, a learning device. If you have never sold before, plunging right into selling services, high-priced items, or business opportunities is like expecting a toddler to climb Mount Everest. Remember, you don't have to make a career of selling this item; it's merely a training device.

What Will I Sell, Who Will My Customers Be?

Business, pared to its most elementary components, consists of three things:

1. A product or service
2. A price for a unit of the product or service that you can deliver
3. A customer

If you possess all three of these items, then you have a business. If you lack any of them, you are out of business until you make up the lack.

There's an infinite variety of low-cost products you could buy at wholesale and sell at retail. This is not a strange thing to do. Every store in the world makes its living on the margin between retail and wholesale price. Most cities have surplus stores offering good-quality end-lot merchandise at bargain basement prices. If your low-cost item is a book, many publishers will give you a discount in exchange for the purchase of 10 copies or so.

A product-related network marketing company could help you here, too. Membership assures you a reliable supply of prod-

uct at a stable price. Additionally, the good companies offer training and support.

Many network marketing companies immediately encourage
you to sell the business opportunity to others. Some people
succeed at this; others do not. We have worked with many clients
in network marketing who were struggling to sell the business
opportunity. In every case, when they learned to sell a low-priced
product, their sales of business opportunities took off. This was
because of the lower emotional intensity and the kiddy-pool
effect we described earlier in this chapter. So, first focus on selling a low-priced product. Your experience with this will be the
most significant contributor to success with selling the business
opportunity.

There is an infinite supply of people. Look around, they're
everywhere. It's actually hard to get away from them. Almost everyone has enough money on hand to buy your low-priced item. Saying "Would you like to buy one of these?" costs you nothing. Doing
so seems strange only if you have never done it before and have not
yet dealt with your terror about selling.

I (PL) quit my job in the computer business in the 1970s and
started teaching seminars. Before quitting I had had some part-time
success with the seminar business, but now that I was relying on it
for all my income, progress was very slow. My selling skills required
improvement. Realizing I needed something easier to sell (the
kiddy pool) as a training device, I hit on the idea of selling books. I
bought 10 copies each of my 5 favorite books from their respective
publishers at a discount and began offering them to my friends and
people I met. I typed up a price list of "Phil's Favorite Books" with
descriptions.

"Here's a list of my favorite books," I would say. "Would you
please take a look? See if there is one that interests you." That was
it. That was all I did at the outset. I was too scared to elaborate. After some practice I improved. For example, I learned to offer two
books. When the customer chose one book, I would point to the
book most similar (or sometimes most different) from the one chosen and say, "How about this one? I think you might like it, too. It is
about such-and-such."

I learned two things from selling these books. First was that I
had allowed my fears to stop me from selling over and over in the
past. Second, there was really nothing to be afraid about. Some
people say yes and others say no. This realization trained my

mind that it was OK for these results to happen and were not about me personally.

Several things occurred. One was that my seminar and teaching business expanded almost immediately. Second was that after a few months, I had customers up and down the East Coast of the United States buying the books. (This was before the advent of online book selling.) I increased the number of titles and added cassette tapes to my line. Third was that, after my manuscript "Money Is My Friend" received its umpteenth rejection and, my friend, Neil Adams asked whether I had considered self-publishing, I thought, "Sure, I can do it. I have money. I know how to sell books." So I went ahead.

This illustrates how personal content of a product you made yourself increases the emotional intensity of selling. As I mentioned, my (PL) most intense selling experience was with my first book, which I published myself in 1979—against the advice of many well-intentioned people who cautioned me of the possibility of ending up with a basement full of books and a heart full of disappointment. The day the first shipment arrived from the printer was a big one for me. I was facing the challenge of having to sell all 2,000 books of the first printing. I remember looking outside my house the day before and seeing my front yard empty. The next day the books arrived, in my front yard and spilling over on to the sidewalk were hundreds of people shouting for attention and waving money at me, wanting my book. The first printing sold out in a couple of hours, with no work on my part.

Now, if you believe this story, you probably also believe a better mousetrap will cause people to beat a path to your door.

The part of the story about self-publishing is accurate. I made up the part about the crowd of people outside my door. The books required more selling effort than that. I sold them to bookstores throughout the United States and Canada for about a year and a half, before and after seminars and while en route between seminar cities. I did most of the selling in person, some by mail and telephone. I continued until the bookstores were generating volume significant enough so regional book distributors were willing to purchase and resell *Money Is My Friend*. Over its first 20 years in print, the book sold more than 400,000 copies in 18 languages.

After the first printing of *Money Is My Friend* arrived, I soon learned that selling my own book was quite different from selling someone else's. It brought the new selling challenge of dealing with an item with high personal content.

Because your experience with the low-priced item will be different from mine, here are some additional examples. In my own example, I used the same product, books, and moved to more and more challenging sales situations. You don't have to do it this way.

A consulting client, a skilled computer programmer, wanted to start his own business. Using the low-priced item idea, he started selling scented candles. He went through the usual fears of "What will people think?" "They will disapprove of me." "I'll never make any money doing this" and the like.

After some success with the $5 candles, he moved to $300 air purifiers. After some success with the air purifiers, he started his own business providing Internet-based patient scheduling for doctors.

When I (PL) lived in Hollywood, several aspiring actors learned the low-priced item method from me and used it to launch their acting careers. They had made no progress securing work in the typical Hollywood rat race of agents, casting calls, and auditions. From selling the low-priced item, they began to understand that lack of selling ability had kept them from parts in the past. They realized that more than acting skill was required to get work as an actor, and they shifted their mentality from waiting to be discovered to forthrightly showing the decision makers why they were the best person for the job. Some of these same people star in movies and TV shows today. Obviously selling yourself and your own talent is way more difficult than the low-priced item. The kiddy pool offers almost guaranteed success at the very beginning when you need it most.

Why Selling the Low-Cost Item Works So Well

Everyone I know who has stuck with the low-priced product has succeeded with it. Here are five reasons it works:

1. You create a success neurology related to selling in which fear no longer means "STOP."
2. Your emotional attachment both to the outcome of each sales encounter and to the product itself are minimized.
3. You maximize your potential market.
4. You maximize your amount of practice.
5. You focus your attention on what you have to offer. (The revenue per sale is too small for you to focus much on that.)

Your personal involvement in selling any item will never go to zero. After a while it will become OK to hear people say no, but your preference for yes will make no at least a little frustrating. The low price makes almost everyone a potential customer. Also, the low price makes the sales cycle—the time lapse between initial contact and completing the sale—very short. This way you receive quick feedback on the effectiveness of your efforts and can make changes quickly, if needed.

When you are first learning to sell, what you need most is practice. At first it seems there are not enough customers. However, if you stay with this, perhaps advertise a little, and ask each satisfied customer for a referral or two, very soon, instead of potential customers, *time* will become your scarcest resource.

Moving beyond the Low-Cost Item

Carrying around a supply of a low-priced item and offering it to individuals, one at a time, is probably not the best long-term business model you can invent. However, by a huge margin, it the best way to learn how to sell. It takes about 30 days to master the low-price sales item. Present your item to 10 people every day and be willing to learn from the people who buy. If you also are willing to learn from those who say no instead of feeling upset about the rejection, then 30 days is a lot more than you will need. Most of us spent many, many years in school learning things far less useful than selling.

Mastering your low-priced sales item offers a wide variety of possibilities that you probably haven't considered before. Some of our clients know beforehand the kind of business they want and use the low-priced item as a warm-up for that business. Other clients have no clear plan until they master selling the low-price item. Acquiring the ability to sell in this manner opens the mental door so you can conceive a practical six-figure project. Fear shuts down your creativity. So, before the 30-day sales training course, back when you were still afraid of selling (can you remember back then?), your mind may have been saying, "Are you kidding? A six-figure project? Why bother coming up with one of those? No matter how good the idea, my fear of selling will get to me anyway, so why bother?"

In my experience with *Money Is My Friend*, I (PL) took the same item and repackaged what I was selling in several steps, as I will explain. Each step was objectively more difficult because the dollar amount increased, but it didn't seem that way to me because of my success with the previous steps. After selling books one at a time to individuals, I took them to bookstores, where I offered them to the book buyer in quantity with wholesale discounts. These transactions were typically 5 to 20 copies. My next step was to offer the book to distributors in the United States, Canada, the United Kingdom, Australia, and New Zealand. These companies typically bought books in three-figure amounts.

Then I sold foreign language rights for *Money Is My Friend* to publishers in Europe and Asia. In these instances, I was selling a higher-priced item, which was actually a business opportunity for the publisher.

Thus I took the same item and moved it step-by-step to the more difficult area of the diagram, as my sales ability increased. It is not just the emotional intensity that changes as you move toward the upper right-hand corner of the diagram. The sales cycle takes longer and the whole thing becomes more complex because there are more steps. Sometimes several people must agree before you can make the sale.

The $5 to $20 item is business at its simplest. It compresses the four basic business processes described in Chapter 9 into one simple operation. Moving to something bigger produces greater emotional intensity and a longer sales cycle.

Learning to Receive

Learning to receive? Yes, that's right, even though most people have never heard those words in the same sentence. Typically, receiving is viewed as a fortuitous, unintentional accident rather than as a skill. Receiving does have a peculiar characteristic that differentiates it from most skills: It is awkward to get practice in receiving. We are not suggesting that you contact your friends and say, "I just read this wonderful book that told me to develop my receiving skill, so would you give me $5,000?" You can do that if you like, but this is not the method we suggest for learning.

Selling is the process of offering others what you have in exchange for their money. Money follows the commands of your mind precisely. People who believe that receiving is bad, people who put themselves last, people who are terrified of being seen as greedy won't sell much regardless of how polished and confident their presentation may be.

The Bible tells us that it is better to give than to receive. Perhaps so, but that does not make receiving bad. Greek philosophy presents a more resourceful perspective about receiving: It is better to be in the position to give than in the position of needing to receive. In fact, if all the receivers stopped receiving, then the givers would be out of business. Giving and receiving are opposite sides of the same coin. You can't have one without the other. In our free economy, you offer to others the goods and services you enjoy producing in exchange for their money. Then you use that money to purchase those goods and services you would rather not produce yourself. It's all part of a natural process.

It is time to examine and change the thinking that may have limited your receiving up to now.

REMOVE YOUR LIMITATIONS TO RECEIVING

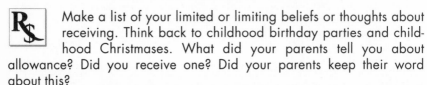 Make a list of your limited or limiting beliefs or thoughts about receiving. Think back to childhood birthday parties and childhood Christmases. What did your parents tell you about allowance? Did you receive one? Did your parents keep their word about this?

Another powerful way to uncover and bring to awareness unconscious beliefs about receiving is to use the Power Affirmations method from Chapter 9. The following affirmations were designed specifically to improve your skills at receiving.

- I love everything about receiving.
- The more willing I am to prosper others, the more willing others are to prosper me.
- Receiving makes me feel good.
- My receiving contributes to my spiritual goodness, and my spiritual goodness contributes to my receiving.
- My receiving benefits everyone.

The Five-Step Sales Map

We have presented the sales map you are about to learn to participants in our Training and to individual consulting clients. In the Training sessions we devote almost two full days to the process, to ensure that each person has plenty of practice with each step. Graduates report that not only are they far more confident when they use it, but it saves them a great deal of time, as well. No longer will you waste time on people who are not interested. Instead, at each step you communicate with a definite outcome in mind. Once that outcome is accomplished, you know it is time to move on to the next step. Such a focus takes into account the value of your own time and respects the value of your customers' time.

There are no hard and fast rules here. Be willing to experiment and make mistakes. Experiment to discover what works best for you. We will make some suggestions about things you might say, but keep in mind that these are only suggestions. Selling is a highly personal process, which is why a prepared script produces only limited results. Being yourself and using your own words are far more powerful.

When I (AF) first started to learn how to sell, I was instructed to use one of several scripts. I picked one. After several months with no success, I decided to choose a different script. Surely the problem was the script, I thought. I talked to several others who were doing well in the organization and asked for their script. I took what they gave me, but after several months of using the new sales script I still had little success. I found the script frustrating to use because whenever a prospect went outside the script I felt lost. My energy was consumed in solving the dilemma of getting back to the script.

Because of my lack of familiarity with selling at the time, it took almost two years before I realized that the script doesn't matter much: It's not what I say; it's how I say it! After I realized this, I memorized my opening only. Then I had a list of questions to qualify each prospect. I was no longer concerned about a script, and I no longer became lost in the process. An important change occurred: I started making sales!

If you are thinking that a script will cure your lack of sales, think again. By focusing on the tools we have provided in this book, you will be able to get rid of that script forever.

The Sales Map is a framework that enables you to apply what you have learned here. If you do everything well in your business, but fail to master selling, your business will not amount to much. But if you master selling and are less than proficient at providing your goods or services, at least you will have lots of customers to practice on until you gain the proficiency you may lack. It all hinges on selling.

You may have some resistance to accepting the importance of selling in business. "This is not fair," some people in our Training sessions have told us. Perhaps it really isn't. But we are not arguing the importance of selling based on fairness. Life isn't fair. Surely fairness is a fine value to hold dear, but insisting that life be fair produces mostly upsets and excuses.

You will be learning to sell in a way that is different from the preconceived notions of convincing and persuading. The foundation of the Sales Map is presenting what you are offering to people who want it or need it, so they make the best decision as to whether it is for them.

The Sales Map is very flexible and works in any sales situation, whether in person, on the phone, or selling to a group.

Memorize the steps in the Sales Map. If you do, you will always know where you are, where you are going, and how to get there. Thus you will never feel lost or uncertain in a sales situation.

People often are surprised at the simplicity of the Sales Map. Can selling really be so simple? Well, the accurate answer is yes and no. While engaged in selling activities, you derive great benefit from everything you have learned in this book so far. You know how to characterize the motivation strategy and the predominant internal representation method of prospective customers. You also know how to tailor your communication to make yourself easily understood, depending on each individual's particular motivation strategy and whether he or she uses predominantly visual, auditory, or kinesthetic internal processing. You know how to put yourself in the other person's shoes from your practice with the perceptual positions.

To prepare yourself and build the most resourceful mind-set, you have designed the purpose of your life so that your behavior is self-directed and not subject to the approval or criticism of others. You have used the Power Affirmations method to quiet negative internal self-talk that may have impeded your progress in the past. You have developed powerful moving-toward motivation using the Baseball Diamond method. You have prepared yourself with SMART goals installed on your timeline, and you have developed a new relationship with your feelings—you are aware now that they no longer mean anything about you. In many ways, you have become a different person from who you were when you first picked up this book.

The Sales Map in Figure 13.3 increases your effectiveness and saves you time no matter what you are selling. You can adapt it for any situation, whether you are selling on the phone, in person, or to a group.

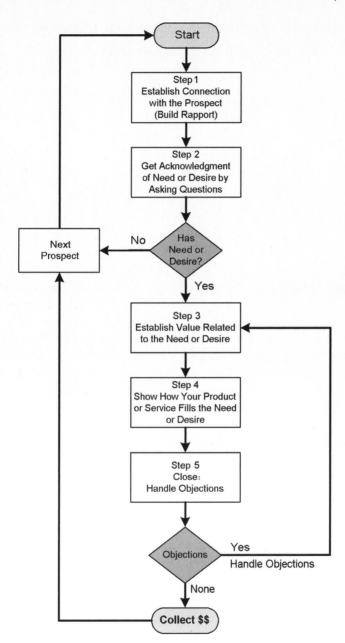

FIGURE 13.3   Five-Step Sales Map

STEP 1. ESTABLISH CONNECTION WITH THE PROSPECT (BUILD RAPPORT)

Put yourself in the other person's shoes. When you receive a call from someone you don't know, your mind spontaneously wonders "Why is this person calling?" and "Why is this person calling me?" The first 20 seconds of your call is to establish a connection with your prospective customer by very quickly answering those two questions, even though they have not been asked out loud. Match the customer's voice pitch, rate, and tempo as well as the representational system they prefer—visual, auditory, or kinesthetic. If you are in front of your prospect, match his or physiology, as well. All these things will build a connection to your prospect.

STEP 2. GET ACKNOWLEDGMENT OF A NEED OR DESIRE BY ASKING QUESTIONS

Make your questions as broad as possible to increase the possibility of an affirmative response. Phrases such as "would you ever" or "have you ever" are good ways to do this. The person with moving-away motivation is more likely to express a need than a desire, whereas the person with moving-toward motivation is more likely to express a desire than a need. Once you understand the broad need or desire, ask questions that define the need or desire more specifically. The more details you can collect, the better. Make note of any unusual word choices the prospect uses at this point. You will be able to use them in Steps 3 and 4.

DECISION POINT: ACKNOWLEDGMENT OF NEED OR DESIRE

If the prospective customer does not acknowledge a need or desire for what you are offering, thank the person and move on. You waste your own time and that of the other person by trying to persuade people who are not interested. Immediately contact your next prospect.

STEP 3. ESTABLISH VALUE RELATED TO THE NEED OR DESIRE

Here you begin the presentation of your product or service with the prospect's need and desire in mind. Present your product or service in such a way that it will fulfill the client's need or desire. If your product or service cannot fill a need or desire, say so and thank the prospect for his or her time. Never sell people something they don't need or desire. Refer the person whose need or desire you cannot meet to someone who can. This is just as good as creating a satisfied customer because of the resulting goodwill and referrals you receive.

STEP 4. SHOW HOW YOUR PRODUCT OR SERVICE FILLS THE NEED OR DESIRE

You must be flexible in this step to focus on the particular features and benefits of what you are offering that will actually serve the person you are speaking with. Present specific benefits that fill the prospect's need or desire or solve his or her problem. Link the need or desire to the benefits of your product or service so that the prospect understands the specific benefits of your product or service.

STEP 5. CLOSE: HANDLE OBJECTIONS

Closing the sale means asking for the order. Do this by asking a question that provides buying instructions.

DECISION POINT: OBJECTIONS

Time and money are the most common objections. You won't prevail in an argument on these topics. Build value in the customer's mind. Remember, an objection is nothing more than feedback telling you the customer does not have enough information to make a decision. Go back to Step 3 and reestablish value by offering a different perspective, then continue through the steps in the map. Go through this loop at least six times before you give up. The top salespeople who make the most amount of money do. Amateurs quit after the first or second no.

Your exact application of these steps depends on the product or service you offer. For example, Steps 3 and 4 will take more time and have greater educational content than shown in the examples if you are selling complex or technical products or services. In situations where a group makes the buying decision, likely you will have to spend more time on Step 5 to deal with objections and obtain buy-in from several people. In many cases, intermediaries are unaware of the requirements and preferences of their bosses who actually make the decisions. Do not rely on intermediaries to describe your product or service to decision makers. During the initial phase of the sales process, make sure all the decision makers are present. If they are not, you will waste a lot of time and will have to do your presentation over again with all the right people involved.

Self-Promotion

You have permission to do this, but only if you give it to yourself. Self-promotion is essential to move ahead. It cannot be very effective if you are too uncomfortable to do it or if it makes you uncomfortable. The key issue is whether you have given yourself permission to reach out to strangers and say good things about yourself. If you don't feel as if you have permission, then go back to the Permission method in Chapter 6 or change the thinking that limits you by applying the Power Affirmations method using any of the affirmations listed at the end of this chapter. Pick the one(s) that produce the strongest emotional reaction for you when you read them. Would you rather be right, or would you rather be rich?

Using the Telephone

The telephone provides the quickest way to reach large numbers of people in a short period of time. For this reason, it is the most common method for direct selling. There is an extensive list of affirmations for dealing with call reluctance at the end of this chapter.

Taking Money from Strangers

To emphasize the importance of reaching out to let people know about your business, we often ask clients to make a list of everyone they know. After you have done this, ask whether this list provides enough qualified prospects for you to create a large and growing income. Almost everyone who completes this exercise concludes that to produce the income they are looking for, they must reach out to strangers as customers.

Even though making effective cold calls may be uncomfortable at first, it is definitely a skill that will pay you high dividends for a very long time. Selling on the phone is generally a bigger challenge than in person, because you receive no visual information from your customer. For this reason, beginning on page 231 we present two annotated scenarios of applying the Sales Map to cold calling. In both cases, the dialogue text presents the actual conversation and the narrative text describes the insights and the process that takes place in the mind of the savvy salesperson.

Although this fact may be obvious, in cold calling you must realize that the person you are about to call is not sitting at home wishing for someone to call and offer products and services. Your call represents an interruption to its recipient. You have about 20 seconds to make this interruption appealing, to make a connection, and to give your prospect a good reason to listen to you. Until you accomplish these things, it is very unlikely that you will hear anything that you wish to hear from your prospect. Therefore, it is a good idea to speak more quickly than usual, without pauses, at the beginning so you can make a connection.

Telephone Answering Machines

Don't waste your time by leaving messages on the answering machines of people you do not know. If you reach an answering machine, hang up; make a note of the time and the day of the week, and call again at a different time and day of the week, because most people operate on a fixed routine. On the third attempt, if you still get an answering machine, briefly state your offer, saying that this will be your only call to that person.

Useful Guidelines about Selling

Selling is an interactive process. You do not control the responses of your customer. Nor do you control the order in which you obtain the information you are looking for. Do not think of the Sales Map as a checklist, but rather a guide of what to do next.

The following are important guidelines that you should deviate from only with very good reasons. Do not embark on a lengthy presentation until you have an acknowledgment of interest in the form of a need or desire from your customer. If you accede to a customer who says, "Just tell me what you have and I will make the decision," then you are turning yourself into a performer who can only hope that the audience approves of your show. You have lost control of the sales process. You'll be far more effective, and save time for yourself and your customer, by seeking an acknowledgment of a particular interest, so you can focus your presentation on the features and benefits that matter to each individual.

Postpone responding to premature questions about price by saying something like "I have a variety of solutions you might consider, and I don't want to discuss price until we know what would work best for you." If the customer persists in knowing prices right at the outset, refer him or her to your Web site. The short way to remember this is: refrain from discussing price until after you establish value.

Selling Dos and Don'ts

Do

- *Have fun with it.* Practice with the low-priced item. Your success will most likely remove the majority of the heavy feelings, primarily dread, from your selling experience. Not only will this make selling more enjoyable, but it will increase your business. Who wants to buy from someone who is uptight and desperate? Do you?
- *Put yourself in your customer's shoes.* Do this by focusing your attention on what you have to offer, not on what you will get. Remember, you are serving the customer rather than persuading.
- *Avoid emotional overload through practice.* Learn with the inexpensive item until you have some comfort and experience with selling. If you are in emotional overload, you won't remember our suggestions.
- *Impart a sense of urgency during your presentation.* Remember, you want customers to perceive what you have as so valuable they can't believe they have gotten along without it so far.
- *Ask questions.* Questions get customers involved, enable you to satisfy their desires, and provide valuable information.
- *Design, practice, and use an elevator speech*—one brief enough to make during a very quick elevator ride. The briefer the better. Its purpose is to attract attention, create interest, and find out whether it is beneficial for you to continue. One we like is: "I teach people how to become wealthy entrepreneurs. Are you interested?"

Don't

- *Don't talk too much.*
- *Don't waste a lot of time on customers who buy on price alone.*
- *Don't sell something you don't care about.*

Using the Five-Step Sales Map to Sell a Service

Next, we present two examples of the Five-Step Sales Map. The first follows the map very closely, while the second adheres more loosely to it.

Sales Dialogue 1 takes you through the entire process with sample dialogue and commentary so you learn the steps. We use this to offer our "Win the Sales Game" and "Win the Money Game" Training sessions.

In this example, we assume we are calling people who would most likely want our services, such as entrepreneurs or sales representatives. You can use this same process with cold calling. With cold calls, you'll probably discover that many people you reach do not acknowledge a need or desire. This means you will only get to Step #2 unless you have prequalified your prospects thoroughly. Move on to the next prospect as shown on the map. Remember that you are sorting, not selling. Sorting is looking for people who acknowledge an interest. Do not waste time persuading people who are not interested.

Because you do not control what the prospect says, we include three possible scenarios.

Sales Dialogue 1

Andy: Hi, may I speak with John Smith, please? (Wait for response.)
Hi, my name is Andy Fuehl from Phoenix, Arizona, and the reason I'm calling you today specifically is to show and tell you about a program we offer to improve your sales results by at least 20 percent. Some of our clients have doubled and tripled their income using our highly effective Sales Map to help them increase their sales results. Are you interested in increasing your sales?

Step 1: Establish Connection with the Prospect (build rapport). Initially qualify your prospect.

This opener gains attention and determines if there is any interest. Include anything you know about the prospect to establish a connection. Mentioning your location also aids in establishing a connection, because it will be something familiar. Here it is critical to match the person's rate of speech and pitch from their first response. Pay close attention, and adjust your rate and pitch to match theirs. Continue to monitor and make adjustments as necessary to maintain the connection.

1. *John:* Yes, I'd like to *hear* more about what you have to *say.*

(Prospect says this is at a medium pace, articulates the words, and his pitch is low. With a positive response such as this, go to step 2.)

The word choice (hear, say) indicates he could be primarily auditory. Respond using auditory language at a steady rate and use the low end of your voice range.

Note: No one is 100 percent auditory. Continue to pay attention because some people change representational systems at different stages of the sales process.

2. *John:* I don't *feel* comfortable taking another one of these sales courses. I have been *burned* by methods they taught when I used them.

This prospect is kinesthetic (feel, burned). He is also moving away from pain.

2. *Andy:* I can appreciate how you *feel.* I have participated in many sales training programs and could not *grasp* how to implement the program fully. If I could give you something that you can really *latch* onto and get a good *feel* for, would that be of interest to you?

I agreed with the prospect and let him know I am on his side. I then asked again using kinesthetic words to build rapport and deliver a message that he can understand.

3. *John:* No, I'm not interested.

This may be a knee-jerk reaction to your interruption. Do not give up at this point.

3. *Andy:* Before I go, may I ask you a question? Are you making all the sales you want? Could you be doing better than you currently are?

You have taken the pressure off by implying you are about to end the call. This question will flush out a true no. If it is a true no, then say: "Thank you so much for your time. If you ever want to improve your sales results dramatically, you can check us out at www.wealthwithoutajob.com."
If it turns out to have been a knee-jerk reaction, continue to Step 2 of the sales map.

Andy: Have you ever taken a sales training course before?

Step 2: Get Acknowledgment of Need or Desire by Asking Questions. Further qualify the prospect in this step.

Determine if the prospect has ever taken something similar.

John: Yes, I have.

If the prospect says no, skip the next few questions and find out more about his current situation. Ask questions about his results and how he feels about the results he has produced thus far. This will flush out the need or desire for the program we are selling.

Andy: What sales training have you taken?

Determine the level of sales training the prospect has—beginner or advanced.

John: Basic sales training.

This tells you the prospect has spent money on training before. If the prospect has never purchased any training, find out why it is important to increase business now. This will reveal how serious he is about improving himself. If he is not willing to invest in himself now, thank him for his time and send him to the Web site for information when he is interested.

Andy: Did you like it?

Determine if the prospect has had a good or bad experience with previous training.

John: It was OK.

Can't tell anything by the response so continue to probe further.

Andy: What did you like most about it?

Find hot button: What did the prospect enjoy?

John: I liked the snacks they provided at the training.

Most likely this prospect has had a negative or neutral experience. He had nothing good to say about the training.

Andy: What did you like least about it?

Find hot button: Search for negatives.

John: The method they taught us was difficult to understand, and my sales didn't improve.

Hot button: Difficult process. Also, the prospect may have a moving away from motivation strategy because he is focused on lack of results. Probe further to make sure.

Andy: Why did you take that training, and what would you like to have seen in that training?

Determine the prospect's motivation strategy for taking the previous course. Is he moving toward pleasure or moving away from pain? Also discover any important things that he is looking for. Take notes and listen carefully.

John: I'm tired of being rejected and making so little money. I really wish I could find a system that is easy to use.

Notice the prospect is moving away from pain. You now know that you must present your offer to relieve his pain. Don't focus on the benefits he will receive by taking the Training, let him know how it will relieve his pain.
    This prospect is also concerned about having an easy-to-use system to generate more sales.

Andy: Let me make sure I fully *grasped* what you want in a training program. If you found a sales training program that is an easy-to-use system that you could get a good *feel* for and it would help you get over being rejected, would that be the type of training course you would be interested in?

We have discovered some ways to serve the prospect and are feeding it back to him to gain acknowledgment of the need or desire.

John: Yes, that's it!

The prospect has acknowledged the need. Now we can continue on to Step 3 of the Sales Map. If the prospect said no or was not sure, you continue asking questions until you find the need or desire. In some instances you cannot find a need or desire. If so, thank the prospect for his or her time and refer the prospect to your Web site. It may be the wrong time, or the prospect may not be ready.

Step 3: Establish Value Related to the Need or Desire

Andy: We have a training program that is a complete system and is easy to use. We have a Five-Step Sales Map that gives you a step-by-step process and helps you know where you are at any point in the sales process. We spend almost two full days on this map, giving you lots of practice along the way so you know how to accomplish each step. Does this *feel* like it may be something you want to learn more about?

We have started to establish the value related to the prospect's needs, desires, and hot buttons. Present the product or service in small chunks, and ask an involvement question at the end. If you keep talking nonstop, you may lose your prospect.

John: Yes, that *sounds* great so far. I am getting a good *feel* for what you are *telling* me.

Notice the prospect is using auditory and kinesthetic words (sounds, feel, telling). Now use both auditory and kinesthetic words to keep your connection with him.

Andy: Great! This training program will give you an opportunity to practice selling in a *safe* environment, and the instructors will give you immediate *feedback* so you will be able to *tell* where you must improve. We have discovered that getting people involved and practicing the skills dramatically *lifts* their sales results. Others have *told* us how much they *enjoyed* taking the class and how *safe* it was to practice working with the tools. Would you like to have a training where you could practice the skill right on the spot and get a good *feel* for the results you can produce?

Continue to build value of the program to serve this prospect using auditory and kinesthetic language (safe, feedback, tell, lifts, told, enjoyed, safe, feel) to keep connected with him. Also get him involved at the end.

John: That makes me *tingle* thinking about this training.

Notice the prospect is using a kinesthetic word now (tingle). To maintain the connection, change over to kinesthetic.

Step 4: Show How Your Product or Service Fills the Need or Desire

Andy: Fantastic! By attending the Win the Sales Game Training, following the sales map and easy-to-use system, and by getting *hands-on* practice in a safe environment, you will stop *feeling burned and rejected* and thus improve your sales results. After you have taken the Win the Sales Game Training and learned how to use the sales map, how will you *feel* when you are able to increase the amount of money you have coming in? What will this allow you to do?

Link the prospect's needs, desires, and hot buttons to the training program. Also use his move away motivation strategy to help him make the decision. The last question links the Training to his feelings (hands-on, feeling burned and rejected, feel).

John: This program *feels* like it might be what I have been *looking* for. I can definitely *see* how more money will make my life more *soothing and satisfying*. How much does this cost?

The prospect is using kinesthetic and visual word now (feels, looking, see, soothing and satisfying). Respond by using both systems. The prospect also sees the value of the service being offered and responds positively.

If he did not respond positively at this point, you did not build enough value in Step 3, you presented it in a different representational system from what the prospect was using, or you did not communicate correctly the link between value and the need or desire. In the last case, make sure you have identified the need or desire. Ask the prospect again if perhaps he is looking for something besides increased income.

Step 5: Close: Handle Objections

Andy: To *see* yourself get involved in the Win the Sales Game Training program and *grasp* all the great tools we use, it will be an investment of only $500. Most trainings of this caliber will cost at least $2,500 to $4,000. We offer this program at a fraction of the cost so everyone can attend and benefit from the information. Would you like to sign up for the May Training, or would you prefer the September Training?

This close uses several tools (see, grasp). It uses a contrast in price comparing it to other seminars, the prospect's representational systems, and an alternative choice question is designed so you have a sale with either answer.

Note: Once you pose the closing question: *SHUT UP!!!* We can't emphasize this enough. Many sales are lost because the person selling keeps selling instead of waiting for the prospect to answer. You do not want to be the first person who speaks at this point.

We will cover a few different outcomes for you to learn the process.

1. *John:* I would like the May Training. The September Training is too late.

The prospect has purchased. Fill out the paperwork immediately to get him processed. (*Note:* Make sure you know and understand the paperwork fully *before* you make any sales calls. Practice ahead of time so you know exactly how to fill it out.)

1. *Andy:* That's great! Would you like to make that investment using your Visa or MasterCard?

Follow through with the payment portion first, then gather any other information later. Finish the transaction, pat yourself on the back, and continue to make calls. You have momentum now, and your excitement will carry over to other prospects you call that day. Take advantage of this. You are a winner.

2. *John:* I don't have the money.

This is a common objection. Objections are a query for more information. The prospect does not have enough information for him to part with his money. Notice that he doesn't say, "Go away. I'm not interested."

2. *Andy:* I can appreciate that, and is that a permanent condition?

Here I agreed with the prospect, to take him off the defensive. My next question interrupts his thinking pattern.

After the prospect answers the question, immediately answer the objection and go back to Step 3 of the Sales Map and continue to build value unless the prospect says he or she will buy.

Most likely the prospect objected here because he doesn't yet perceive enough value. After you establish the value, continue the process as before. Go through this loop at least six times before you give up unless the client gets angry or hostile. Most people give up too soon. You don't want to be one of those. The prospect is still interested in finding out more about what you have.

3. *John:* That's too expensive.

Again, this response means the prospect does not understand the value of what you are offering.

3. *Andy:* Compared to what?

Answer the objection and determine what the prospect is comparing your offer to. Be sure to get a specific answer.

Most likely objection is just a smokescreen for an objection your prospect has not mentioned yet.

Once you find out the real objection, go back to Step 3 of the Sales Map and follow the flow chart again until you get a yes.

4. *John:* I don't have the time.

Time and money are similar objections. Both mean that the prospect does not value what you are offering sufficiently to give up the time. No one wants to spend valuable time on something we see no value in.

4. *Andy:* I can appreciate that and earlier you told me that your results are not where you want them to be. Can you afford not to change what you are doing currently?

Again, we agree with the prospect and use what he told us earlier. Then wait for his response and go back to Step 3 on the Sales Map.

If a prospect has not purchased what you are selling and you have gone through the loop and have offered your close at least six times, refer him or her to your Web site. Most likely you will not be able to serve this person right now. Don't waste time. Move on to the next prospect.

In Sales Dialogue 2, you are Bill Smith, a home improvement contractor. The purpose of your call is to find out whether your potential customer qualifies for your services and whether you both would benefit from your personal visit to his or her home. Notice in this dialogue that the prospect does most of the talking. Bill gets this result by asking questions and ending each of his comments with a question. Notice, also, that Bill does not allow himself to be stuck in making a canned presentation. He engages the prospect by finding out what matters to him or her and by asking for commitments as the process moves along.

Bill has just completed a kitchen renovation for Mr. and Mrs. Benson at 12 Country Lane. After the job was done, he asked the Bensons for the names, addresses, and phone numbers of friends, neighbors, and associates who might also be interested in his services.

While taking a break from his work, he walked around the neighborhood writing down the names and addresses of the people living in the area and making notes about the houses he saw in the neighborhood. By using the phone book and directory assistance, Bill has compiled a list of prospects for cold calling.

In the prospecting portion of your business, it is essential that you gather lots and lots of prospects, even more than you could contact. If you have too few contacts, you'll seem desperate. Prospective customers will detect that desperation and avoid you.

Obviously the Bensons' referrals would be easier to connect with, but we want to use cold calling as an example.

Bill checks the National Do Not Call List to eliminate names that appear there. Although perhaps not its original intention, this list will save you time by identifying people who probably won't buy.

Understand that this is an example only. Selling is far too dynamic a process to use canned questions. Use the questions in the following dialogue as a guide.

Sales Dialogue 2

Bill: Hello, my name is Bill Smith, and my company is offering home improvements to boost both the comfort and the value of your home. I just installed a beautiful new kitchen for Mary and Tom Benson on Country Lane in your neighborhood. It is my twentieth kitchen so far and I think it is one of my best. Do you own your home?

Step 1: Right at the beginning, connect with something familiar to your customer, his or her own neighborhood. Build credibility here by mentioning your experience and the pride you take in your work. And ask the most important question: whether the prospect owns a home. If the answer to this question is no, say thank you and good-bye. Call the next person on your contact list.

Here you are sorting and looking for qualified prospects.

Bill: Have you ever thought of improvements that could add to the value and the comfort of your home?

Phrase this question as broadly as possible to increase the possibility of an affirmative response. Use it to build the connection to the prospect and to further qualify.

Note: You do not control the other person's response, so you must have mental flexibility here. Four possible prospect answers and four possible responses follow.

1. *Prospect*: We've been discussing finishing the basement.

1. *Bill:* What would you like to change about your basement?

You are now on Step 2 of the Sales Map. This question is designed to discover the prospect's motivation strategy. If you hear answers like "The basement is a mess, it leaks and there is mildew" or "My wife has been nagging me about it," then you can be pretty sure this person has a need and is moving away from pain as a motivation strategy. If you hear something like "We want a place for our kids and their friends to hang out at home" or "I want a space for my business, which has outgrown the kitchen table," your customer has a desire and uses moving toward pleasure motivation.

2. *Prospect*: We are putting our house on the market next week.

2. *Bill:* I understand. Has your real estate agent pointed out some small improvements that could add thousands to your selling price or help your house to sell more quickly?

Just because you got a negative response is not necessarily a reason to give up. Be flexible. Try a different approach.

3. *Prospect*: No, we are not interested.

3. *Bill:* OK. What about some repairs that haven't gotten done?

Same as previous example.

4. *Prospect*: Who do you think you are, interrupting my dinner?

4. *Bill:* Wow! It must feel terrible to think like that. I hope you feel better soon. I won't call again. Bye now.

Some people are like this. Do not allow them to bring you down to their level of discontent and rudeness. Immediately contact the next person on your list. If you do not, this negative state will cause you to give up. Keep calling until you get a positive response before ending the calling day.

Bill: For most people, their home is their largest investment. What would be important to you in the improvements you are thinking about?

Step 2: Continue asking questions to find the need or desire. At this point, you have uncovered your customer's motivation strategy. Next, you want information about his or her method of internal representation (primarily visual, auditory, or kinesthetic processing?). Listen carefully for the sensory indicators. The answer to this question is likely to give you the information you are looking for. If the prospect answers is, "I would need to see a detailed proposal with some alternatives," the processing system is visual; if the answer is, "It would have to sound right to me," the prospect is auditory; or the answer is, "I want the basement to be conformable," then the prospect is kinesthetic.

Pay close attention here and take notes. Your prospect is telling you the standards you must meet to get the sale.

Bill: Have you used a home improvement contractor before? If, yes: How did that work out?

The answer here provides useful information about the prospect's thinking and a useful lead-in for your next comments. Pay close attention to the prospect. If the prospect had a good experience, then emphasize that he or she will have a good experience using your service later on in the presentation. If the prospect had a bad experience, probe further to find out what happened. Use this description later to help the prospect understand how you will handle it differently so the bad experience won't be repeated.

Bill: Have you considered doing this project yourself?

Bill has been burned by a do-it-yourselfer who took the ideas and design Bill drew up and did the work himself. In general, it is useful for you to learn about alternatives prospects have considered and discarded to understand the precise nature of their needs and desires.

Bill: So I am not wasting your time, do you have financing available for this investment?

Bill will spend an hour in travel time for this appointment and several hours at the prospect's house. This question is designed to discover how serious the prospect is about renovating the basement. The good connection Bill made with the prospect at the beginning facilitates discussion of potentially sensitive issues like payment.

Prospect: How much will this cost?

Since you are paying close attention, you notice that the question has not been answered yet. So answer the prospect's question and then ask yours again, in a different way.

Bill: That is impossible to say without looking at your basement. After our meeting, I can (show you) (tell you) (give you a feel for) several different alternatives. I have refinished many basements. One was a $20,000 job and some were as low as $6,000, but I won't quote you a price until you know what you are getting, so you can make an informed decision. In any case, the renovation will be a much better investment and much more economical than renting office space. Wouldn't you agree?

The sentence about office space links to the prospect's already stated desire. This is Step 4 of the Sales Map. Bill has made a good point here and has been talking for a long time, so he pauses to ask a question.

Bill: Quite often my customers use a home equity line of credit for improvements that raise the value and the comfort of their home. Is that something that you might consider?

It is far too early to be closing the sale and far too early to be concerned about exactly how the prospect will pay for the project. First build the value of what you are offering. You are looking for willingness on the part of the prospect to discuss financing possibilities. If the prospect is unwilling, you may have a suspect (a person with no intention of buying).

Bill: What is your time frame for completing this project?

Bill wants to make sure he can meet the prospect's requirements regarding time and also is checking to see whether the prospect has a sense of urgency about it. If the prospect has little or no urgency, Bill gives the preparation of this price quotation a low priority.

Bill: Let me give you an idea of how I prefer to work. I will pay you a visit at your convenience so (I can show you some alternatives for your basement) (I can tell you about some possibilities for your basement) (you can get a feel for the alternatives). I will (show you) (tell you about) (toss around) alternatives to fit your budget.

Would Thursday at 8:00 P.M. or Saturday at 10:00 A.M. be more convenient for you?

Take charge by offering alternatives convenient for *you*. This alternative question leads to the prospect saying yes either way.

Bill: OK, I look forward to meeting with you.

Fast-forward to personal appointment at the prospect's home.

Bill is prepared with an attractive photographic portfolio of before-and-after pictures of several of his past basement renovations. Each bears the name, address, and phone number of the homeowners who have consented to serve as references for him. Bill phones the day before and leaves a message confirming the appointment.

Bill: Hi, Mr. Prospect. Thanks for meeting with me today. I like this neighborhood. Your lawn looks great. How do you keep it so green?

Notice that Bill starts at the beginning of the sales map, reestablishing his connection with the prospect. Anytime there is a gap in time between conversations or meetings, always go back to Step 1 of the Sales Map and build the connection. If you don't, you will have a difficult time making the sale. Remember, people like doing business with people like themselves. Don't you?

Bill: Now, I remember when we spoke on the phone, you mentioned the importance of using your basement for your business. Is that still the case?
   Can we take a look at it?

Bill has summarized his previous conversation and informally checked whether the prospect still has the desire mentioned on the phone. This is Step 2 of the Sales Map. If, in the interim, the customer has taken a job outside his home, for example, Bill wants to know this right away. This doesn't necessarily mean he has lost the sale; the prospect may have an alternate reason for renovating his basement. Make sure you know what the need or desire is and have the prospect acknowledge it.

(After looking at the basement, they return to the kitchen table.)

Bill: Do you have an idea how you want the finished basement to look and feel?

Here Bill is linking ahead to the prospect's desire. This is Step 4 of the Sales Map. Bill shows the prospect samples of paneling and flooring material based on prospect's taste.

The prospect chooses the materials he wants, and Bill returns to the basement to take measurements.

This is Step 3 of the Sales Map. Bill builds value by helping the prospect pick the materials and illustrates what it will look like, thus specifically identifying the value that Bill adds to the job.

Bill: I will be presenting you with a detailed price quotation. Now, do you have financing available for the project, or do you want me to suggest reliable financing sources I have worked with before?

Prospect: I have a line of credit I can use for this.

Anyone in a business offering high-ticket, custom products or services quickly realizes the importance of qualifying any prospective customer as precisely as possible.

By failing to do so, you waste time and energy preparing customized proposals and designs for people with no intention or means to buy. In his initial call Bill has already asked questions about paying for the renovation.

Bill: It will take me a couple of days to prepare the price quote for your new basement office. I can deliver it to you on Tuesday or Wednesday at 7:00 P.M. Which would be more convenient?

Again offer the prospect a choice, either of which means he or she has accepted your offer.

Bill remains quiet until the prospect agrees to the time for the next meeting.

Prospect: Can't you just mail it to me?

Bill: No, because I want to be able to answer any questions you have.

Prospect: Wednesday would be better.

This is a test close and is Step 5 in the Sales Map. If the prospect is not ready to make a decision at this point, ask more questions.

Bill: Will you be in a position to make a decision at that point?

Fast-forward to closing meeting.

What do you think would happen if Bill were to arrive and say something like, "I am afraid to tell you that your basement will cost you $8,000?"

Do you think he would make the sale? Of course not. Then Bill goes through the features of his price quote before naming his price.

Remember to use Step 1 of the Sales Map. You must reestablish a connection with the prospect. If you do not, you risk the chance the prospect will decline your offer.

Bill then goes through Step 3 of the Sales Map to build the value of what is being offered before presenting the price. If the value was not established first, it will not matter how little Bill's quote is. Anything will seem too much.

Bill: This includes the complete waterproofing system we discussed with a five-year guarantee, the tile we discussed in gray for the floor (showing sample). This has a five-year guarantee. I did not include the imported tile, which you said you did not want, because it would have added $2,500 to the price. But it does include the knotty pine paneling. OK?

By going through the different features with the prospect and showing samples, you get the prospect and his or her senses involved in the process. This will build emotional ties to what you are offering.

Bill: The quotation works out to $7,100. I can start work as soon as Monday. Are you ready for your new basement office.

The last sentence is the closing question, even though we don't use a question mark. Bill knows to state it like a command, so his voice goes down instead of up at the end of the sentence. Practice your closing question. Say, "Get off the couch." Use the same downward pitch at the end of the sentence you would use in saying that to your beloved pet. Then practice it with your closing questions.

1. *Prospect:* How about $6,900?

Bill has read and understood the information in Chapter 11 about negotiation, so he has left himself some wiggle room in his price quotation. Earlier he established $6,600 as his rock-bottom price. He also knows that if he agrees to the prospect's lower offer without getting anything, even something small, in return, the prospect could be motivated to go even lower.

1. *Bill:* You have a deal at $6,900, but it would require a deposit of 60 percent. Can I get a check from you.

Use the same downward inflection of your voice on this closing question, too.

2. *Prospect*: Not so fast. I don't think I will be ready for you to start then.

2. *Bill:* OK, my schedule is clear starting on September 15. Can we agree on September 15, or would October 1 be better for you.

Use the same downward inflection of your voice on this closing question, too.

2. *Prospect*: September 15. I'll get my checkbook.

Professional Telephone Affirmations
- I love to talk on the phone.
- I forgive my mother (father) for disapproving of me for talking on the phone.
- Now that I am grown up, I can make all the phone calls I want.
- It is OK for me to phone people.
- It is OK for me to interrupt people.
- It is OK for me to bother people.
- It is OK for me to argue with people.
- I've been hung up on before.
- It is OK for me to pretend that approval has value.
- "No" means I decline your offer, I love you, I admire you, I respect you, and I am open to future offers.
- The phone company is my friend.
- The phone company wants me to use the phone.
- The telephone is my most valuable business tool.
- I love to pay my phone bill.
- I can call whoever I want.
- I love talking about ( ).
- I love telling people about ( ).
- Everyone I talk with is greatly interested in ( ).
- Anyone who can afford a telephone can obviously afford what I am offering.
- The people that I talk with can make up their minds quickly.
- It is OK for me to say "I don't want to talk with you any longer."
- I always have time for my phone calls.
- Learning to sell is much easier than commuting.

- I live in a safe and friendly (universe) (state) (city) (town) filled with people who support my purpose and give me what I want.
- I am proud of what I have to offer people.
- Now that I am grown up, it is OK for me to ask strangers for money.
- It is OK for me to pretend that selling is difficult.
- Sales is a highly pleasing career for me.
- I have nothing to lose and everything to gain by selling.
- I'd rather put up with a little discomfort than struggle with my crummy job.

Sales Affirmations
- I love to sell.
- I love my clients and they love me.
- My customers buy from me whether they like me or not.
- Even though I have fears, reservations, and a few other limiting notions, I feel successful at selling.

14

PUTTING IT
ALL TOGETHER
INTO A PLAN

A plan is the natural mental response we experience to any challenge. People can learn to use their natural creativity to develop planning ability. Avoid common problems by planning and use the five essential elements of any plan.

Plans are important. You could say that your current situation is the result of many plans you chose in the past, both consciously and unconsciously. Typically, the unconsciously chosen plans cause those results that are less than pleasant. Here you will learn to make conscious plans to accomplish goals that are expressions of your true purpose.

In our Trainings, participants apply the methods in this chapter and develop a written plan for an income-increasing project of their choice, the skills to carry it out, and the ability to plan any additional projects.

Planning is not taught in school, but it is easy to learn once you deal with common mistakes and misconceptions.

A goal without a plan is a dream that won't come true. Failure to plan is planning to fail. Sure, dreams sometimes come true all by themselves, but this mostly happens in the movies. In real life, a goal is most often accomplished by carefully planning it out and then following the plan, adjusting for new information and unanticipated events as they occur. Having your planned activities laid out all the way to the fruition of your goal aids you in focusing on the task at hand; writing your plan frees you from having to remember all the steps involved.

Planning is easy because everyone has a natural ability to do it. Earlier we mentioned that feelings are an increase in physical energy in response to a challenge. Your body automatically provides the energy you need to deal with any challenge. Similarly, a plan results from the natural increase in *mental* energy in response to a challenge. Whenever you are confronted with a challenging problem, your mind naturally begins to figure out and evaluate various solutions. The planning method you will learn in this chapter builds on your mind's natural ability.

For example, if you are driving to work and a tire on your car goes flat, your mind immediately begins to make a plan to minimize the lateness of your arrival. You may consider abandoning the car and taking a taxi, changing the tire yourself, or telephoning for a repair service to help you. None of these alternatives is perfect. Each has different disadvantages. There is no ideal solution. The best choice depends on your personal values about punctuality and money, as well as the resources available to you.

Written plans are not required even for complicated tasks if you have done them before. The first time you give a formal dinner party for 10 guests, you would want to plan it out in detail and write your plans down to ensure that you remember everything. After giving a few successful dinner parties, you wouldn't need the written plan anymore. At this point your plan might consist only of a guest list and a menu.

A written plan is required to accomplish any significant goal that is new to you. The bigger the project, the more you need a plan. The more people involved, the more you need a plan. The length of the plan depends on the complexity of the job. The plan of the Apollo project to send men to the Moon and return them safely filled many, many thick books.

Go back to the SMART goals you made in Chapter 8 and choose one of these to make your plan. You will miss the very important emotional involvement if you don't pick a goal that matters to you. The challenge of the plan is to create a map or a path from where you are now to the destination you desire.

Common Problems with Planning

By far, the most common difficulty people have with planning is *fear*. But there are also:

- Too much focus on numbers
- Inadequate access to creativity
- Plan's lack of harmony with your true purpose

Planning is scary. It's about the future, so you should expect fear to be present. This is normal. You may have intense emotions about events in your personal history, but those emotions are probably sadness or resentment. Those events are over. Fears are about things that haven't happened yet. Remember, the fear is there to help you deal with the challenge. Don't avoid it. Let it help you by letting the fear be OK. (Refer back to the hairy elephants in Chapter 7, if necessary.)

Too much focus on numbers is a common problem. Many times, if you ask business managers for their plan, you will be presented with a detailed spreadsheet that lays out anticipated receipts and expenditures. Unfortunately, this is not a plan; it cannot serve as a guide to action. The spreadsheet is a budget only. A budget is a good thing to have, but it is not a plan.

A budget can measure the progress of a plan's execution, but by itself it does not serve as a guide to the sequential action required for success. A plan does that. Clearly an understanding of the numbers is an important part of a plan, but more is required for success.

Another common problem is inadequate access to creativity. A plan is about the future. The logical, analytical function of your mind is best suited for analyzing the cause and effect of what already exists. Because the future doesn't exist yet, the analytical portion of your mind is poorly equipped to deal with it.

Your mind's creative function is best equipped for dealing with the future. If you use the analytical part of your mind to design your plan, you will inevitably become stuck. When the participants in our Training sessions make their plan, we tell them it's very easy to know when you are stuck. You gaze off into the middle distance, most often glassy-eyed and slack-jawed, awaiting inspiration to come along to guide you. "Don't hold your breath waiting for inspiration," we advise. Instead, put your creativity to work immediately. The Discovery Writing technique from Chapter 8 is ideally suited to planning. Start by using these topics to make lists that can help you.

- 20 early steps in my plan
- 20 people who could help me
- 20 people who have done something similar before
- 20 places I could look for information
- 20 ways I could avoid the next step altogether
- 20 things I know could never work

Making such lists enables you to access the creative function of your mind and then call on your analytical function to evaluate the alternatives.

Still another problem is a plan's lack of harmony with your true purpose. It is difficult to get very excited about expressing your inherited purpose. You didn't choose it, so the amount of satisfaction it can deliver is severely limited. Purpose, values, goal, and plans function in a hierarchy like a chain of command or an organizational chart. Your true purpose is a statement of how you intend to express your most important values. Each goal becomes a specific expression of your purpose and each plan is a method to accomplish that goal. Figure 14.1 presents the hierarchical chart.

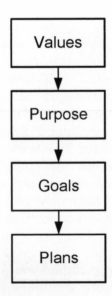

FIGURE 14.1   Hierarchy of Your Goals

Dealing with Time

Any plan is somewhat similar to a schedule. In a plan you are establishing priorities about time.

Most parents decide time issues for their children. My mother (PL) fed me on a schedule given to her by the pediatrician. It was always a rush. She shoveled in the food faster than I wanted it. Later, when I mastered the spoon, she told me that I ate too fast. (I know, tough childhood.) I concluded that other people make the decisions about time and speed, that they do so in an inconsistent manner, and that my preferences about time and speed are less important than theirs.

You do not need an experience like this to convince you that other people are in charge of time. Most parents put their children to bed when the parents are tired. In school, other people determine the schedule; determine how many years you must attend to reach graduation. Military training, of course, takes this to an extreme. At a job, your employer determines your work schedule, time off, and vacations. You may influence the schedule a little, but the negotiation is probably not on an adult–adult basis.

To succeed with planning, you may need to place yourself in charge of time. The interactive affirmation process in Chapter 9 can help with this a great deal.

Which Goals Do You Plan For?

During the next five years, changes will occur in your life. Who will decide what these changes are? Will they be changes you made or things that happened to you? If you have no goals and no plans to carry them out, the changes are likely to be determined by someone else or by outside forces. You will not be satisfied with changes you do not consciously ask for. This is the magic of goals. If you allow yourself to think about it, there are many, many things you want: things you would like to accomplish, changes you want in your relationships, in your health, things you want to learn. Having written goals gives you the opportunity to make the improvements you prefer.

Goals focus your time and energy on those desires that are most important to you. Without goals, it is easy to waste time and energy on things that don't matter very much. (Television and surfing the Web are currently popular time-wasters.) Another possibility is that someone else, with a clearer sense of purpose, will hire you to aid in accomplishing his or her goals. Whether this is satisfying for you depends on whether that person's desires are in harmony with yours. The prevalence of the Thank Goodness It's Friday (TGIF) mentality indicates such harmony is infrequent.

Requirements of a Plan

Time management is actually a misnomer. You don't really manage time, but rather your activities. All the time management courses in the world will not help very much if you don't have an organized and detailed approach for using your creativity to solve problems. Without this, your efforts will lack focus and direction and are likely to be driven by the desires of others.

Perfectionism and Creativity Are Natural Enemies

There is no such thing as a perfect plan. Do not wait for yours to be perfect before you begin working to achieve it. There is not even a best plan. There is a wide variety of ways to accomplish any goal. Different plans will work better for different people. Even after you have written your plan, you'll be changing it from time to time to accommodate new information and unanticipated events.

Five Requirements for a Successful Plan

There are only five requirements for a successful plan.

1. It must be written.
2. It must be in chronological order, starting now and continuing all the way to the end.
3. The completion of each step must leave you ready to begin the next step.
4. It must be in harmony with your values and your true purpose.
5. It must include personal growth activity.

If you are like most people, you already have some plans. Some may be written in detail, and others may be vaguely formulated. Use the requirements just listed to improve any plans you have already made. You may discover that you want to discard some of those plans because they are no longer in harmony with your true purpose.

Let's consider the requirements for a successful plan in more detail.

PLANS MUST BE WRITTEN

Writing your plan makes the result more real in your mind and imposes a degree of rigor and thinking it through like nothing else does. Having it written enables you to make the changes that will be necessary in an organized manner. Having the plan in written form also facilitates checking it for completeness, making improvements, communicating steps to others in a timely manner, and, most important, detecting as early as possible the effect of any changes on future steps. Using a computer is convenient because the plan is then easy to modify.

PLANS MUST BE IN CHRONOLOGICAL ORDER

Your plan must begin now. (Well, tomorrow morning may be soon enough.) If your plan does not take you from your current situation to your desired result, then it is most likely a dream that will not come true. Do not delay starting for any of the million or so reasons why it seems better to wait until you have:

- More money saved
- Paid your bills
- Raised your self-esteem
- Gotten married, divorced, whatever

There is magic to beginning. The boldness becomes energizing and self-fulfilling. If you are not willing to begin immediately, you are procrastinating. Right here at the beginning of the planning process is the time to deal with your priorities. Either your goal matters to you or it doesn't. If it doesn't matter enough to begin to take action, then you are much better off forgetting about it for now and putting your time and energy into some other goal that matters more to you. This does not make you a bad person or lazy.

Nevertheless, it will be no easier for you to deal with your own resistance, self-limiting patterns, upsets, or other emotional conflicts next week. It only seems so. There is no time like the present. Make up your mind now. Choosing is not complicated. Thus, it is better for your peace of mind to discard a goal for now than to insist that you should do it, while at the same time taking no action.

Your plan must take you all the way to the end. If, for example, your goal is to buy a new car and pay cash for it, then the final step must be you handing over the cash to the car dealer and driving home from the car lot.

COMPLETION OF EACH STEP MUST LEAVE YOU READY TO BEGIN THE NEXT ONE

This requirement ensures that your plan is complete. If your plan is complete from beginning to end, then the accomplishment of each step places you in a position where you are ready to begin the following step. Such is the nature of steps. If this is not the case, there are steps missing in your plan. Knowing this, you see where steps must be added to make it complete. It is much better to find out ahead of time that steps are missing than to discover at the last moment that you have forgotten something.

PLANS MUST BE IN HARMONY WITH YOUR VALUES AND YOUR TRUE PURPOSE

If you are not certain about your true purpose, you will spend your time and energy expressing the purpose of someone who is. Perhaps you notice that you have made little or no progress on some plans that you have already made or are working on. It is difficult to accomplish something that is not in harmony with your values and your purpose because of the internal conflicts.

PLANS MUST INCLUDE PERSONAL GROWTH ACTIVITY

By "personal growth," we mean any activity that enhances your peace of mind, your emotional well-being, your creativity, or that helps you to resolve the conflicts from your past. The accomplishment of any significant, long-held desire will change you—not your essence, but your perception of yourself, others' perception of you, and your perception of others. In this way, accomplishment contributes to your personal development. It is hard for people to make significant accomplishments unless they resolve internal conflicts that hold them back. Any sort of personal growth activity that aids you directly in the resolution of internal conflicts and childhood conditioning is certain to facilitate your accomplishment of any significant project.

Sample Plan

Here is the beginning of a sample plan someone wrote to expand a proofreading and editing business. This plan is modeled to include the four distinct business processes from Chapter 10:

1. Finding prospective customers
2. Presenting your product or service, so prospects buy

3. Producing your product or service, delivering it and collecting payment
4. Follow-up

Date	Purpose	Activity
Jun 12		Get business license, checking account, and merchant VISA account
Jun 14	Prospecting	Research magazines to reach writers and publishers with advertising
Jun 14	Closing	Update answering machine's outgoing message
Jun 15	Prospecting	Write my elevator speech for use in phoning
Jun 15	Prospecting	Write out what to say about my prices
Jun 17	Prospecting	Start phoning local advertising agencies
Jun 17	Personal	Write daily Power Affirmations to enhance my sales results
???	Closing	Respond to ad agencies that are interested
Jun 18	Prospecting	Research Internet to find publishers who need proofreaders
July 19	Prospecting	Place ads in magazines
July 20	Prospecting	Make calls to magazines and book publishers (during lunch hour)
Undated	Producing	Research various kinds of proofreading software
Undated	Referrals	Solicit existing and past customers weekly for additional business from them or those they know

Clearly there are holes here to be filled in once the business gets rolling and work for customers must be scheduled. Nevertheless, this a good basic plan; not much more is required to get started.

When you start making your plan, you only have two known points: the starting point and the desired destination. You go through the planning process to map out the best route for you. Remember that there are thousands of ways to accomplish anything. Your plan doesn't have to be perfect. Be determined about your goal and flexible about your plan. Besides serving as a guide for action, a plan increases in your mind the possibility of success.

QUICK PLANNING METHOD

As mentioned, goals and plans are different. A goal answers the question What? and a plan answers the question How? In this exercise you put your goals and plans in a Quick Planning method you can use every day to keep yourself moving.

Copy the following chart or use the space provided.

Massive Action 20 steps to accomplish my desired outcome	Desired Outcome	Why?
1. _____		
2. _____		
3. _____		
4. _____		
5. _____		
6. _____		
7. _____		
8. _____		
9. _____		
10. _____		
11. _____		
12. _____		
13. _____		
14. _____		
15. _____		
16. _____		
17. _____		
18. _____		
19. _____		
20. _____		

First, fill in the center column, "Desired Outcome," using one of your SMART goals. Be sure to include the completion date.

Next complete the "Why?" column. Write down how you will feel when this goal is completed. Actually feel it in your body. Make the sensation even more intensely pleasurable now. See the job done and hear the sounds of celebration. Who says you must wait for celebration? Celebrate now! Go ahead, it's OK.

Next set your timer for two minutes. In the "Massive Action" Column, write down 20 steps that move you closer to your desired outcome. If you have not done the warm-up lists described in Chapter 8 at least once, go back and do these now. They help you learn how to silence your analytical mind. Remember, write as fast you can. Do not think while you are making this list. Think only after the list is done. Make your list now! No procrastinating. You're doing great! Now keep up your momentum.

Now that your list of 20 steps is done, circle those that actually move you toward the result you want.

Completing Your Plan

If your desired outcome is a significant goal, then the circled items on your list represent only the beginning of a plan. Copy the circled items on to a separate sheet of paper in chronological order. A plan is complete when finishing each step places you in a position to begin the next step.

Look over your chronological list of activities that move you toward your desired outcome. Check to see that all steps move you forward. If there are gaps, where one step does not leave you ready to begin the next, then use Discovery Writing to create the missing steps. Keep going until your plan is complete and meets the criteria described in this chapter.

Summary of What You Learned

We left the method for making your plan to last, so that you had the chance to learn the methods we presented. By learning the methods and gaining confidence in using them, you will make bolder and more decisive plans.

Now it is time to review the skills and information you have learned.

In Chapter 4, you learned the benefits of accepting responsibility for your results. You also learned how results are caused by behavior and behavior is caused by your internal state of being, which in turn you control by changing your physiology and psychology. Additionally, you built a powerful and reliable motivation strategy with the Baseball Diamond method.

In Chapter 5, you learned the three steps to change awareness, acceptance, and action. In Chapter 6, you declared the purpose of your life so you have greater satisfaction and sense of direction. In Chapter 7, you learned to develop a more empowering relationship with your feelings by understanding that they exist as an increase in energy in response to a challenge. In Chapter 8, you established SMART goals and learned how to perceive time more productively, the power of changing your perception of unpleasant past events to reduce their emotional impact, and to use your creativity. You also created a business definition. In Chapter 9, you learned to cultivate the thinking that moves you ahead with Power Affirmations, and Chapter 10 presented the basic elements of a successful business.

In Chapter 11, you learned about the obstacles that may have prevented you from successful negotiation in the past, and in Chapter 12, you learned what to listen for in sales situations and how to tailor your communication most effectively for each person you deal with. In Chapter 13, you learned the benefits of learning to sell in the kiddy pool and the Five-Step Sales Map to guide your decision making and communication when selling.

None of this information will produce results for you unless you take massive action. Massive action means more than is required. Herein lies a significant benefit of doing work you love. Massive action would be drudgery in work you don't like.

Meet the Authors Every Week

You are not alone. Even after you have finished reading, we are available to help and answer questions. Join us on the phone for our weekly teleclass where we present topics in this book (and some that are not) and answer your questions. There are monthly special guest speakers.

This class has been packed since day one. Call in early to reserve your spot. You may call in with questions as early as five minutes before the hour.

The free weekly eZine is available to you at:

www.wealthwithoutajob.com

So is the Entrepreneurs Country Club, the Internet-based, members-only club with an exclusive discussion board and lots of special offers and discounts.

Every Wednesday Night!

9:00 P.M. Eastern
8:00 P.M. Central
7:00 P.M. Mountain
6:00 P.M. Pacific
4:00 P.M. Hawaiian (in winter)

Call 646-519-5860 ID: 2791#

or

212-461-5860 ID: 2791# at the times above to listen in.

Gain valuable practice with the methods in this book and with others that do not lend themselves to written presentation by attending the Wealth Without a Job full-day course FREE. As our way of saying thank you to our readers, we reserve a limited number of free seats at each Wealth Without a Job course. First come, first served. Find the schedule and get your free ticket at the Readers Section of our Web site, www.wealthwithoutajob.com. The Readers Section is password protected. To access it you must enter:

Username: reader
Password: iwantmore

We look forward to meeting you.

APPENDIX

HOW TO
FEEL BETTER
INSTANTLY
WITHOUT YEARS
OF THERAPY

Our minds do not relate to reality directly. Instead, we interpret reality through a variety of internal prisms and filters, or internal representations. We constructed these representations from our past experience and from conclusions we reached, as well as from what people told us about life and about ourselves. In many cases, the internal representations that you use to interpret reality are not conducive to your maximum effectiveness, happiness, and resourcefulness. Why? Some were constructed during childhood, when your power and authority were limited by the constraints of other people who controlled your life back then. Also, some of the important internal representations that shape your behaviors and outlook were constructed in response to a crisis. Even though the crisis is over, the one-time intensity of the associated emotion tends to hold your conclusion in place. It is as if some part of your mind believes that the conclusions made from a past emergency situation are necessary for survival.

Information reaches our mind through our five senses:

1. Seeing
2. Hearing
3. Kinesthetic (feeling)
4. Tasting
5. Smelling

Remember that your mind is busy interpreting reality during all of your waking hours. Everywhere you go, you take yourself with you.

In many of the exercises, we ask you to recall past experiences and the visual, auditory, kinesthetic, taste, and smell memories that go with them. In our Training sessions, sometimes participants tell us, "I can't visualize very well. I always have trouble with it." Change this internal representation immediately by noticing the degree to which you are able to visualize. Everyone has had an experience like this one: You go to a party with a friend. You excuse yourself to visit the rest room and, upon your return, you are *able* to find your friend. To do so, you must visualize what your friend looks like when you return and scan the crowd to find a person whose appearance conforms to your internal representation. Even if your internal image is somewhat faulty—if you remember the friend wearing a blue outfit and actually he wore a gray outfit—you can still find him. Our internal representations are almost never perfect; they don't need to be. If seeing Paris were the same as visualizing it, surely fewer people would go. Even after you have visited Paris, your internal representations of it do not precisely express how it looks.

Sometimes in our Training sessions people say, "I can't imagine that." This is not a matter of ability but rather of willingness. Your mind has the capability to imagine anything. It is completely free to think anything. Even better than anything you have imagined before—or worse, too, for those who want to go in that direction.

Two steps in increasing your ability to visualize and to gain access to the internal representations you have recorded from all of your senses are:

1. Notice the ability you already have.
2. Increase your willingness for your mind to be free.

HOW TO FEEL BETTER INSTANTLY WITHOUT YEARS OF THERAPY

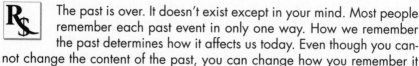 The past is over. It doesn't exist except in your mind. Most people remember each past event in only one way. How we remember the past determines how it affects us today. Even though you cannot change the content of the past, you can change how you remember it and, thus, change how it affects you. People do this unintentionally all the time. For example, I (PL) served in the military during the Vietnam War. In those days, members of the armed forces complained about military life, constantly counting the days until their discharge. Today, many of the same people remember that same military experience fondly.

VCR Visualization Method

 This is a powerful and speedy technique to change your personal representations. You may have only one way to represent these; here we will give you a new way. Take the time and do the exercise now.

You have in your mind a VCR. This VCR is superior to any of the VCRs generally available, which record only sights and sounds. The VCR in your mind is able to record feelings, tastes, and smells, as well as sights and sounds. We'll be using this internal super-VCR.

Now, recall a mildly upsetting event from your personal history and rate the intensity of the upset on a scale of 1 to 10.

Note: If you are doing this exercise for the first time, do not choose the worst thing that ever happened to you. It is much easier to learn this and other techniques as well as in this book when you start with something easy and then progress. Learn the techniques first. Then apply them to more dramatic experiences. Your results will be greatly enhanced.

Imagine yourself seated in an empty theater. Make this experience as real as possible. Imagine the chair holding you up, its arms supporting your elbows, and the empty screen before you. Once you have this, move your point of view to the projection booth. From the projection booth, look down and see yourself seated in this empty theater.

In the projection booth there is a super-VCR that records all the sights, smells, sounds, feelings, and tastes on the theater screen.

Now, on the screen let yourself see the movie of this past event you have chosen while at the same time recording on the VCR everything that appears.

Include on the tape the *sounds* related to this event—the things you said, the things others said, and the background noises, too. Notice the details of the sounds, including loudness, pitch, and tone. Notice and record any internal dialogue you experienced as the event unfolds.

Record the *sights*—what you saw of the event as it unfolded, recalling colors and textures.

Record the *feelings* you experienced and perhaps even those you think others experienced. Notice how the feelings changed as the event unfolded—how they changed in intensity, in location, in temperature or in any other way. Also notice and record how your body position or posture changed as the event unfolded.

Record also any *tastes* or *smells* associated with this event and how they changed in nature and intensity as the event unfolded.

Now play this tape you just recorded in your mind in *reverse* chronological order (from end to beginning) and notice how you feel about it.

Now take the same tape and play it in reverse chronological order a little faster than normal speed (from end to beginning). The people talk backward, walk backward, and even drive backward. Everything happens in reverse. Notice how this feels.

Now take that the tape and play it in reverse two or three more times, except faster than normal speed. Not so fast that it is blurry, but fast enough so that the movement is jerky like an old Charlie Chaplin movie. Notice how this feels. It should take you no more than five seconds for each reverse playing of the tape.

Now recall the event normally. Rate the intensity of the experience again from 1 to 10. Repeat until the intensity is reduced to 1 or 2.

If you do not experience a dramatic reduction in the intensity associated with your memory of the past event, take a careful look at the tape to find out what you omitted. Likely you omitted input from one of your five senses. Then make a more complete tape and redo the visualization. You'll experience a significant reduction in intensity.

ABOUT THE AUTHORS

Phil Laut

Phil Laut is the world's foremost teacher of money psychology. In 1979 he brought to international attention the link between a person's thoughts, attitudes, and feelings and his or her bank account. This occurred with the publication of *Money Is My Friend*, the groundbreaking best-seller. *Money Is My Friend* has sold more than 400,000 copies in seventeen foreign languages: Chinese, Croatian, Czech, Dutch, French, German, Hungarian, Icelandic, Italian, Korean, Portuguese, Russian, Serbian, Slovak, Slovenian, Spanish, and Turkish, as well as in English.

He has taught thousands of people to free themselves from the shackles of limited thinking, regardless of its origin, and led them to the income they want from satisfying work. Find out about his unique Emerging Entrepreneur Consulting Program. He has taught in more than sixteen countries throughout the western hemisphere, Europe, and the Pacific Rim. Before involving himself in the personal growth field, Phil was a financial controller at a major U.S. computer manufacturer. During the Vietnam War, he served as commanding officer of a Coast Guard patrol boat. He is a graduate of Harvard Business School and the U.S. Coast Guard Academy. Phil lives in Charlotte, North Carolina.

Andy Fuehl

Andy Fuehl, author of *Profiting in Turbulent Times* is a sought-after teacher and consultant who helps people create effective entrepreneurial businesses. Andy believes that a well-trained entrepreneur can achieve success in any economic condition.

Andy has worked extensively with Phil Laut in devising and presenting their Wealth Without a Job workshops internationally. He has dedicated his life to instructing individuals in the use of Performance Enrichment Technology to achieve excellence both personally and professionally.

Andy earned an MS from Illinois Institute of Technology and is a Certified Neuro Linguistic Programming, TimeLine®, and Hypnotherapy Master Practitioner. He resides in Phoenix, Arizona, with his lovely wife Tamar.

Contact us both:
info@wtmgame.com
1-888-258-4282

Live Trainings

All our trainings are highly interactive. Lecture is kept to a minimum while exercises, role-playing, and laboratories provide a true hands-on learning experience.

Win the Money Game

This training is specifically designed for new entrepreneurs and people concerned about job security in today's uncertain economy. It is a jam-packed two-day course where you will learn to:

- Enhance your entrepreneurial skills and mind-set
- Identify and overcome obstacles that have held you back

- Understand your feelings and channel them for success
- Build the motivation that will move you ahead

Each participant returns home with a written plan to accomplish the moneymaking project of his or her choice, the skills to carry it out, and the ability to plan additional projects.

Win the Sales Game

This intensive two-day program is designed for entrepreneurs and sales professionals who want to excel. You will master the Five Step Sales Map. With one-on-one guidance and practice, you will learn to develop a true understanding of what motivates your prospects and how to use that knowledge to increase your success ratio. With our exclusive sales laboratories, you gain practice in the safe environment of the training and return home to confidently use what you learned.

Wealth Without a Job

Our full-day workshop is designed for anyone who wants a guided tour of how to apply the information in this book to his or her personal and professional life.

You will learn to:

- Free yourself of performance limiting past events
- Appreciate the boundless possibilities of free enterprise
- Place the responsibility for your financial success in the right hands—yours!
- Discover why you'll have greater satisfaction and more money with your own business.

Visit www.wealthwithoutajob.com for additional information.

Books

Money Is My Friend by Phil Laut—The world's best book about money because of its unique emotional approach. 400,000 copies sold and printed in 18 languages.

Profiting in Turbulent Times by Andy Fuehl and Brad Hoeck—Discover the dynamic relationship among environment, behaviors, capabilities, beliefs, identity, and vision. See how you can leverage these factors to achieve your own pinnacle of success.

Audio Programs for Car or Home

Fill your drive time with positive messages. You'll be surprised how listening to uplifting, success-oriented messages can prime you for excellence.

Money Masters II—Eight CD set recorded live at Breakthroughs to Success Training in Los Angeles. Learn from Phil Laut, Jeffery Combs, Lisa Kitter, Jerry Clark, Anne Sermons Gillis, David Martin, and Frederic Lehrman. Top wealth creation experts guide you toward a new understanding of the role money plays in your life.

Prosperity Mind-Set—Cassette tape with Phil Laut—For network marketers, independent businesspeople and anyone who works for him- or herself.

Money Is an Intentional Creation of the Mind with Phil Laut—Two hours recorded live at the Unity Church in Minneapolis. This program will teach you how anyone can learn to sell, and how your thoughts and feelings determine your bank balance.

AUDIO TAPES AND CDS FOR HOME USE ONLY

These audio programs are not recommended for vehicle use because they require a high degree of listener involvement.

Why Wait: Hypnosis for Selling with Active Confidence (Two CD set) by Andy Fuehl and Douglas Raymond—Sales superstars use Active Confidence. Boost your results quickly and easily by making your selling anxiety free.

Earn, Receive, and Accumulate Money with Sean Collins—Unique Dual Channel Recording Technology produces rapid advancement in your income.

Principles of Personal Financial Success with Phil Laut—The ultimate in internal organization, this program will get your purpose, goals, and plans organized in a manner that makes you unstoppable.

Entrepreneurs Companion Set (Two CD set) Mind-set Affirmations for vehicle listening and dual channel affirmations for home listening. Visit www.wealthwithoutajob.com for additional information.

INDEX